Instructor's Resource Manual

to accompany

Operations Management
for Competitive Advantage

Ninth Edition

Richard B. Chase
University of Southern California

Nicholas J. Aquilano
University of Arizona

F. Robert Jacobs
Indiana University

Prepared by
F. Robert Jacobs
Indiana University

**McGraw-Hill
Irwin**

Boston   Burr Ridge, IL   Dubuque, IA   Madison, WI   New York   San Francisco   St. Louis
Bangkok   Bogotá   Caracas   Lisbon   London   Madrid
Mexico City   Milan   New Delhi   Seoul   Singapore   Sydney   Taipei   Toronto

McGraw-Hill Higher Education

A Division of The McGraw-Hill Companies

Instructor's Resource Manual to accompany
OPERATIONS MANAGEMENT FOR COMPETITIVE ADVANTAGE
Richard B. Chase, Nicholas J. Aquilano, and F. Robert Jacobs

3 4 5 6 7 8 9 0 HAM/HAM 0 9 8 7 6 5 4 3 2

ISBN 0-07-239273-8

www.mhhe.com

McGRAW-HILL/IRWIN/

Instructor's Resource Manual to accompany Operations Management for Competitive Advantage, 9/e by Chase, Aquilano, and Jacobs..

Please use this postage-paid form to report any errors that you find in this material. Be as complete as possible noting specifically which changes should be made. We will address them in subsequent printings and future editions. Thank You.

NOTE: Extra copies of this form appear at the end of this manual.

Attention: R. T. Hercher

Name _____   School _____

Office Phone _____

Please fold and seal so that our address is visible.

ACKNOWLEDGEMENTS

I am indebted to S. Thomas Foster, Jr. for his significant contribution to this Instructors Resource Manual. Prof. Foster of Boise State University wrote the Instructors Manual for the 7th edition and some of that material is included in this document.

Thanks to Louis A. Le Blanc, of the University of Arkansas, Little Rock for the generous contribution of three classroom exercises to this manual.

Finally, thanks to Gail Korosa of McGraw-Hill/Irwin for her ideas concerning the organization and formatting of the manual.

F. Robert Jacobs

INSTRUCTORS RESOURCE MANUAL
TABLE OF CONTENTS

INTRODUCTION

Clearly, teaching Operations Management (OM) can be a significant challenge. This is particularly true in a school dominated by Accounting or Finance majors. We have found that, if designed correctly, the OM course can easily be one of the most popular. Students like the "hands-on" orientation of the topics and can see the direct applicability of the material. The purposes of this instructor's resource guide are twofold. First, it is designed to help in the development of an Operations Management course. Our second purpose is to provide some ideas for innovative ways that a particular topic can be presented.

In our many talks with instructors using *Operations Management for Competitive Advantage*, we have been surprised with the variety of ways the book is used. The book is widely used by both Graduate and Undergraduate courses. The book is used for both introductory courses and for more specialized courses. Some instructors teach a more quantitative course, while others focus on the managerial material. Only a few instructors cover the topics in the order presented, and we do not know of any instructor who covers the entire book in a single course. Instructors seem to select what they feel is important and interesting. Many instructors augment the book with supplemental material such as Harvard cases and articles.

Thank you for using our book in the past and considering this new edition for the future. Operations management is a dynamic discipline, with new concepts appearing frequently. The challenge for a textbook is not only to capture these concepts but also to anchor them to the existing body of knowledge in an understandable way. It goes without saying that the basics must be covered effectively as well.

Discussion of 9th Edition Revisions

In developing the revisions for the 9th edition, we have been very careful to make the sections and chapters as modular as possible. This allows you to drop things out, or rearrange topics as you see fit. Actually, our discussions concerning the current line up of chapters were extensive, but we realized that no matter what we ended up with, it was a compromise. We know from experience, that the current line up works well.

We have continued to innovate in the edition. The major revisions to be found are:

- A new organization focuses time and coverage on key operations issues such as Project Management (Chapter 3), Process Analysis (Chapter 4), and Supply Chain Design (Section Three). Technical coverage of linear programming and transportation are relocated into a new Supplement at the end of the text call Linear Programming Using Excel Solver. Additional Supplements at text end are Financial Analysis and Operations Technology. These can be covered, or not, at your discretion.

- New strategy material focuses on developing a competitive advantage through operations.

- A new chapter on Process Analysis (Chapter 4) gives specific tools and methods for analyzing a manufacturing or service process. Students will have a concise yet complete understanding that can then be applied throughout the rest of the course.

- Three hot topics in business today are Electronic Commerce, Supply Chain Management and Enterprise Resource Planning Systems. These topics are studied in the book from the view of the operations function with up-to-date high-level managerial material to clarify the "big picture" of what these topics are and why they are so important to business today. In the Electronic Commerce area for example, we introduce the term "E-Ops" to provide a structure for presenting numerous applications of Electronic Commerce in operations throughout the book.

- Managerial briefings open two key sections of the text and provide students with an executive-summary style introduction to the concepts of Electronic Commerce (Section 3) and Enterprise Resource Planning (Section 4).

- Technical notes detail how operations-related problems such as Learning Curves, Waiting Line Management, Layout, and Location are solved. These are concise treatments of the many decisions that need to be made in designing, planning, and managing the operations of a business. Many spreadsheets are included on the Student CD, Website to help clarify how these problems are quickly solved.

- Quality Management (Chapter 7) has been shortened and a more global perspective has been developed with coverage of the European Quality award.

- Statistical Process Control (Technical Note 7) has been reorganized to de-emphasize inspection. The technical notes starts with process capability, Taguchi and 6-sigma. Process monitoring tools are then developed.

- The new Supply Chain Strategy chapter (Chapter 8) moves this material beyond the planning and control aspects of Supply Chain Management that dominated the SCM material in the last edition. An interesting postponement case (Pepe Jeans) is included in the new chapter.

- The use of the transportation model for facility location (Technical Note 9) is now included. The Excel Solver is explained in the technical note for solving the problem. A new case (Applichem – the Transportation Problem) that allows the application of Excel Solver is included in the Technical Note.

- Forecasting (Chapter 11) has been updated to now use a more conventional presentation of exponential smoothing with trend.

- The Aggregate Planning chapter (Chapter 12) includes a new case exercise (Bradford Manufacturing) that demonstrates the interface between Aggregate Planning and Master Scheduling. Students solve the aggregate plan using Excel Solver.

- Inventory control (Chapter 13) has been simplified and shortened. Z statistics are now used for safety stock calculations, rather than the E(z) statistic.

- A new case (HP Deskjet in Chapter 13) that demonstrates inventory pooling is included. This ties inventory control to the supply chain strategy material.

- MRP (Chapter 14) has been shortened and a step-by-step explanation of the MRP explosion process included.

- A new E-OPS game, played over the Internet, allows students to experience the importance of coordinating purchasing, production and sales. This case in included in the Enterprise Resource Planning System managerial briefing starting Section Four.

- A new simulation exercise (Understanding the Impact of Variability on the Capacity of a Production System) that makes use of John McClain's (Cornell University) simulation spreadsheet is included in Technical Note 15 - Simulation. Both of John's simulation spreadsheets, LineSim and CellSim are now included on the CD with the book.

- The Consulting and Reengineering Chapters (Chapter 16) have been combined for a more concise presentation of this material.

- Synchronous Manufacturing and Theory of Constraints (Chapter 17) has been shortened.

- The Student CD, Website has been updated with new tutorial animations, expanded Excel tools, enhanced quizzes, greater use of the Internet, and integration with the text. Two commercial software packages are included – Tree Age DATA and Primavera SureTrak. We are also including

Premium Solver from Frontline Systems. Logos in the text indicate Excel spreadsheets, cases, simulations, and other assets located on the CD.

- New Internet Enrichment Exercises provide a medium for Internet research.

- Key terms are now introduced in the chapter outline then defined at the end of each chapter.

- New advanced problems are included in chapters where appropriate.

- Additional cases, classroom exercises, test questions, and updates are available on two websites supported by the authors of the book. The address of the McGraw-Hill hosted site is http://www.mhhe.com/chase and the address of the site directly supported by professor Jacobs is http://www.pom.edu/pom.

In this edition of the book we have continued our emphasis on showing both manufacturing and services perspective on all the topics. In addition, we have stressed a global perspective and where appropriate shown how the concepts apply in a global context. A final emphasis of the book is to show the importance of cross-functional integration of the topics. Special icons are used by the book to highlight services, global, and cross-functional material.

Opening vignettes set the stage for the material in each chapter. Most of these vignettes have been updated with current examples. The book includes 32 cases (11 of which are new this edition), solved problems at the end of chapter, formula summaries, new and revised problems, and updated bibliographies. Many spreadsheets are included on the Student CD, Website packaged with the book that corresponds to the exhibits, solved problems, and cases. Each spreadsheet is marked in the book with a CD logo.

We have included in the Instructor's Edition of the book annotations to help teach the course. Titles of video segments from the Operations Management Video series are noted where they could enhance the text topic. Check answers are placed in the margin next to end-of-chapter problems.

The support package for *Operations Management for Competitive Advantage* includes:

- Student CD, Website packaged free with the text, includes Excel templates and data files, PowerPoint slides on key concepts for each chapter, practice exams, links to text-referenced websites, electronic tutorials, industry applications software, and video clips of key operations function for student interest. The electronic tutorials are on EOQ, Aggregate Planning with SAP R/3, the Drum-Buffer-Rope Concept, and Using the Excel Solver for Transportation Problems.

- Instructor's CD (ISBN 0072392770) places all the supplements, including the Instructor's Solution Manual, Instructor's Resource Manual, the Test Bank, and presentations including PowerPoint, over 50 video clips, and all the text figures, on one, easy-to-use CD tool. The presentation platform allows you to build customized classroom presentation using the resources from the CD.

- Instructor's Solution Manual (ISBN 0072392746) prepared by Ross Fink of Bradley University, contains worked solutions to text problems. A handy grid at the beginning of each chapter indicates what problems correspond to specific topics in the text and their level of difficulty.

- Instructor's Resource Manual (ISBN 0072392738) prepared by the authors, includes sample course syllabi; suggested cases, videos, case teaching notes, teaching tips, spreadsheets, and PowerPoint slides for each chapter.

- Test Bank (ISBN 0072392754) created by Marc Schniederjans of the University of Nebraska, provides true/false, multiple-choice, and solve-for-the-answer problems. The test bank is also available in a computerized version that allows you to generate, add, and edit questions, save and reload tests, and select questions based on the level of difficulty. The computerized version is available on the Instructor's CD.

- Study Guide (ISBN 0072392797) prepared by Marilyn Helms of the University of Tennessee at Chattanooga, helps students prepare with an overview of each chapter, key terms, a review quiz, and problems and exercises that parallel text problems.

- Operations Management Video Series consisting of 27 segments of about 10 minutes each, covers quality, inventory, lean production, CIM, process and services. These videos show students OM concepts at work in real companies such as Honda, Motorola, Toyota, and United Airlines.

- Internet version of the Beer Distribution Game (http://www.pom.edu/beer/) that can be played with teams of students in a classroom equipped with Internet access. This game is used to demonstrate Supply Chain System dynamics and is a great exercise for use with the new Chapter 8: Supply Chain Strategy.

- E-Ops Game (http://www.pom.edu/ebus/) is a new Internet based exercise that allows the student to experience what it is like to run a business in Internet time. Students take on the role of purchasing, manufacturing and sales in a fast-paced game where the goal is to make as much money as possible. The game is designed to work with Section Four: Planning and

Controlling the Supply Chain. This game can be played in or out of the classroom, and can be played by individuals or by teams of students.

COURSE SYLLABUS IDEAS

Session Timing

The following schedules give ideas for how an introductory course can be set up using the text. Proper timing of the topics is important for undergraduate or graduate level courses. Two schedules are provided, one for a typical 45-session course (meets 3 times per week for 55 minutes) and the other for a 30-session course (meets 2 times per week for 75 minutes). If you are faced with the problem of not having the time to cover the entire book, we suggest that you take complete topics out of the syllabus, rather than trying to rush through a topic.

45 Sessions – 3 per week - 55 minutes each

Theme		Topic	Ch
The Nature and Context of Operations Management	1	Introduction	1
	2	Operations Strategy and Competitiveness	2
	3	Case: Compaq verses Dell Computer Case: Los Angeles Toy Company	2
	4	Project Management	3
	5	Case: The Campus Wedding (A & B)	3
Product Design and Process Selection	6	Process Analysis	4
	7	Product Design and Process Selection - Manufacturing	5
	8	Case: Paper Clips	IRM
	9	Product Design and Process Selection – Services	6
	10	Case: Kinko's copier Stores Case: AOL's Move to Flat-Rate Pricing	6
	11	Waiting Line Management	TN6
	12	Quality Management	7
	13	Case: Hank Kolb	7
	14	Statistical Quality Control Methods	TN7
	15	**First Midterm**	
Design of Facilities and Jobs	16	Strategic Capacity Planning	9
	17	Case: Shouldice Hospital	9
	18	Just-In-Time Production Systems	10
	19	Facility Location	TN9
	20	Facility Layout	TN5
	21	Case: Soteriou's Souvlaki	TN5
	22	Job Design and Work Measurement	TN4
	23	Learning Curves	TN2
Supply Chain Management	24	Supply Chain Strategy	8
	25	Beer Distribution Game	IRM
	26	Forecasting	11
	27	Forecasting	11

7

28	Aggregate Planning	12
29	Aggregate Planning	12
30	**Second Midterm**	
31	Inventory Control	13
32	Inventory Control	13
33	Case: Finish Line	IRM
34	Material Requirements Planning	14
35	Material Requirements Planning	14
36	Case: Nichols Company	14
37	Enterprise Resource Planning Systems	MB

	38	Operations Scheduling	15
	39	Operations Scheduling	15
	40	Simulation Case: Understanding the Impact of Variability on the Capacity of a Production System	TN15
Revising the System	41	Operations Consulting and Reengineering	16
	42	Operations Consulting and Reengineering	16
	43	Synchronous Manufacturing and Theory of Constraints	17
	44	Review and Wrap-up	
	45	Final Exam	

30 Sessions – 2 per week – 75 minutes each

Theme		Topic	Ch
The Nature and Context of Operations Management	1	Introduction	1
	2	Operations Strategy and Competitiveness	2
	3	Project Management	3
	4	Case: The Campus Wedding (A & B)	3
Product Design and Process Selection	5	Product Design and Process Selection - Manufacturing	5
	6	Product Design and Process Selection – Services	6
	7	Case: Kinko's copier Stores Case: AOL's Move to Flat-Rate Pricing	6
	8	Waiting Line Management	TN6
	9	Quality Management	7
	10	Case: Hank Kolb	7
	11	Statistical Quality Control Methods	TN7
	12	**Midterm**	
Design of Facilities and Jobs	13	Strategic Capacity Planning Case: Shouldice Hospital	9

	14	Just-In-Time Production Systems	10
	15	Facility Location	TN9
	16	Facility Layout Case: Soteriou's Souvlaki	TN5
	17	Job Design and Work Measurement	TN4
	18	Learning Curves	TN2
Supply Chain Management	19	Supply Chain Strategy	8
	20	Forecasting	11
	21	Aggregate Planning	12
	22	Inventory Control	13
	23	Case: HP – Supplying DeskJet Printer in Europe	13
	24	Material Requirements Planning	14
	25	Case: Nichols Company	14
	26	Enterprise Resource Planning Systems	MB
	27	Operations Scheduling	15
Revising the System	28	Operations Consulting and Reengineering	16
	29	Synchronous Manufacturing and Theory of Constraints	17
	30	**Final Exam**	

9

Session Resources

For undergraduate courses, the book provides all of the material needed for an introductory level course. Usually the undergraduate course is more "problem" oriented than a graduate course. Every chapter and technical note in the book contains at least one "problem" to serve this focus in the course.

Typically the graduate course has a more "managerial" focus (although, we are now seeing many undergraduate courses with a mixed "problem and managerial" focus). Business cases can be used to illustrate the managerial implications of a particular topic. Many short cases are available in the book and in this Instructors Resource Manual. Some instructors prefer to use more comprehensive cases such as those published by the Harvard Business School. To aid in the selection of these cases, the following table is provided which shows the most popular Harvard Business School cases that can be used with each chapter and supplement in the book.

Also available to instructors using the book is an Instructor CD that contains an expanded set of video clips and all of the exhibits from the book. In addition a program is available on the Instructor CD, Website that assists in putting together an electronic slide show using video clips, PowerPoint slides and the exhibits from the book.

Finally, we have included suggestions for videotapes that can be used with each topic. These are professionally produced and show real world applications of the various topics in the course. Keep in mind that your students have a set of video clips on the CD-ROM that comes with the book. The clips are segments from these tapes where specific concepts are defined. You may want to use some of these video clips in class to quickly introduce a topic.

These tapes are from the Irwin/McGraw-Hill videotape series and can be requested through your Irwin/McGraw-Hill book representative (they are free!).

(See the Appendix for tape and video clip details.)

CASE TEACHING NOTES AND EXTRA CASES

Chapter 1 – Introduction to the Field

Overview

Chapter one provides an introduction to the field of operations management. The importance of this introduction should not be discounted as many students enter the introductory POM course with little prior knowledge of the subject. Demand for POM majors is consistently increasing as more companies seek employees with knowledge about JIT, quality and continuous improvement. This course focuses on the core activities of the firm-be it services or manufacturing. During this course, the student will become familiar with the design and management of a firms supply chain. This course should round out a sound management preparation for non-POM majors and provide POM majors with a solid foundation of principles leading to greater in-depth knowledge of the field.

Major Points of the Chapter

- An understanding of POM is essential to the student's development as a manager.
- POM provides a systematic means of observing organizational processes.
- POM tools can be applied in a variety of jobs and industries-including all services.
- POM focuses on the core, conversion processes of the firm. This is where value is added for the customer.
- POM is essentially a 20th century discipline.

Teaching Tips

We have included a case titled "Fast Food Feast" that is a good case to get the course started. Students are asked to visit two fast food restaurants and compare the processes used to make hamburgers.

An alternative case is the "Wyatt Earp – Buffalo Hunter" case that is very good for breaking the ice. Students find it quick reading and discussion of the process, technology and environmental issues flows easily.

It is easy to spend 10-15 minutes in class discussing the Purchasing Managers Index spreadsheet. You can have students look for this when it is announced each month in the Wall Street Journal during the semester or quarter.

Cases, Exercises and Spreadsheets (Source)

PMI_Data.xls (Spreadsheet on CD-ROM),

"Fast Food Feast" (Book)

"Wyatt Earp – Buffalo Hunter" (IRM)

Videos/Clips (Source)

"Services" (Vol. 1)

"Lean Production" (Vol. 1)

CASE

The Purchasing Managers Index (PMI) – Teaching Note

This exercise is a result of an interest in showing that the performance of companies from an operations standpoint can have a profound impact on the stock market. Every month Wall Street eagerly waits for the numbers published by the Purchasing Managers Association in their PMI index. Through this exercise, students will learn what this index is, and can get a good idea for how employment levels, productivity, and inventory levels have changed over recent years. It also gives students an opportunity to practice spreadsheet skills in the context of the Operations Management course.

A spreadsheet is available on the Student CD, Website-ROM that contains recent PMI data. Students will find it interesting to visit the Purchasing Managers Association home page at http://www.napm.org/ to get the latest information relating to the index. Actually, updating the data from the web site may be difficult for students who are not familiar with importing data into Excel spreadsheets. An updated spreadsheet, with the most recent data, is available on the book web site at http://www.pom.edu/pom.

This exercise could be discussed in class or the students could be asked to prepare a short memo that answers the discussion questions.

Typical data contained in the spreadsheet on the CD-ROM is as follows:

PMI Index

	1992	1993	1994	1995	1996	1997	1998	1999
January	47.30	55.80	56.00	57.40	45.40	53.30	53.00	49.50
February	52.70	55.20	56.50	55.10	46.00	53.40	53.40	52.40
March	54.60	53.50	56.90	52.10	47.10	54.70	54.20	54.30
April	52.60	50.20	57.40	51.60	49.40	53.90	52.50	52.80
May	55.70	51.20	58.20	46.70	49.40	56.50	51.40	55.20
June	53.60	49.60	58.80	45.90	53.80	55.70	49.70	57.00
July	53.90	50.20	58.50	50.70	49.70	57.70	49.20	53.40
August	53.40	50.70	58.00	47.10	51.60	56.00	48.90	54.20
September	49.70	50.80	59.00	48.10	51.30	54.30	49.10	57.80
October	50.30	53.40	59.40	46.70	50.30	55.90	48.40	56.60
November	53.60	53.80	59.20	45.90	52.60	54.70	47.00	56.20
December	54.20	55.60	56.10	46.20	54.50	53.40	45.30	55.50

Seasonally Adjusted Indexes -- 1992, 1993, 1994, 1995, 1996, 1997, 1998, 1999

13

	New Orders	Production	Employment	Supplier Deliveries	Inventories	Prices	Export Orders	Imports
Jan-92	49.60	50.40	40.60	48.70	44.10	45.40	51.90	47.00
Feb-92	58.30	58.70	43.90	49.30	44.00	45.90	54.70	47.20
Mar-92	63.30	59.70	43.70	50.30	44.30	48.10	54.70	49.80
Apr-92	59.10	57.80	45.00	47.40	43.20	51.10	53.40	52.10
May-92	60.90	61.20	49.50	50.00	47.00	55.00	56.20	53.90
Jun-92	59.80	57.60	46.60	50.80	43.10	53.90	53.10	49.10
Jul-92	59.50	57.40	45.50	52.50	46.90	56.20	55.20	49.70
Aug-92	58.80	56.80	47.30	50.30	45.80	53.70	53.30	48.60
Sep-92	51.10	53.90	45.10	51.20	42.30	51.60	55.80	46.70
Oct-92	53.80	54.70	44.70	48.60	42.40	46.40	53.80	47.70
Nov-92	58.80	58.60	47.10	51.30	42.10	42.10	52.90	48.00
Dec-92	61.00	57.90	45.90	51.50	45.00	48.00	53.10	51.40
Jan-93	63.00	61.50	46.90	52.30	43.30	49.80	53.40	49.40
Feb-93	59.70	63.50	47.00	51.70	42.60	53.90	53.20	49.50
Mar-93	58.10	56.70	47.10	52.70	45.60	53.60	52.30	49.40
Apr-93	53.00	51.60	44.80	52.80	44.70	54.60	53.50	50.10
May-93	55.20	55.00	43.60	51.50	44.80	50.40	54.20	47.40
Jun-93	51.60	53.10	43.20	50.40	46.50	50.60	52.40	49.80
Jul-93	53.80	52.70	43.60	51.00	45.50	51.40	50.10	48.70
Aug-93	55.30	53.90	41.90	51.80	44.40	52.30	52.60	49.40
Sep-93	52.60	55.20	44.50	51.30	46.20	49.00	51.70	49.90
Oct-93	58.90	56.10	46.00	50.70	48.60	50.90	54.10	49.40
Nov-93	60.40	57.50	45.50	50.90	45.50	52.70	55.00	51.50
Dec-93	62.40	61.70	47.10	51.50	43.20	53.10	53.80	50.30
Jan-94	63.50	59.70	47.50	54.40	43.90	58.90	55.30	52.40
Feb-94	62.20	60.20	48.70	57.00	44.60	63.00	58.30	51.90
Mar-94	62.80	63.40	48.20	55.40	43.00	52.90	55.20	51.80
Apr-94	62.70	61.40	50.10	57.20	45.90	53.50	56.90	51.80
May-94	61.60	62.70	51.40	60.20	47.60	67.80	54.90	53.40
Jun-94	65.00	62.00	49.50	60.30	48.30	69.70	57.80	55.20
Jul-94	64.20	62.30	52.30	58.10	45.10	71.60	56.70	51.10
Aug-94	63.00	60.20	51.40	61.60	44.90	75.20	57.70	51.30
Sep-94	62.70	62.80	52.50	62.50	46.10	80.30	60.00	53.00
Oct-94	63.00	63.30	51.10	64.90	47.60	84.10	58.50	53.70
Nov-94	61.50	63.90	51.60	64.70	47.30	84.50	56.10	53.20
Dec-94	58.90	59.50	46.70	64.80	45.00	87.10	58.40	52.60
Jan-95	59.70	60.90	51.90	62.70	45.20	86.00	59.10	52.20
Feb-95	56.60	57.40	50.00	60.70	47.00	81.70	58.70	53.00
Mar-95	51.90	54.80	48.10	56.90	47.00	78.90	56.90	52.00
Apr-95	52.20	54.10	47.40	56.30	44.20	74.50	55.60	49.80
May-95	44.00	49.90	43.70	53.30	43.30	70.50	56.30	47.90
Jun-95	43.50	46.10	46.50	51.80	43.00	64.70	56.10	49.30
Jul-95	52.70	51.60	48.10	51.30	46.50	58.60	56.40	53.30

Aug-95	46.50	49.10	45.00	49.10	45.50	48.50	53.70	51.80
Sep-95	49.40	50.50	45.50	50.00	40.30	48.80	52.60	49.40
Oct-95	47.50	47.00	45.90	48.40	42.20	46.50	52.20	49.50
Nov-95	48.60	45.00	44.50	45.30	43.30	44.50	54.70	44.20
Dec-95	45.90	46.90	46.20	47.50	43.10	40.30	56.50	49.50
Jan-96	43.90	45.50	45.10	47.80	46.50	39.70	50.30	48.20
Feb-96	46.30	45.80	44.40	49.50	43.40	38.70	51.50	48.10
Mar-96	49.40	47.70	44.40	49.70	40.00	39.90	51.00	48.00
Apr-96	52.40	51.70	44.80	49.40	44.20	41.50	51.70	47.70
May-96	52.40	53.10	45.10	49.90	38.50	50.60	57.50	48.70
Jun-96	60.00	55.80	48.40	52.70	42.80	48.20	53.40	48.90
Jul-96	52.20	52.20	46.40	50.80	40.80	44.10	53.10	52.00
Aug-96	54.40	54.90	47.50	51.90	42.30	46.90	55.20	50.00
Sep-96	55.10	53.80	47.10	50.00	43.50	50.80	55.30	50.90
Oct-96	52.20	55.00	46.00	50.90	40.30	46.10	56.50	52.80
Nov-96	56.20	57.40	47.40	51.10	42.40	46.00	54.50	52.90
Dec-96	59.60	58.90	48.40	52.10	44.40	51.00	55.70	51.20
Jan-97	56.40	58.90	49.50	49.60	43.10	52.10	56.10	52.40
Feb-97	58.50	59.30	45.50	52.00	41.30	55.60	54.60	51.70
Mar-97	59.50	57.30	50.70	53.20	43.60	51.40	57.30	49.90
Apr-97	56.90	56.80	52.10	53.40	41.70	51.20	55.60	52.90
May-97	63.10	56.90	52.00	54.80	46.90	49.10	55.00	53.60
Jun-97	60.90	57.40	52.00	54.70	44.70	49.10	54.20	54.90
Jul-97	61.70	64.30	51.40	54.70	45.90	51.90	55.40	53.30
Aug-97	59.80	60.70	51.50	55.20	43.20	52.50	55.00	53.90
Sep-97	55.90	57.20	51.30	55.00	46.80	54.70	50.20	52.80
Oct-97	59.60	58.40	52.70	55.00	46.70	54.30	52.30	51.80
Nov-97	56.00	58.40	53.20	55.00	44.10	50.90	52.60	53.10
Dec-97	54.40	56.10	51.10	54.30	46.50	50.40	49.80	55.40
Jan-98	56.30	54.00	50.60	52.90	45.90	45.60	46.20	54.00
Feb-98	56.10	55.30	50.90	52.50	46.60	46.00	48.60	51.30
Mar-98	56.30	57.50	51.60	53.10	46.60	44.70	48.10	54.20
Apr-98	55.80	53.40	49.50	52.40	46.10	42.10	49.20	55.40
May-98	52.20	53.50	51.00	51.30	44.60	41.70	47.40	53.60
Jun-98	51.70	51.50	47.60	51.10	41.50	39.10	46.80	52.40
Jul-98	52.00	50.80	44.70	50.30	43.90	38.00	45.10	49.30
Aug-98	50.20	49.70	46.80	50.20	45.10	37.50	44.00	51.40
Sep-98	50.00	52.20	45.80	51.00	42.80	34.80	44.90	52.70
Oct-98	46.80	51.50	45.20	50.10	49.50	35.00	42.30	51.30
Nov-98	46.50	48.50	44.70	50.00	44.70	33.40	42.80	49.70
Dec-98	46.40	46.80	40.90	48.70	41.90	31.10	44.70	49.90
Jan-99	51.30	53.10	44.80	50.90	42.30	32.50	49.80	49.40
Feb-99	57.20	56.90	45.00	50.60	44.20	35.90	54.00	52.30
Mar-99	58.20	59.60	48.00	52.50	44.60	43.20	51.70	55.30
Apr-99	54.80	57.60	49.50	49.40	46.60	49.90	51.60	53.40

May-99	58.9	59.2	53.5	51.9	42.2	52.2	52.4	54.6
Jun-99	61.7	63	51.9	53.1	44.1	53.5	53.3	52.9
Jul-99	54.4	58.2	49.6	54.2	44.4	54.7	50.4	51.6
Aug-99	56.6	56.7	53.4	51.1	46.6	59.8	54.2	53.9
Sep-99	64.4	61.7	51.5	55.9	43.2	67.6	56.6	55.7
Oct-99	59.5	58.3	52.8	56.6	51.1	69.4	52.4	54.3
Nov-99	59.9	57.4	52.2	55.9	50	65.3	54.5	51.2
Dec-99	55.5	58.7	54.3	56.9	47.2	65.7	53.4	51.4
Jan-00	60.4	55.9	52.7	55.2	53.4	72.6	52.6	51.9
Feb-00								

Discussion Questions:

1. How have employment levels in manufacturing companies in the United States changed over the past three years?

This question is answered by plotting the employment levels from the data given in the spreadsheet. The spreadsheet contains the following sample plots of data: a plot of the PMI index, a plot with employment and production data, and a plot of the ratio of inventory to sales. Using these examples, students should be able to extend the analysis.

The following is a plot of the employment and production data.

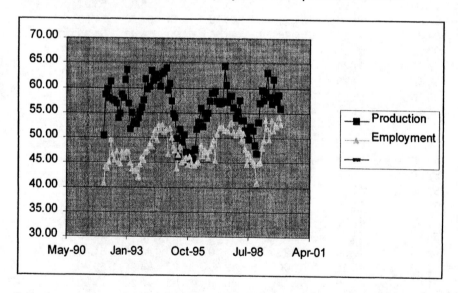

Draw your own conclusion here, but it does appear that employment is going up over the past four years. Additional analysis could be done the most obvious being the plotting of the ratio of production to employment.

2. Have manufacturing companies been successful in reducing inventories?

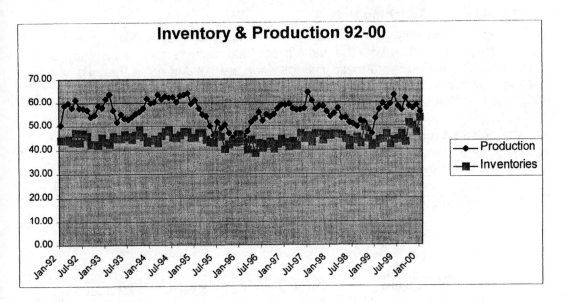

It looks like, at least recently, that inventory has been reduced while production has increased.

3. How do inventory levels fluctuate with new orders (sales)?

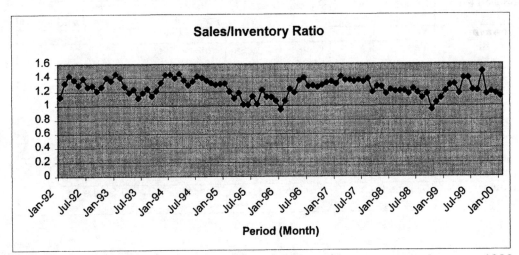

This is an interesting plot. Between December 1993 through January 1996, sales went down relative to inventory. In 1996, the ratio returned to the levels prevalent in 1992 and 1993.

CASE

Fast Food Feast – Teaching Note

This is a good exercise to get the students thinking about processes. Students are generally very familiar with the various fast food restaurants and it is easy to get them talking their preferences. The following are a set of notes that can be used to organize a session that discusses this exercise. It is useful to make this assignment 2-3 weeks prior the first class for the course.

For McDonald's we have included data on their old process which was designed around a burger bin, where inventory was carried and their new "Made for You" system that is currently being installed in all of their restaurants.

The following is a board plan for the process comparison, a flowchart depicting McDonald's old process, and a second grid comparing the performance criteria across the firms. A set of questions that can be used to develop the discussion are then given.

Process/Step	McDonald's – Old	McDonald's – New	Burger King	Wendy's
Burger Prep	Grill (80 seconds)	Grill	Chain – Broiled	Grill
Burger Inventory	Yes	Yes (moisture control)	Yes	Yes
Buns	Toaster	High Speed Toaster (10 seconds)	Chain – 2x speed of hamburgers	Heated
Bun Inventory	Yes – not heated	None	Yes – heated	Heated
Sandwich Prep	2 lines	2 lines - heated	2 lines – specialized	2 lines - specialized
Microwave	Yes	No	Yes	No
Burger Bin	Yes	Usually No (peak times)	Small – Yes	No
Control System	Manual – Production Mgr/Computer for specials and drive through	Computer – even controls the bin	Manual/Speakers – computer for specials	Computer
Drinks	Delivered	Self Served	Self Served	Delivered
Number of cash registers	5	5	2	2
Customer Queue	Multiple lines	Multiple lines	Snake	Snake

The following is a diagram of McDonald's old system. Process maps of these restaurants are given in Chapter 4 (p. 98).

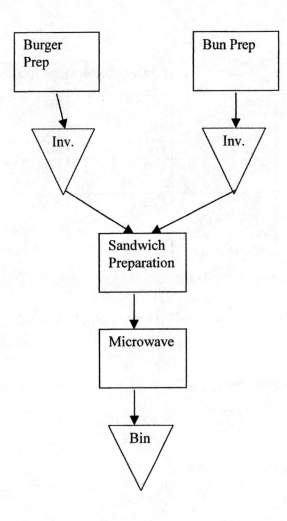

The Basic Process

Take order → Get Drinks → Get Food → Take payment and make change

Criteria	McDonalds – Old	McDonalds – New	Burger King	Wendy's
Capacity	High	High	High	High
Quality	Low	High	Low	High
Flexibility	High	High	Low	High
Order Accuracy	High	High	Low	High
Speed	Fast	Slow? Technology may compensate	Fast?	Slow

What do these different fast food restaurants sell? Does each of them sell something different?

McDonalds:
Speed - Goal 3.5 minutes door to delivery.
Did somebody say McDonalds?

New McDonalds:
Made for you.
Will save $15,000 in waste annually.

Wendy's:
Quality

Burger King:
Flexibility
Have it your way?

Organization of the case part of the session:

What are these fast food restaurants selling? Are there differences?

What is different about the operations of these restaurants?
Processes ----   Back room and visible areas.
Technology
Service Speed
Overall Capacity
Flexibility

How are the operations controlled?
Manual
Computer

Do their processes and control systems match up with their marketing?

Marketing
What do they sell? What are the implications from an Operations standpoint?
Are there any "order winners?" Are there any "order qualifiers?"

Processes and technology
How do these stores make hamburgers? Did you notice any differences?

Variability
What are sources of variability that these stores must deal with?

Quality
How do these businesses ensure quality?

Management control
How are the processes controlled? What other things need to be controlled?

Supply Chain
What does it take to support these stores?

End with a summary and how all this fits with the rest of the course.

EXTRA CASE

Wyatt Earp - The Buffalo Hunter
F. Robert Jacobs, Indiana University

The legend of Wyatt Earp lives on largely based on his exploits as a gunfighter and Marshall of the frontier West in the 1880s. The classic tales of the shootout at the O.K. Corral in Tombstone or his sawed-off shotgun duel with Curly Bill are possibly the most celebrated gunfights of frontier history and can not fail to stir the reader's imagination. Wyatt lived to be over 80 years old, long enough to recount his story to Stuart Lake for the book <u>Wyatt Earp: Frontier Marshall</u>[1] (published by Pocket Books).

Apparently, Wyatt was quite a financial success long before he became a marshal. He learned how to hunt and shoot buffalo when only 15 years old. By the time he was 20, the Kansas City and Caldwell buffalo hunters knew him as one of the best in the west. His methods for hunting buffalo were very different from the established practices of the time.

Outside the marshal's office in Caldwell, veteran hunters would meet to compare the season's hunt. Success was measured solely by animals killed and cash received for the hides and meat. Wyatt realized that what was important was the gain after expenditures for horses, wagons, supplies, and skinners' wages were considered. Any hunter could boast of the money in his pockets at the end of a season, but few could say accurately how much was gain.

The Ways of the Veteran Hunters

The buffalo hunter of 1871 set out for the range with five four-horse wagons, with one driver, the stocktender, camp watchman, and cook; and four others to skin the kill. The hunter provided horses, wagons, and supplies for several months. Money received for hides and meat would be divided into two equal parts; one went to the hunter, and from his share, he paid all expenses. The second was again split into as many shares as there were drivers, skinners and helpers with each getting a share as his seasonal wage. It was believed that no really top-notch buffalo hunter would stoop to skinning the animals he shot. Each person in the party had a specific assigned job, and none would do something below their level of dignity.

The weapon of choice at the time was the Sharps "Fifty" rifle. These rifles, which all right-minded buffalo hunters carried, weighed more than twenty pounds. The gun shot a slug of lead two inches in length, a half-inch in diameter, weighing approximately an eighth of a pound. The Sharps was the best weapon

1. ————————————

1Parts of this case are from Chapter 5, "The Buffalo Range."

obtainable for long-range shooting, but notable among its drawbacks were the cost of ammunition and the fact that the rifle's accuracy was seriously affected by continued rapid fire. To prevent damaging the rifle, the wise user, ran a water-soaked rag through the barrel after every second or third shot and let the metal cool.

Wyatt recounted that "early white hunters had followed the Indian practice of shooting buffalo from the back of a horse galloping full tilt at the edge of a stampeding herd. In skin hunting this did not pay. Shooting from horseback could not be as accurate as from a stand, and the animals killed during a run would be strung for miles across the prairie, making a lot of travel for the skinners, with the added certainty that many hides would be missed. Also, every buffalo left alive would be stampeded clear out of the country in a day's hunt, and the killers would have to move camp or wait for another herd.

"In stories about Buffalo Bill Cody and other Western characters who went into the circus business, I've read of a single horseman holding a bunch of buffalo stock-still by riding around and around them for hours and shooting as he rode. That was an impossibility. Two minutes after the horseman started his riding and shooting, there would not have been a buffalo within rifle range. Buffalo would stampede instantly at the sight or smell of a man on horseback; they would ignore a man on foot, or eye him in curiosity. That was why hide hunters shoot from a stand.

Wyatt goes on to recount the methods of current hunters. "A Hunter would drag his Sharps to a rise of ground giving a good view of the herd, pick a bunch of animals, set his rest-sticks[2] and start shooting. He aimed to hit an animal on the edge of the bunch, the leader if possible, just back of the foreleg and about one third of the way up the body. If the slug went true, the animal would drop in his tracks or stagger a few steps and fall. Strangely enough, the buffalo paid no attention to the report of the rifle and very little, if any, to one that fell.

"A first-class hunter would kill with almost every shot, and if he was good, he could drop game until some buffalo still on his feet chanced to sniff closely at one that had fallen. Then it was up to the hunter to drop the sniffer before he could spread his excitement over the smell of blood. If he could do this, the slaughter might continue, but eventually the blood scent became so strong that several animals noticed it. They would bellow and paw, their frenzy would spread to the bunches nearby, and suddenly the whole herd was off on a wild run. The hunter could kill no more until he found conditions suitable for another stand.

1. ————————————————

[2]A shooting rest was two sticks tied together, X-fashion, set in the ground to support the rifle while the marksman aimed and fired.

"Where large parties of hunters were working the plains by such methods in fairly close quarters, the periodical scarcity of buffalo was a certainty. With the best of luck, a single hunter might kill one hundred buffalo in a day, from several stands. That would be all that four skinners could handle. I found that the average bunch would stampede by the time thirty or forty had been killed. Only the best of hunters could average 50 kills a day, thirty to forty was more common.

Wyatt Earp's Buffalo Hunting Method

The first flaw which Wyatt Earp saw was that the average hunter outfitted in expectation of killing one hundred buffalo a day, and selling each animal's hide and meat for two to five dollars, depending upon size and quality. In place of five wagons and twenty-odd horses, Wyatt purchased one wagon, four sound animals for harness and one to ride. He engaged an experienced skinner in a straight profit-sharing scheme. Wyatt was to finance the hunt; the skinner would drive and cook; and, greatly to the disgust of older hands, Wyatt was to assist in skinning and butchering. At the end of the hunt, Wyatt was to keep the team and wagon, deduct all other expenses from the gross receipts, and share any net equally with his skinner.

In contrast to the use of the Sharps rifle, Wyatt killed buffalo with a shotgun. Wyatt was well acquainted with the buffalo's idiosyncrasy of stampeding at the sight or scent of a man on horseback, but generally ignoring one on foot. He intended to make use of this in reaching shotgun range of the herds. He purchased a breech-loading gun, with apparatus for reloading shells, and this, with a supply of powder, lead, and caps, was to constitute his hunting arsenal. He loaded a single one-and-one-half-ounce slug to the shell. He knew that at any range under one hundred yards he could score as accurately with his shotgun as any rifleman.

Wyatt described his approach: "My system for hunting buffalo was to work my way on foot nearer to the herds than the rifle users like to locate. The shorter range of my shotgun made this necessary, but I could fire the piece as rapidly as I wished without harming it. I planned to get within fifty yards of the buffalo before I started shooting, and at that range pick off selected animals. I would shoot until I had downed all the skinner and I could handle that day. I figured to offset the danger of a stampede by finishing my kill before the animals smelled blood and then working the herd away quietly in the direction I wanted it to go. To do this, I would stand up, wave my coat in the air, and shout. The buffalo would probably move away quietly if I got them started before they scented blood. Then the skinner and I would get to work. In practice, my idea worked out exactly as I had calculated it would.

"Some people called my method foolhardy. To me, it was simply a question of whether or not I could outguess a buffalo. The best answer is that there never was a moment during my three seasons as a buffalo hunter when I was in danger from a stampede, nor a day when I hunted that I did not have a profitable kill. My lowest score for a single stand was eighteen buffalo, the highest, twenty-seven. I shot one stand a day, which meant twenty to thirty-five dollars apiece for the skinner and myself every day we worked. That was cash in hand, not hopes.

"No wonder the average buffalo hunter was glad that the code forbade him to skin his kill; skinning was hard, dirty work. My skinner kept out of sight with the wagon until I had finished shooting. Then he came on the job. In skinning a buffalo, we slit down the inside of each leg and along the belly from neck to tail. The legs and a strip along each side of the belly-cut were skinned out and the neck skinned all the way around. The head skin was not taken. We gathered the heavy neck hide into a bunch around which we looped a short length of rope, and a horse hitched to the other end ripped the hide off. We did it every time this way.

"In camp, we dusted the hides and the ground nearby with poison to keep off flies and bugs, and pegged out the skins, flesh-side up. In the dry prairie air, first curing took but a day or so. The hides were then turned, and, after they had cured so water would not injure them, they were stacked in piles, hair-side up, until we hauled them to a hide buyer's station, or a buyer's wagon came to our camp.

Wyatt Earp - The Legend

The success of Wyatt Earp's venture against cherished customs became legend to the ranks of the buffalo hunters. Time after time on checking tallies, the lone hunter found that, while some had killed greater numbers than he from the given stands, or had larger seasonal totals, his daily count of hides was well above average. Rudimentary arithmetic proved that his profits were much higher.

Wyatt recounts the inevitable demise of the great buffalo herds: "With all the buffalo I saw in the days when they roamed the range, I shall never forget a herd we sighted in the fall of '71. We had seen a few small bunches, but none that I stopped for, as I wanted to make camp as permanent as possible. We had crossed the Medicine Lodge when the plenticity of buffalo sign indicated that we were closing on a sizable herd. I went to a rise possibly three hundred feet above the creek bottom. The sight that greeted me as I topped the hill soon disappeared for all time.

"I stood on the highest point within miles. To the west and south, the prairie rolled in mounds and level stretches pitted with buffalo wallow as far as I could see, twenty or thirty miles. For all that distance the range was packed with grazing buffalo.

"... I signaled my skinner to join me. 'My God!' he said, 'there must be a million.'

25

"It might give a better idea of the results of buffalo hunting to jump ahead seven years to 1878, when Bill Tilghman, Bat Masterson, and I went buffalo hunting for sport. We traveled due west from Dodge City more than one hundred miles along the Arkansas River, south to the Cimmarron, and east to Crooked Creek again, at the height of the best hunting season over what in 1871 had been the greatest buffalo ground in the world. Grass was as plentiful and as succulent as ever, but we never saw a buffalo. The herds were gone, wiped out."

Discussion Questions:

- Compare Wyatt's buffalo hunting to the approach used by the old timers?
- What are the key elements of business success from an operations perspective?
- Relate these ideas to Wyatt's approach.
- Were the buffalo hunters irresponsible in killing off the great buffalo herds as they did?

EXTRA CASE

Wyatt Earp – The Buffalo Hunter! - Labor Productivity, Operations Technology, Quality, Environmental Impact – Teaching Note

This useful case will not become dated. The goal with this case is to have students recognize what is needed to compete successfully in a business from an operations standpoint. The impact of labor productivity, operations technology, quality, and the environment, are stressed in the case discussion. Parallels can easily be drawn between the buffalo hunting business of the old West and business today. Students with virtually any background can quickly understand the buffalo-hunting situation. US students will be familiar with the Wyatt Earp character, and a surprising number of foreign students have viewed the original television series.

Case Discussion Questions:

- Compare Wyatt's buffalo hunting to the approach used by the old timers?
- What are the key elements of business success from an operations perspective?
- Relate these ideas to Wyatt's approach.
- Were the buffalo hunters irresponsible in killing off the great buffalo herds as they did?

Session Outline:

(First 10 minutes of the class)

You might start the class with a clip from <u>Tombstone</u>. The scene showing the shootout at the O.K. Coral is good. Others have used a clip from Kevin Costner's <u>Dancing with Wolves</u>.

(Next 5 minutes)

Following this, begin the class with the question: Who is this Wyatt Earp character? What is he best known for?

This should get the class going. Those not familiar with the legend will learn that Wyatt was an interesting character.

(Next 20 minutes)

Compare Wyatt's buffalo hunting approach to the approach used by the old timers?

Why was Wyatt's approach superior?

Cover all the details here:

Size of the hunting party. 6-7 persons verses 2.

Type of firearm: Sharps "Fifty" rifle verses shotgun.

Ammunition carried: The heavy bullets verse reloads for the shotgun shells.

Method of shooting: Long-range verses short range.

Control of the herd: Random, try to quickly shoot curious buffalo verses control the movement of the herd.

Job assignments: Very specific, no sharing of responsibility verses sharing of duties.

Daily kill goal: 100 buffalo, unreachable verses 25, which could be regularly accomplished.

Method of compensation: Hunter responsible for covering costs verses profit split after expenses.

(Next 20 minutes)

What are the keys to business success from an operations perspective?

Introduce the concepts of people, plants (the location), process, parts (ammunition, salt, food, etc.), plan. Further, stress the importance of low cost, high quality, and predictability of the process.

Relate these ideas to the details of Wyatt's approach.

Point out how Wyatt ensured quality with his approach. Recall the procedure used for skinning and field curing the buffalo. Show how this procedure guaranteed the quality of his skins.

In addition, students will realize that the basic ideas, which were important back in the days of Wyatt Earp, are still just as important.

(Last 10 minutes)

End the class with a discussion of environmental responsibility.

Were the buffalo hunters irresponsible in killing off the great buffalo herds as they did?

Teaching Points – Use to close the class (Important)

- Innovation
- Strategy
- Technology
- Quality
- Procedure/Repetition
- Social Responsibility
- Environmental Impact

Chapter 2 - Operations Strategy and Competitiveness

Overview

In recent years, the world has witnessed a revolution in manufacturing. In large part, this has occurred as companies have recognized the strategic importance of the operations management function. This recognition began with Wickham Skinner's 1969 article "Manufacturing-The Missing Link in Corporate Strategy." Strategic considerations in operations management include capacity planning, facility planning, technology planning, workforce development, quality planning, production planning and workplace organization. For an additional reading in the operations strategy area, a good beginning is *Manufacturing Strategy* by Terry Hill (published by Irwin/McGraw-Hill). Using the Hill approach, companies identify order-winning criteria in an effort to obtain alignment between marketing and operations strategies. The text chapter also provides a discussion of the four stages of service firm competitiveness. This underlies the belief that operations management in service firms will become of greater strategic importance.

Major Points of the Chapter

1. Harvard University researchers performed much of the early work in operations strategy: Skinner, Abernathy, Hayes, Clark and Wheelright.
2. Quality has been an essential competitive variable for many firms; first as an order winner, and now as an order qualifier.
3. Strategic Fit – this is making all the activities that make up a firm's operations fit the strategy being followed by a company. An activity map, as shown in Exhibit 2.1 is useful for depicting this.
4. Some good examples of how Wal-Mart has become the dominant discounter in the United States are given.
5. The United States economy cannot support itself solely on its service industry. Strong service *and* manufacturing industries are needed.
6. Services operations strategy is the final strategic frontier. It is interesting to note that General Motor's largest supplier is Blue Cross/Blue Shield.
7. Various measures of productivity are developed at the end of the chapter.

Teaching Tips

An interesting exercise is to debate the concept of factory focus. While Skinner felt that manufacturers should adopt a focused approach (hence the advent of "Skinner walls" and "plants within plants"), others are now arguing that firms can simultaneously achieve different strategic objectives such as quality, speed, and low cost. The question is then asked: Where does organizational learning fit into this discussion?

Many have found "The Great Nuclear Fizzle at Old B&W" to be a great case to use to introduce this topic. The case is included in *Manufacturing Strategy – Text and Cases*, T. J. Hill (Irwin/McGraw-Hill), 1997.

For a more modern comparison of two businesses that compete in the same industry, the case "Compaq Computer versus Dell Computer – Business Model Comparison" has been included in the book. Since the strategies being employed by these two companies is continually changing, this is given as an Internet exercise. The case should generate some good discussion.

Cases, Exercises and Spreadsheets (Source)

"Compaq Computer versus Dell Computer – Business Model Comparison" (Book)

"Los Angeles Toy Company" (Book)

Productivity_Measures.xls (CD-ROM)

"Great Nuclear Fizzle at Old B&W" (Hill)

"American Connector Co (A) (HBS 9-693-035)

"McDonald's Corp" (HBS 9-693-028)

Videos/Clips (Source)

"Lean Production" (Vol. I)

"Improving Operations Methods" (Vol. II)

"Reengineering at Caterpillar" (Vol. III)

"Value Driven Production at Trek" (Vol. IV)

"Valuation of Operations at ABCco" (Vol. VI)

"Lean Production/Flexibility)" (CD-ROM)

"Operations Strategy and Goals" (CD-ROM)

"Value" (CD-ROM)

"Focus Factory" (CD-ROM)

CASE

Compaq Computer versus Dell Computer – Business Model Comparison – Teaching Note

Probably the best way to approach this is to just go to the two company's web sites and observe differences between these companies. Clearly, Dell has a much stronger focus than Compaq. Compaq's major acquisition of Digital has given it a strong capability in the high-end server computer market. This augments the desktop computer segment that Compaq has been the industry leader in for years. Some might argue that trying to serve both markets is difficult.

It is difficult to answers the discussion questions, since the answers may change over the next three years. The following are some thoughts on what to expect when looking at current data:

1. Compare the two companies based on the major operations priorities: cost, product quality, deliver speed, delivery reliability, coping with changes in demand, flexibility, and new product introduction speed.

Here the big thing to consider in how different the high-end server market that Compaq serves is different from the personal computer market. The personal computer market is dominated by price, whereas product quality (features such as product reliability and speed) may be more important in the high-end server market.

2. What are the operations competitive advantages of Compaq compared to Dell?

Dell has the big advantage with the direct linking of the order taking website with their assembly process. Further, Dell's focus on personal computers gives them a big advantage in inventory management.

3. Compare the annual financial statements of Compaq and Dell? The most current statements are available from the web sites of these companies. From an operations standpoint (i.e. look at cost-of-sales data), which company seems to be stronger? Why?

Dell's inventory turn is 50 turns per year, whereas Compaq runs about 14 turns per year.

4. Which company do you think is best positioned to be successful in the first five years of the 21st century? Why do you feel this way?

This is a very, very open ended question. Dell is strong financially due to the amazing focus on personal computers and the "direct" delivery approach. Compaq has a strong product lineup for corporate buyers and can offer a better "full service" capability to corporate customers. These are both strong business models for being successful in the future.

CASE

Los Angeles Toy Company – Teaching Note

How consistent is the Jay Leno doll order with the current capabilities and focus of LATC?

There is a significant amount of inconsistency between current capabilities and requirements to produce the Jay Leno doll. There is a mismatch between the current workbench based, specialized assembly and the need for high volume production. Absent the synthesizer, the assembly is similar to doll and puppet assembly that has traditionally been performed.

Should LATC (a) manufacture the doll itself, (b) subcontract the work to a Tijuana, Mexico manufacturing plant that specializes in high-volume production (at a cost of $8 per doll to LATC-, or (c) look for another product more in line with its capabilities?

The agency that holds the license to Jay Leno products wants a decision right away, as does the Mexican supplier.

The advantages of LATC producing the doll are:

Assuming a conservative wholesale price of $14/doll, the contribution to the company would be 50,000 × $7, or $350,000.

The company will have to expand its production capability at some point if it is to compete in a wider toy market, and this product seems to be a good one to start out with to make the big leap.

The advantages of subcontracting to Mexico are that they make almost as much money without the production headaches. They, of course, still bear the risk of the product not being purchased at anywhere near the $14 wholesale price, or of it not being of good enough quality that the retailers will want to buy it.

Perhaps the most desirable alternative is to subcontract and go after a product more in line with their capabilities. The downside is that the subcontractor may not deliver a good product, and hence LATC would have a loser in its product line, and/or there is simply no other toy that calls for castle and puppet making expertise.

Technical Note 2 – Learning Curves

Overview

This technical note describes the concept of learning curves and how to estimate them. Guidelines for when learning curves should be applied are also given. The concepts of individual and organization learning are covered. Organization unlearning is also briefly discussed.

Major Points of the technical note

1. Future performance can be predicted when some observations are collected and subjected to learning curve analysis.

2. Learning rates differ within the same group (e.g., people) as well as across groups (e.g., between people and material).

Teaching Tips

None

Cases, Exercises and Spreadsheets (Source)

"Analog Devices, Inc.: The Half-Life System" (HBS 9-190-061)

"Eli Lilly and Co.: Manufacturing Process Technology Strategy – 1991" (HBS 9-692-056)

Chapter 3 - Project Management

Overview

Project management skills are needed in today's working environment. Workers find themselves increasingly involved in a variety of simultaneous projects. After discussing project management and how it differs from traditional management, in purpose, structure and operation, this chapter deals with critical path methods in three contexts-time-based models, time/cost models, and limited resource models. Under time-based models, we discuss classical PERT and one of the standard approaches to CPM. There is a discussion and example of time/cost trade-off using CPM network and a brief discussion of PERT/cost. Under limited resources, we consider the similar though distinct problems of workforce leveling and resource allocation.

Major Points of the Chapter

1. Virtually every major organization has numerous projects underway at all times.

2. Project management organization and procedures are still not used fully.

3. The work breakdown structure should display a logical division and hierarchy of the elements of a project.

4. Three alternative project organizations are pure project, functional, and matrix.

5. The matrix organizational form offers advantages of functional division while maintaining benefits of project responsibility.

6. Critical path scheduling focuses attention on those activities in a project network that are the most critical in completing a project on time.

Teaching Tip

Have your students use the Primavera Sure Trak program on the Student CD, Website-ROM to solve the Campus Wedding Case. This program is fully functional. The only restriction is the number of tasks that can be in the project network. This limit is set at 25 for the version on the Student CD, Website-ROM. The Campus Wedding Case is a sure winner.

Cases, Exercises and Spreadsheets (Source)

"The Campus Wedding" (Book)

Project Management at CPAone" (Book)

"Boeing 767: From Concept to Production (A)" (HBS 9-688-040)

Project_Management.xls (Spreadsheet on CD-ROM)

Primavera SureTrak (CD-ROM)

Videos/Clips (Source)

"Return of the Jedi" – Opening scene –Vader: "I'm here to put you back on schedule" (Video Store)[3]

"Project Management Building the Alton "Super Bridge"" (Vol. VI)

1. ———————————

[3] Thanks to Dwight Smith-Daniels for this idea.

CASE

The Campus Wedding Case – Teaching Note

We need to offer special thanks to Clay Whybark for permission to publish this case. Students seem to be able to identify with this case easily. This is a great session. You can play off your experts in class (those that are married and the women), and have some fun trying to decide just how the activities leading up to the wedding need to be done. The easiest way to run the class is just to follow the discussion questions. Students should be encouraged to use the Sure Trak project management software to solve the case. Using the software will take a little more time, than analyzing the case manually, but they will get a good idea of how commercial software to support project management works.

The "A" case

1. Given the activities and precedence relationships described in the (A) case, develop a network diagram for the wedding plans.

The following table contains the activities, expected activity times, and crashing information.

Activity	Duration (days)	Predecessor Activities	Crash Cost	Crash Time
1. Reserve Church	1			
2. Church Notice Wait	17	1. Reserve Church	$100	10
3. Decorate Church	3	2. Church Notice Wait		
4. Travel from Guatemala	10		$500	2
5. Fit Dress	2	4. Travel from Guatemala 11. Sew Dress		
6. Choose Cake	2			
7. Jack's Catering Lead Time	10	6. Choose Cake		
8. Rehearsal Dinner	1	7. Jack's Catering Lead Time 18. Get Bridesmaids Gifts		
9. Order and Receive Lace	8	10. Choose Pattern	$25	5
10. Choose Pattern	3			
11. Sew Dress	11	9. Order and Receive Lace	$120/day	Can be crashed 5 days.
12. Clean and Press Dresses	2	5. Fit Dress	$30	1
13. Order and Receive Invitations	12	14. Choose Invitations	$35	5

Activity	Duration (days)	Predecessor Activities	Crash Cost	Crash Time
14. Choose Invitations	3			
15. Invitation Lead Time	10	16. Take to Post Office	$200	8
16. Take to Post Office	1	17. Address Invitations		
17. Address Invitations	4	13. Order and Receive Invitations 19. Prepare Guest List	$25/day	Can be crashed 2 days.
18. Get Bridesmaids Gift	1			
19. Prepare Guest List	4			
20. Wedding	1	3. Decorate Church 8. Rehearsal Dinner 12. Clean and Press Dresses 15. Invitation Lead Time		

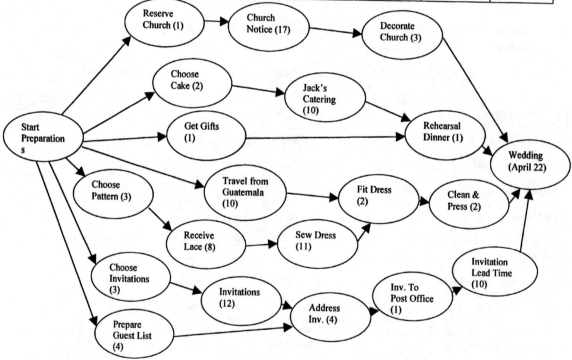

2. Identify the paths, which are critical.

There are 7 paths through the network. The paths and their length are as follows:

PATH 1: Reserve Church (1) – Church Notice (17) – Decorate Church (3) – Wedding (1) -- length 22 days.

PATH 2: Choose Cake (2) – Jack's Catering (10) – Rehearsal Dinner (1) – Wedding (1) – length 14 days.

PATH 3: Get Gifts (1) – Rehearsal Dinner (1) – Wedding (1) – length 3 days.

PATH 4: Travel from Guatemala (10) – Fit Dress (2) – Clean & Press (2) – Wedding (1) -- length 15 days.

PATH 5: Choose Pattern (3) – Receive Lace (8) – Sew Dress (11) – Fit Dress (2) – Clean & Press (2) – Wedding (1) –length 27 days.

PATH 6: Choose Invitations (3) – Receive Invitations (12) – Address Invitations (4) – Inv. To Post Office (1) – Invitation Lead Time (10) – Wedding (1) – length 31 days.

PATH 7: Prepare Guest List (4) – Address Invitations (4) – Inv. To Past Office (1) – Invitation Lead Time (10) – Wedding (1) – length 20 days.

Some assumptions are in order: (1) we assume that we can start tomorrow (April 1), (2) everyone works 7 days a week.

Path 1, 5 and 6 are all critical. Path 5 and 6 will have to be crashed to meet the wedding date of April 22.

3. What is the minimum cost plan that meets the April 22 date?

For path 6, we would reduce the time to Receive the Invitations (13) to 5 days (cost $35) and hire help to Address Invitations (17) to reduce this time to 2 days (cost $50). This would reduce the path length to exactly 22 days at a cost of $85.

For path 5, we would reduce the time to Receive Lace (9) to 5 days (cost $25), reduce Clean & Press (12) to 1 day (cost $30), and hire Mrs. Watson 1 day to reduce Sew Dress (11) to 10 (cost $120) days. This would reduce the path length to exactly 22 days at a cost of $175.

The minimum cost to have the wedding on April 22 is $260.

A lively discussion can be had concerning whether you would really want to implement the minimum cost plan.

The following is output from Primavera Sure Trak.

Description	Rem Dur	Gantt Chart
Prepare for Wedding	**31**	
Reserve Church	1	Mary
Church Notice Wait	17	
Decorate Church	3	Mary, Mother
Get Bridesmaids Gifts	1	Mary
Choose Cake	2	Mary, Mother
Jack's Catering Lead Time	10	Jack's C
Rehearsal Dinner	1	Fath
Travel From Guatemala	10	Jane
Choose Pattern	3	Mary, Mother
Order and Receive Lace	8	
Sew Dress	11	Mother
Fit Dress	2	Mother
Clean and Press Dresses	2	
Choose Invitations	3	Mary, Mother
Order and Receive Invitations	12	
Prepare Guest List	4	Mother
Address Invitations	4	Mary, Mother
Take Invitations to Post Office	1	Mary
Invitation Lead Time	10	
Wedding	1	

Legend: Early bar, Progress bar, Critical bar, Summary bar, Progress point, Critical point, Summary point, Start milestone point

The Campus Wedding (B) – Teaching Note

1. Given your answers to the (A) case, describe the effects on the wedding plans of each incident noted in the (B) case.

1. *On April 2 the Chairman of the Vestry Committee at the church was left unimpressed by the added donation and said he wouldn't reduce the notice period from 17 to days.*

This is not a problem, since that path would not delay the wedding.

2. *A call to Guatemala revealed that the potential bridesmaid had several commitments and could not possibly leave the country until April 10.*

This creates a major problem. She will have to fly up at an additional cost of $500.

3. *Mother comes down with the four-day flu just as she started on the guest list.*

This is not a problem, since you have to wait on the invitation anyway.

4. *The lace and dress materials are lost in transit. Notice of the loss was delivered to the Jackson home early on April 10.*

This is the showstopper! There is no way to order the lace and to get it in time to sew and fit the dresses. One thing they can do is to purchase the material locally. Someone in the class should come up with this idea.

5. *There was a small fire at the caterer's shop on April 8. It was estimated that the shop would be closed two or three days for repairs.*

This should not create a problem.

CASE

CPAOne – Teaching Note

The accounting students in your class will like this assignment.

1. What are the major milestones associated with this project? What additional information would you need to develop a PERT chart?

Assigning the project to a partner is the official start of a project. The first milestone is to decide whether or not to refuse to do the audit. The next milestone, if the partner decides to pursue the audit, is to complete the proposal. The next milestone is when the client accepts or rejects the project. The final milestone is when the project is completed.

To develop a PERT chart for the project, each task must be clearly identified together with the person responsible. Each task would have time estimates associated with its completion. Many of the tasks can be done simultaneously in this type of project, so the more people that can be assigned to the project, the quicker that it can be completed.

2. What are the project director's managerial responsibilities?

The project director is responsible for writing the proposal, defining the project tasks, and estimating the time to complete each task. During the project, the project director must review progress on the project on a regular basis, and work with the project team and the client to resolve problems when they occur. After completion of the project, the project director is responsible for any follow up work that might be required, such as meeting with the IRS if needed.

Chapter 4 – Process Analysis

Overview

This chapter has been designed to help students analyze a business process. Many may find this chapter useful when used Harvard process analysis cases such as Benihana, Cranberry Cooperative, Donner and others. The goal is for students to learn basic process flowcharting and process analysis. Examples are used that the students may be familiar with such as a casino slot machine, bread-making, a restaurant, and a transit bus operation.

Major Points of the Chapter

1. Definition of what a process is and basic process measures such as cycle time and utilization.

2. An introduction to process flowcharting with some familiar "fast food" restaurant examples.

3. Concepts such as buffering, blocking, starving and bottlenecks are introduced.

4. Make-to-order verses make-to-stock are defined.

5. The relationship between common process measures is shown.

6. Little's Law is defined.

7. Three common examples are developed: Bread-making, restaurant, and transit bus operation.

8. Ideas for how process throughput time can be reduced are discussed.

Teaching Tip

This chapter is probably best assigned as a reading together with a case. Some of the Harvard cases mentioned above are good for process analysis. The case in the book titled "Analyzing Casino Money-Handling Processes" can also be used.

The problems given in the chapter are good for assignment as a problem set that can be turned in for grading. The problems are challenging and vary enough so that if the student completes them, he/she should be able to analyze most cases. The "Advanced Problem" can be given as extra credit as it takes some time to analyze.

Cases, Exercises and Spreadsheets (Source)

Bottleneck_Simulation.xls (Spreadsheet on CD-ROM)

Java_Slot_Machine (This game is on the CD-ROM)

Videos/Clips (Source)

"Flow Charting" (CD-ROM)

"The Manufacturing Process" (Vol. I)

"Reengineering at Caterpillar" (Vol. III)

"Product Design & Manufacturing at TriState Industries (Vol. VI)

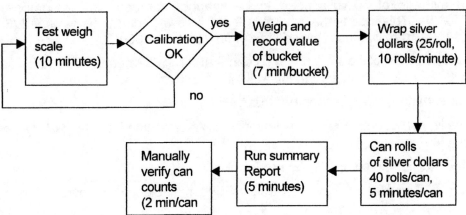

CASE

Analyzing Casino Honey-Handling Processes – Teaching Note

Case Questions:

1. Draw a diagram of the drop process. How long should it take to empty 300 silver dollar slot machines?

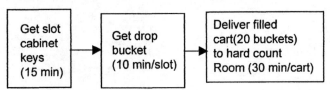

Getting the slot cabinet keys only needs to be done one time and takes 15 minutes.

Getting the drop buckets will take 3,000 minutes (300 x 10).

To empty 300 slot machines, 15 carts need to be delivered (300/20), and delivering the 15 carts will take 450 minutes (15 x 30).

Total time to complete the process will be 15 + 3,000 + 450 = 3,465 minutes.

This 57 ¾ hours of work.

This assumes that only 1 team is doing the work.

2. Draw a diagram of the hard count process. How long should this process take to complete for 300 silver dollar slot machines? Assume that each slot machine has an average of 750 silver dollars when it is emptied.

Let's assume that the weigh scale test is ok. This will take 10 minutes.

To weigh and record 300 buckets takes 2,100 minutes (300 x 7).

47

An average of 30 rolls need to be wrapped for each bucket processed (750/25). This means that a total of 9,000 rolls will need to be wrapped (30 x 300). At 10 rolls/minute this will take 900 minutes (9,000/10).

Rolls are then placed in cans. To can 9,000 rolls 225 cans need to be filled (9000/40). At 5 minutes/can this will take 1,125 minutes.

The summary report is then run that takes 5 minutes.

Finally, can counts are manually verified. At 2 minutes/can this will take 450 minutes.

The total time to complete the process is

$10 + 2,100 + 900 + 1,125 + 5 + 450 = 4,500$ minutes or 76.5 hours.

3. The casino is considering the purchase of a second coin-wrapping machine. What impact would this have on the hard count process? Is this the most desirable machine to purchase?

Actually, the slowest process that involves a machine is the weighing process. The company should look into a second scale.

Technical Note 4 - Job Design and Work Measurement

Overview

This technical note discusses many of the current trends in job design. Some of these trends include implementing quality control in jobs, cross-training workers, employee involvement, team involvement in work, information technology's impact on work, use of temporary workers, automation of heavy manual work and increased emphasis on job satisfaction. These trends place pressure on management to pay close attention to job enrichment, worker interaction with machinery, and interaction with co-workers. The chapter points out that many companies such as UPS, NUMMI, and Lincoln Electric have benefited as a result of skilled use of standards. Many students are generally opposed to using work measurement standards. However, the discussion in the second teaching tip below actually demonstrates that students often prefer standards.

Major Points of the Chapter

1. Work standards are the foundation of capacity and production planning.

2. Work measurement techniques, particularly flow diagrams and work sampling, are widely used in services as well as manufacturing.

3. Standard hour plans are the most common type of wage incentive plans; profit sharing plans are growing in importance.

Teaching Tips

Tip 1

Get a pegboard and select teams of three men and three women to fill the board as fast as they can. The women's team generally wins unless the men use the principles of motion economy. This keys off discussion methods, timing, job design, and learning curves.

Make sure you practice before going to class since students will surely coax you into doing it also. Play defensive – "I can't do that," "Haven't done it in years," etc.

Tip 2

Bait the students by asking the, "How many of you would like to work in a work measurement environment?" No one will respond in the affirmative. Next, offer them two scenarios:
1. "I come in the first day of class and offer you no syllabus, no scoring scheme and promise to give each student the grade I feel he/she

deserves at semester's end based on how I feel. There might or might not be a test and possible tests might or might not be scored."
2.   "On the Fist day of class I offer you a syllabus outlining the tests, papers and requirements for the class. In the end, you will be graded based on a percentage of these objective requirements."

90% of the class will typically prefer option 2. Then say rhetorically, "I thought you didn't like work measurement!" Discuss.

Cases, Exercises and Spreadsheets (Source)

"Teamwork at Volvo" (Book)

"Jeans Therapy – Levi's Factory Workers Are Assigned to Teams, and Morale Takes a Hit" (Book)

"Fabritek Corp." (HBS 9-669-004)

"Measure of Delight: The Pursuit of Quality at AT&T Universal Card Services (A)" (HBS 9-694-047)

Videos/Clips (Source)

"Incentive Pay" (CD-ROM)

"The Original Tapes of Frank and Lillian Gilbreth" (Library)

"I'm Alright, Jack" – Scene showing employee reaction to time study that requires it be done with binoculars (Video Store)[4]

1. ————————————

[4] Thanks to Dwight Smith-Daniels for this idea.

CASE

Teamwork at Volvo –Teaching Note

1.   What is the difference between teams at the Kalmar plant and self-managed teams at Uddevalla?

The Kalmar plant is much older with more experienced workers. The Volvo approach appears to be learning dependent. Given this orientation, it will take the Uddevalla workers much longer to achieve the performance level of the Kalmar plant.

2.   How important is empowerment in Volvo's Uddevalla facility?

Empowerment is important as the Uddevalla plant uses the "stall built" system with teams. The teams set break times, vacations and schedules. This provides a fertile framework for learning based improvement to occur. Empowerment is central to this philosophy of manufacturing.

3.   Why do you think there is resistance to the team approach at Uddevalla? How can Volvo overcome this resistance?

Although the case doesn't describe much resistance to the changes, some workers resist empowerment because of lack of trust of management. Other employees resent being given additional responsibility without additional pay. Management's job is to then engender trust and build pride of workmanship. It sounds like Volvo is doing this.

4.   The Uddevalla plan was closed in 1996. Why was it never able to produce cars as inexpensively as the Ghent plant? (Hint: remember that Uddevalla is in Sweden and Ghent is in Belgium.)

Answers will vary. Much depends on the learning rates at the two plants. The potential for rapid improvement should have been great for Uddevalla than for Kalmar due to the newness of the effort. Volvo found that they had more capacity in Europe than they needed and had to close one of the plants. The Kalmar plant was much larger and had a much lower labor cost, therefore it was kept open.

CASE

Jeans Therapy – Levi's Factory Workers Are Assigned to Teams, and Morale Takes a Hit – Teaching Note

1. What went wrong with Levi's move to teams in their plants?

Employees were used to a culture that encouraged individual productivity and this was well supported by the old piece rate system. The move to the new group incentive system was probably not well implemented by the company. It's interesting that the main motivation for the change was the safety problems caused by repetitive-stress injuries. The company felt that by sharing tasks workers could do different tasks thus reducing the incidence of this type of injury. The more productive workers were not able to make as much money under the group structure, thus creating many problems.

2. What could Levi's have done differently to avert the problems?

This may have been a good time to actually reengineer the processes. It the problem was really repetitive-stress injuries, then an effort should have been made to redesign these processes to eliminate the movement that cased the injuries. Redesigned processes that better supported group work may have been a better approach. This should have probably been more of an engineering effort, rather than something that employees were "empowered" to do. The workers could have been used to "fine tune" the new processes after they had been developed and implemented in new work cells.

3. Devise a team incentive plan that you think might work.

The incentive plan should have been based on the number of jeans produced, but worker skill levels should have been considered as part of the formula. Those workers that have better skills (i.e. can do more job and produce fewer defects) should be paid at higher pay rate levels.

4. Do you think the need to move jeans production offshore was inevitable? Could Levi's have done anything to avert the problem of increasing labor costs?

It probably was inevitable that production would have to move offshore. Some type of clear strategy that related to sourcing the "high end" versus "low end" jeans may have been developed. Also, all kinds of "Made-in-America" marketing schemes may have been possible. Probably, some effort should have been put into automation as a way to reduce the labor content of the work. It would be interesting to see if computer made jeans might be possible. If anyone could have justified the development of the technology, Levi's would be the company.

Chapter 5 - Product Design and Process Selection-Manufacturing

Overview

Companies such as Honda have successfully competed through skillful application of the concepts in this chapter. In recent years, product development has changed in important ways as the customer has been made part of the design process. End products are being designed with manufacturability in mind. Another important concept has been the adoption of "design teams" and "concurrent engineering." This chapter also introduces the popular Quality Function Deployment topic. With the team approach, process engineers, product design engineers, marketers, customers, suppliers and other stakeholders are involved simultaneously to design products. Tom Peters tells of Ingersoll Rand Corporation's reduction in speed of concept to market from 4 years to 1 year for a hand grinder. This chapter also emphasizes the importance of process flow analysis in improving production processes.

Major Points of the Chapter

- Speed of "concept to market", is an important competitive variable for today's manufacturer. Concurrent engineering is used to speed the product design process.

- Product design is moving away from "designing for engineers" to "designing for customers."

- Quality Function Deployment is an important method for getting the voice of the customer into product design specifications.

- Designing a product that will be easy to manufacture or assemble reduces the overall cost of the product.

- The design and analysis of manufacturing systems starts with mapping the flow of materials and describing operations.

- Manufacturing management includes coordination of support groups as well as supervision of direct production activities.

- Four types of processes used in manufacturing include job shop, batch, assembly line, and continuous flow.

- The globalization of product markets presents unique challenges to manufacturing companies today.

Teaching Tip

Take small items such as some ballpoint pens to class. Toss them to different people in the room. Then ask the questions.

What do you have to know to make these?

What do you have to know to make them *at a profit?*

This starts the class thinking about the myriad of things one needs to know (and will find out about) in POM.

Cases, Exercises and Spreadsheets (Source)

"The Best Engineered Part is No Part" (Book)

"Paper Clips" (IRM)

"BMW: The 7-Series Project (A) (HBS 9-692-083)

"Quantum Corp.: Business and Product Teams" (HBS 9-692-023)

Videos/Clips (Source)

"Reengineering at Caterpillar" (Vol. III)

"The Manufacturing Process" (Vol. I)

"Washburn Guitars" (Vol. III)

"Quality Product & Process Design at Detroit Diesel" (Vol. IV)

"Production Tour of the Vision Light System at Federal Signal" (Vol. IV)

"Product Design & Manufacturing at TriState Industries" (Vol. VI)

"Product/Process Matrix" (CD-ROM)

"Assembly Line Process" (CD-ROM)

"Batch Process" (CD-ROM)

"Continuous Process" (CD-ROM)

"Job-Shop Process" (CD-ROM)

"Manufacturing Flexibility" (CD-ROM)

"Creating Customer Value" (CD-ROM)

"Quality Function Deployment" (CD-ROM)

CASE

The Best-Engineered Part is No Part – Teaching Note

1. What development problem has the NCR approach overcome?

NCR has achieved or overcome the following:

- Less components
- Less suppliers
- Less assembly time
- Eliminating screws & fasteners
- Faster speed of concept to market
- Lower cost
- Better on-time delivery
- No "over the wall" syndrome

Extra Case

PAPER CLIPS - Those Useful Little Things[5]
F. Robert Jacobs, Indiana University

One of the most useful problematic things to deal with when you're trying to keep pieces of paper together, is how this is to be done. Paper, by its very nature is not adhesive, and requires something more to allow it to remain in a group.

Many solutions have actually been tried, some of which involve different types of chemical or water-based adhesive, called "glue", and others which attempt to place the corners of the paper into a position where they cannot possibly move on their own. The most permanent method involves binding the paper together by making holes in it and threading string through the holes.

In between, there are various methods that touch on both sides, and vary from being more and less effective.

The most popular method is the "paper clip", which is basically a small curved length of metal shaped into a clip. This is always a temporary arrangement, however, as the paper clip is not quite strong enough to hold paper together against all the elements. Also, it is certainly not strong enough to hold something together without getting caught on something else entirely, and going off on its own merry way, at some point very early into its task.

Another major disadvantage of paper clips is thickness of what can be bound. The amount of paper that you can actually place inside a paper-clip and expect to leave in there is not very great at all. In fact, a few sheets are about it, before the clip starts to bend, or in extreme cases, snap.

In fact, paper clips only serve two real purposes in the modern world. The first is that of a lock-pick in spy films, and the second, which may have its roots in the first, is something that somebody can pick apart and unravel when they have nothing else to do.

THE GEM PAPER CLIP

For whatever reason, the most successful paper clip design, and the one that has become virtually synonymous with "paper clip," was never patented. Indeed, the concept of what has come to be known as the Gem clip clearly existed in the late nineteenth century because a patent was issued to William Middlebrook, of Waterbury, Connecticut, for a machine for *making* paper clips.

1. ────────────

[5] A historical account of the paper clip is given by Henry Petroski in <u>Invention by Design: How Engineers Get from Thought to Thing</u>, Harvard University Press, 1996, pp. 8-42.

Middlebrook's 1899 patent incidentally shows that the Norwegian Johan Vaaler, who is normally credited with its invention, is not correct (the Vaaler patent was filed in 1901). While Vaaler and other turn-of-the-century inventors were in fact patenting all manner of shapes and sizes of paper clips, Middlebrook was patenting the means for forming the Gem clip economically. There could be many shapes of clip that can hold a pile of papers just about as well as, if not better than, a Gem, but the ability to manufacture the clips reliably and in large quantities is what would make or break a company.

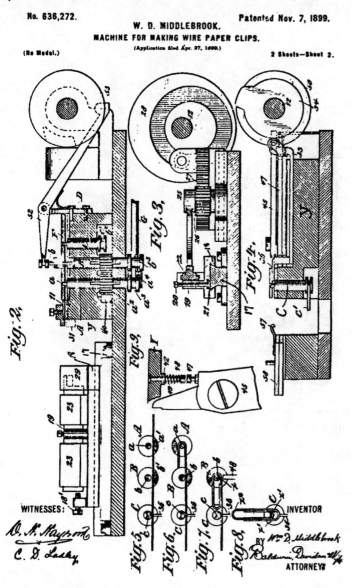

No. 636,272.

W. D. MIDDLEBROOK.

MACHINE FOR MAKING WIRE PAPER CLIPS.

Patented Nov. 7, 1899.

(Application filed Apr. 27, 1899.)

(No Model.)

2 Sheets—Sheet 2.

Middlebrook's Machine for making paper clips (1899).

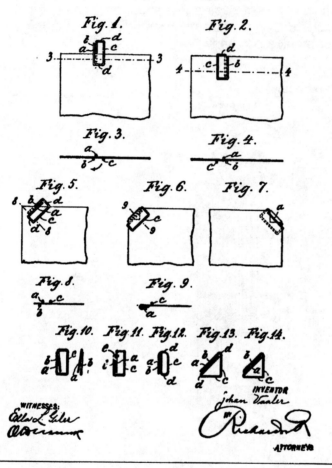

Johan Vaaler's paper clip patent (1901).

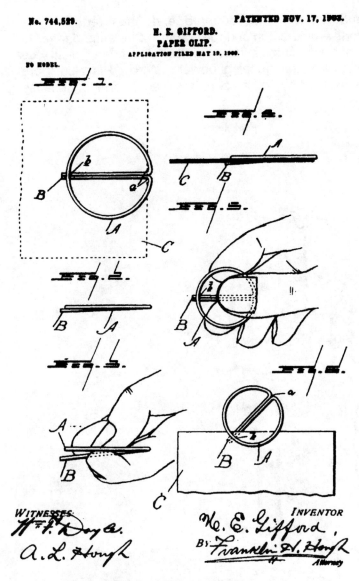

No. 744,529.

PATENTED NOV. 17, 1903.

H. E. GIFFORD.
PAPER CLIP.
APPLICATION FILED MAY 19, 1900.

NO MODEL.

An "improved" design by Gifford (1903).

IMPROVEMENTS IN PAPER CLIPS

Inventors are always looking for things to improve, and for about a century the Gem has been the main target of criticism in patents for new and improved paper clips. For example, one clear challenge to the Gem was patented in 1934 and has come to be known as the Gothic clip, because its loops are pointed more to resemble Gothic arches than the rounded Romanesque ones of the Gem. Henry Lankenau's patent application for the "perfect Gem" also listed ease of applying to papers as one of the invention's advantages. More importantly, the Gothic clip has longer legs that extend almost to its squared end, thus reducing the possibility that their sharp ends would catch and tear paper. Since the danger of tearing papers or the pages of books is minimized with this clip, it can typically be made of heavier wire to give it better gripping power. While it is also more expensive, the Gothic clip is favored by some users, such as librarians, because of its distinct advantages.

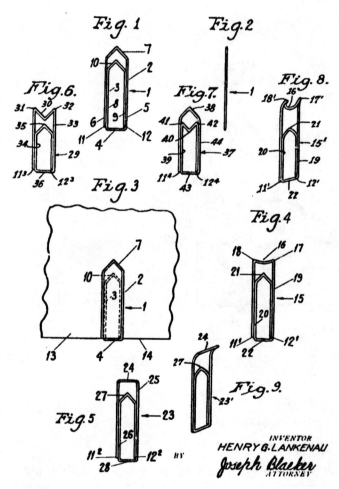

Dec. 25, 1934.   H. G. LANKENAU   1,985,866
                                    PAPER CLIP
                              Filed Nov. 23, 1933

INVENTOR
HENRY G. LANKENAU
Joseph Blacker
ATTORNEY

Lankenau's Gothic clip design.

There are other ways to improve the paper clip, and among the most often tried is economizing on raw materials, a common object of engineering design and manufacturing. After the capital investment that goes into the machinery to make paper clips, the wire that is used is the single most controllable factor in determining cost and hence price. Starting with a piece of wire just ten percent shorter than what the competition uses to fashion its Gems can translate into an advantage in the office products catalog, especially if saving pennies on every box of paper clips is more important than how the clips look to a supply manager who orders them by the millions.

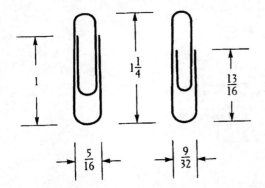

The standard Gem clip and a recent "economical" imitation.

DESIGNING A BETTER PAPER CLIP

A favorite pastime of some office workers is to doodle in wire by reshaping paper clips into all sorts of fanciful, and sometimes grotesque, new forms. Try your hand at deconstructing a Gem and designing a new paper clip.

How is your design an improvement on the Gem? List as many features as possible and evaluate your design against the Gem.

Does it have any less desirable qualities, such as reduced gripping power? Inventors often claim their improved designs for paper clips have superior gripping power to that of the prior art.

How could you determine in an objective way which of two paper clips has the greater gripping force under comparable conditions?

United States Patent [19]

Michelson

[11] Patent Number: 4,949,435

[45] Date of Patent: Aug. 21, 1990

[54] **PAPER CLIP**

[76] Inventor: Gary K. Michelson, 438 Sherman Canal, Venice, Calif. 90291

[21] Appl. No.: 257,849

[22] Filed: Oct. 14, 1988

[51] Int. Cl.⁵ B42F 1/02
[52] U.S. Cl. 24/67.9; 24/546
[58] Field of Search .... 24/67.9, 67 R, 67.3, 24/67 CF, 545, 546, 547, 548, 549, DIG. 8, DIG. 9, DIG. 10; D19/65

[56] **References Cited**

U.S. PATENT DOCUMENTS

184,626	11/1876	Jewett	24/546
395,473	1/1889	Bartley	24/67.9
715,992	12/1902	Cox	24/548
743,017	11/1903	McGill	24/545
795,048	7/1905	Maguire	24/67.9
1,334,233	3/1920	Dinwiddie	24/547
1,336,626	4/1920	Hall	24/547
1,783,099	11/1930	Ries	24/546
2,642,638	6/1953	Larrabee	24/67.9
2,822,993	2/1958	Sponsel	24/67.9
4,286,358	9/1981	Levin	24/67 R

4,665,594	5/1987	Wagner	24/546

FOREIGN PATENT DOCUMENTS

317844	9/1902	France	24/67.9
1439151	4/1966	France	24/370
709353	5/1954	United Kingdom	24/67.9

OTHER PUBLICATIONS

Horders Inc. Cat. #56, 1952, One Sheet "Paper Clips and Fasteners".

Primary Examiner—Victor N. Sakran
Attorney, Agent, or Firm—Lewis Anten

[57] **ABSTRACT**

An improved paper clip is disclosed consisting of a single piece of wire bent so as to have a straight top spine portion, two straight side leg portions substantially perpendicular to each end of the top spine portion and bent portions extending from, each side leg portion diagonally at approximately 45 degrees in the direction of the top spine portion. Each bent end portion extends from more than ½ the diagonal distance from the end of the side leg portion to the top spine portion.

1 Claim, 2 Drawing Sheets

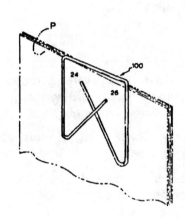

Technical Note 5 - Facility Layout

Overview

A problem faced by every company is designing an effective layout. As business requirements change, layouts are subsequently changed. This is true for manufacturing and services alike. This chapter discusses layouts for new facilities and existing facilities for both service and manufacturing companies. Product, process, group technology (GT), and fixed position layouts are common manufacturing layouts. No particular type of layout is inherently good or bad, and layouts are often reflective of the organizational makeup of individual firms. Tools such as CRAFT and FactoryFLOW can be used by organizations to improve layouts. For services, the "servicescape" approach is explained. It is good to reflect on the JIT tenet that unnecessary transportation is wasteful and should be avoided. This chapter can also be taught in concert with Supplement to Chapter 5 on queuing models.

Major Points of the Chapter

1. Process layout and assembly line balancing decisions both present complex combinatorial problems and therefore call for computerized heuristic approaches to deal with them.

2. Good facility layout is key to achieving an effective production system.

3. Assembly line balancing provides a good background for studying balancing problems at all levels of manufacturing.

4. FactoryFLOW software and CRAFT-based software packages are useful in improving layouts.

5. Sometimes, magnet boards with templates are very useful for trial and error approaches to layout.

6. "Servicescape" is a term that refers to the environment surrounding the delivery of a service. As such, the "servicescape" affects the service experience of the customer.

Teaching Tip

Ask your students to map the layout of a single room in their house or apartment. Gather in the papers and redistribute them to other students in the same class. Ask the students then to act as consultants and recommend changes to improve the room layouts. Short reports can be returned in a week or so. The original owners of the layouts should evaluate these recommendations. Be careful to include details such as outlets, vents, windows, etc.

Cases, Exercises and Spreadsheets (Source)

"Soteriou's Souviaki" (Book)

"State Automobile License Renewals" (Book)

"Travel Intensity Matrix - Job Shop Layout Analysis" (IRM)

"Assembly Line Balancing – Helgeson-Bernie Rank Positional Weight (RPW) Technique" (IRM)

"Metreke Cards" (HBS 9-672-073))

Videos/Clips (Source)

"The Manufacturing Process" (Vol. I)

"Layout Improvements and Equipment Strategies" (Vol. II)

"Production Tour of the Vision Light System at Federal Signal" (Vol. IV)

"Value-Driven Production at Trek" (Vol. IV)

"TriState-Converting to JIT Part 1 and 2 (Vol. V)

"Facility Layout" (CD-ROM)

"Workcells" (CD-ROM)

"Focus Using Group Technology" (CD-ROM)

CASE

Soterious' Souvlaki – Teaching Note

1. The following two matrices show the importance of proximity for the kitchen equipment and dining are features. Use systematic layout planning (with numerical reference weightings) to develop a floor layout for the kitchen and the dining are for Soteriou's Souvlaki.

The Kitchen

	Grill	Prep. Table	Refrig.	Vertical Broiler	Display Case
Cash Register	X	A	X	U	A
Grill	-	A	A	U	E
Prep. Table	-	-	I	A	U
Refrig.	-	-	-	U	X
Vertical Broiler	-	-	-	-	U
Display Case	-	-	-	-	-

The Dining Area

	No Smk.	Smoking	Drinks	Salad Bar	Waiting Area
Cash Register	U	U	I	I	A
No Smk.	-	X	E	E	U
Smoking	-	-	I	I	U
Drinks	-	-	-	U	U
Salad Bar	-	-	-	-	X
Waiting Area	-	-	-	-	-

Following is the SLP solution:

Optimal Kitchen Layout using SLP - Optimum value 84

Storage Case	Preparation Table	Refrigerator
Cash Register	Vertical Broiler	Grill

Optimal Dining Layout using SLP - Optimum value 44

No Smoking Section	Cash Register	Waiting Area
Salad Bar	Drink Machines	Smoking Section

Suggested Layout of Soteriou's

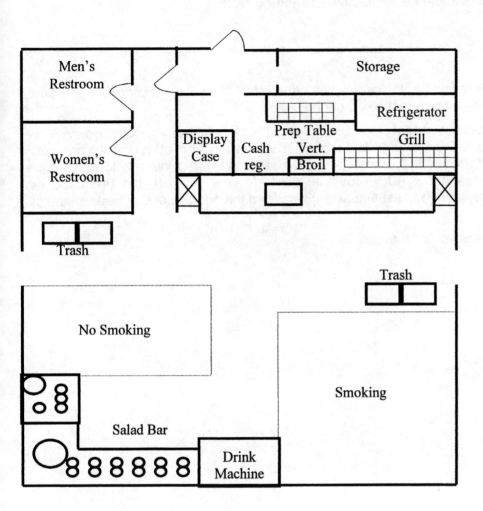

CASE

State Automobile License Renewals – Teaching Note

1. Since task 3 has a 60-second cycle time, the total output for the system is 60 per hour.

2. The bottleneck would then be found at step 4 with a 40-second cycle time. Therefore output would be 90 per hour.

3. It is possible to produce 120 units per hour with only one additional clerk. Since a 30 second cycle time is associated with an output of 120 units per hour, combining tasks 3, 4, and 5, and optimally assigning 4 workers to these tasks results in a (60 + 40 + 20)/4=30 second cycle time. If the tasks are not combined, then the best output resulting from the addition of one clerk is 90 units per hour.

4. See the answer to Question 3.

Travel Intensity Matrix - Job Shop Layout Analysis

The clinic of a university is being moved to a larger building. As head administrator, you have to make plans - a rough sketch is sufficient - of a new floor plan. The following departments are to be incorporated in the new building.

- Receiving and records, supplies storage
- Examining rooms
- Testing carrels
- Immunization
- Lavatory
- Two-bed ward

From the medical records of clinic operation, the traffic flows between departments during an average week are given below.

Traffic Flows Between Departments

From	To	# Patients	From	To	# Patients
A	B	22	C	A	1
A	C	11	C	B	6
A	D	1	C	D	6
A	E	5	C	E	3
A	F	6	C	F	9

The following physical arrangement is a possible starting layout for the clinic.

Department A	Department B	Department C
Department D	Department E	Department F

Analysis by Travel Intensity Matrix

1. Identify most intensively used department by summing each row, summing each column, and combining these traffic sub-totals for each department.

69

2. Locate most intensely used department or workstation in the center or at least as close to the center of the layout as possible.

3. Calculate non-contiguous and non-adjacent moves across the layout. The objective is to minimize these long movements.

Travel Intensity Matrix – Job Shop Layout Analysis – Teaching Note

Travel Intensity Matrix

	A	B	C	D	E	F	ΣRow	ΣColumn	Total
A	-	22	11	1	5	6	45	5	50
B	4	-	15	6	7	2	34	32	66
C	1	6	-	6	3	9	25	29	54
D				-	1	10	11	13	24
E		2			-	12	14	16	30
F		2	3			-	5	39	44

From the above matrix, the most intensely used department is B, since it has the most traffic both in and out (66 patients a week on average). Place Department B in the middle of the starting layout with less busy departments on the perimeter. The grid below can serve as a possible starting layout as B is "in the middle' of the floor plan and other busy departments (like A and C) are immediately on each side of B. There is a hallway along the length of the clinic separating sets of three departments.

Department A	Department B	Department C
Department D	Department E	Department F

With reference to the initial clinic layout above, the non-contiguous and non-adjacent moves are from Department A to Department C, and back from Department C to Department A, from Department A to Department F, and back from Department F to Department A, etc. The following table lists all the non-contiguous and non-adjacent moves for the initial layout of the clinic.

Non-Contiguous and Non-Adjacent Moves for Initial Layout

Department Pairs	# Moves	Department Pairs	# Moves
AC	11	DC	0
CA	1	CD	6
AF	6	DF	10
FA	0	FD	0
	18		16

34 total non-contiguous and non-adjacent moves in the initial layout.

Since the objective of the travel intensity matrix approach to job shop layout analysis is to minimize the total of non-contiguous and non-adjacent moves, several of the departments in the initial layout need to be relocated in order to reduce the number of undesirable or long moves from 34.

Relocate Departments A and C (put A in the former place of C, drop C down across the hallway where F formerly was) and Departments D and F (put F in the place of E and move E in the spot where A vacated) as done in the following second layout. This relocation is to lessen the long moves across the clinic and place high-traffic department close to one another.

Department E	Department B	Department A
Department D	Department F	Department C

Recalculate the non-contiguous and non-adjacent moves for this second layout of the clinic.

Non-Contiguous and Non-Adjacent Moves for Second Layout

Department Pairs	# Moves	Department Pairs	# Moves
DA	0	EA	0
AD	1	AE	5
DC	0	EC	0
CD	6	CE	3
	7		8

15 total non-contiguous and non-adjacent moves in the second layout.

This second layout reduces the number of long and undesirable moves by about 55 percent to 15 non-contiguous and non-adjacent moves. Can the layout be improved beyond this second layout? There are many more possibilities, but this layout may be hard to beat!

The number of unique possible layouts is calculated by 6! (six factorial), or 720 unique possibilities. If the number of departments increased by one or two, what is the effect on the number of potential unique layouts and the importance of such layout analysis techniques such as the travel intensity matrix?

Assembly Line Balancing
Helgeson-Bernie Rank Positional Weight (RPW) Technique

Task	Performance Time	Preceding Task
U1	6	None
U2	2	U1
U3	5	U1
U4	7	U1
U5	1	U1
U6	2	U2
U7	3	U3, U4, U5
U8	6	U6
U9	5	U7
U10	5	U8
U11	4	U9, U10

Problem Statement:

- Efficiency in current balance is 59 percent

- Assume a cycle time of ten (10) will result in an adequate level and rate of output.

- Can the line be re-balanced?

Note: It is much easier to understand the precedence relationships by referring to the "directed" graph of tasks!

Helgeson-Bernie RPW Technique

1.   Calculate the positional weight (PW) for each work station. PW is the time at a station plus the sum of all the times [work station times] after it.

2.   Rank operations (high to low) by their PW

3.   Assign tasks to work stations.

4.   Assignment is constrained by: a) accumula᠁ ᠁ ᠁   ᠁ ᠁ ᠁   ᠁ ᠁ time; and, all precedence must be observed.

Assembly Line Balancing
Helgeson-Bernie Rank Positional Weight (RPW) Technique – Teaching Note

1.   Calculate positional weight (PW): the time of a particular work stations plus the Σ of the times after the station.

Task	Positional Weight
U1	46
U2	19
U3	17
U4	19
U5	13
U6	17
U7	12
U8	15
U9	9
U10	9
U11	4

2.   Rank tasks by positional weight (PW)

U1   U2   U4   U3   U6   U8   U5   U7   U9   U10   U11

3.   Assign tasks to work stations, constrained by accumulated time $\leq$ cycle time and all precedence must be observed.

Station #1	Station #2	Station #3	Station #4	Station #5	Station #6
U1 U2 U6	U4 U5	U3 U7	U8	U9 U10	U11
6 + 2 + 2	7 + 1	5 + 3	6	5 + 5	4

Efficiency is the sum of all the times at the workstations divided by the number of workstations times the cycle time (Σ times / NC, where N is the number of stations and C is the cycle time). The cycle time is the maximum time at any station on the line.

Efficiency for the re-balanced line is 46/6(10) = 46/60 = .77 or 77, percent.

The minimum number of stations (minimum N) for a line is: Σ times / C. For this problem, the minimum number of station is: N = 46/10, or 4.6 stations.

Chapter 6 - Product Design and Process Selection - Services

Overview

The contemporary view of services is that the customer is the focal point of all actions in a service organization. This means that all strategic and tactical decisions must be made with the customer in mind. This view places the customer at the center of the services triangle including the service strategy, the service systems and the people providing the service. Service strategy begins by selecting an operations focus, such as treatment of the customer, speed of delivery, price, variety, quality or unique skills that constitute a services offering. This chapter can be very enjoyable for students. After all, we are all experts in services and know what we like. It is important to tap this intuitive knowledge and structure the student's thinking by using the models in the chapter.

Major Points of the Chapter

1. Services are big business.

2. Everybody is an "expert" on services because of our constant interaction with them. That is, we know what we like and don't like about them.

3. Two broad organizational contexts of services are recognized: service businesses and internal services.

4. Services can be classified according to the degree of customer contact inherent in service delivery.

5. Exhibit 6.9 shows how an automotive service operation was fail-safed (poka-yoke) to improve quality.

6. The Service-System Design Matrix illustrates trade-offs between sales opportunity and production efficiency in service businesses.

7. As companies become more technology driven, the need for personal attention increases. Wal-Mart and Lands End (see opening vignette) are examples of high-tech companies with a homey feel.

Teaching Tips

The McGraw-Hill/Irwin video on "Service Systems and the Service-System Design Matrix" is particularly useful.

The film Five Easy Pieces starring Jack Nicholson shows a classic sequence involving ordering a special meal at a roadside café. The video is now in video stores and makes a great introduction to services.

Teams of students are assigned to call a number of companies that provide a similar service. After choosing a generic question or request, the teams will call these different companies (5 or 6). When calling, a log of the calls is kept including number of transfers, final respondent, attitude of respondents and overall satisfaction with the response. Phone call results are then reported to the class......or

Each student is assigned to write a letter of complaint to a company early in the semester. A response from the company is requested in the letter. Students can then share responses with the class throughout the semester.

Cases, Exercises and Spreadsheets (Source)

"Kinki's Copier Stores" (Book)

"AOL's Move to Flat-Rate Pricing" (Book)

"Benihana" (HBS 9-673-057),

"Burger King Corp" (HBS 9-681-045)

"McDonald's Corp (Condensed)" (HBS 9-681-044)

Videos/Clips (Source)

"Service" (Vol. I),

"Service Systems and the Service-System Design Matrix" (Vol. II).

"Service System Design Matrix" (CD-ROM)

"Five Easy Pieces" – The restaurant scene (Video Store)

CASE

Kinko's Copier Stores – Teaching Note

1. Can general operational standards be developed and implemented in all or a majority of the Kinko's shops?

   Yes. The technology is the same for all shops and the types of jobs performed by the customers. Differences in culture exist in different areas causing a need to handle the behavioral problems differently.

2. Discuss the idea of grouping copiers in machine centers so that certain copiers are available for specific tasks.

   At Kinko's this functional layout is useful in that it allows customers to perform different jobs simultaneously.

3. How do the different services offered (private copying versus copying services provided) present separate problems for management.

   First, there is the problem of capacity (e.g., how much is allotted to what?). This makes layout decisions more challenging as there is a need for different machinery for each task. This provides a need for front room and back room operations (even though at Kinko's the back room is clearly visible to the customer). The problem is not unlike a manufacturer with high volume and low volume production lines in the same facility. Pricing is different for each type of service.

4. Kinko's Professor Publishing apparently did not pan out. What do you think might have been the cause?

   As anyone in academia knows, it is getting more difficult to procure the needed copyright releases in a timely fashion. Professors might procrastinate until the last minute to provide materials to Kinko's making it difficult to obtain releases on time. This program creates a capacity problem in that there is a huge demand on resources during the beginning of every semester. However, this service is still available at most Kinko's copiers.

CASE

AOL's Move to Flat-Rate Pricing – Teaching Note

1. Should AOL be held accountable for its inability to provide immediate access to its network?

   Sure they should, especially if it can be proved that they intentionally oversold the capacity of their networks. It's important that a company that provides a service that is essential to the success of other companies and individuals provide what customers expect. The company needs to be clear about what customers should expect during the peak times. They might even provide statistics relating to expected probability of getting a line during the peak and off-peak times.

2. Compare the case of AOL with that of airline companies who regularly oversell their seats.

   It seems that airline companies are very careful to not overbook in a reckless manner. This is probably what upset AOL customers, it seemed that they had not forecast what the impact would be of their new pricing strategy.

3. Suggest a policy that AOL should use that relates the capacity of their systems to the number of potential users.

   AOL should use sophisticated queuing models (as described in the supplement), to develop ratios of customers in a particular area to the size of the modem pool serving the area. They will probably have to put limits on the amount of time that a customer can use a modem at a time (a one-hour limit, for example).

4. Should the government get involved in this?

   Let's hope that the government not get involved. One might think that the legal profession would keep AOL honest.

Technical Note 6 - Waiting Line Management

Overview

The objectives of this technical note are (1) to describe how to model waiting line situations and (2) to demonstrate how the standard formulas for waiting line situations can be used to provide information for staffing, location, and layout decisions. Since services are frequently waiting line situations, waiting line discussion provides a good follow-up to design of service. For a typical introductory OM class, coverage of queuing structures, Poisson and exponential distributions, and working through some of the simple models is about as far as one can go in a 75 minute session. If time exists for a second session, we recommend that finite queuing be discussed along with one or two of the more advanced models. In the course of the discussion, we like to point out that simulation is the alternative approach to studying those waiting line problems where the basic Poisson assumptions do not hold, or where problems involve multiple phases.

Major Points of the Chapter

1. Waiting lines are a fact of life and exist almost everywhere.

2. The objective in solving a waiting line problem is to balance the cost of waiting with the cost of adding additional resources.

3. In service systems, in order to provide service with reasonably short wait times, the utilization of the server may be quite low.

4. One of the main issues in waiting lines is the priority selection process: what priority rule or procedure should be used to select the next customer to be served or product to be worked on.

Teaching Tips

We usually have a lot of fun teaching waiting line theory. We joke about having the idea of waiting lines as part of our culture. If more than 3 people ever stand behind each other in public, everyone else will get in line also.

Example of our culture

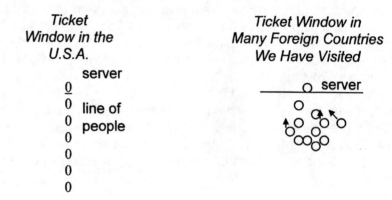

Which waiting line format would you prefer?

Another example follows: *Tellers in a bank*

Which do you prefer?

Most students will choose the single line. Ask them why? Actually, banks tried the single-line theory in the late 60's but they failed. People would drive up to the bank and instead of seeing 3 people in front of 5 tellers, they saw a lobby full of people, since the single line creates that illusion. Banks abandoned the idea. In the early and middle 70's, customers were ready to accept the idea.

You can play similar games with quick check-out cashiers in the supermarkets and ask if students really think they're a good idea and how they affect efficiency. (Note that the quick check-out cashier is always the slowest cashier in the place. Stores use the quick check-out lane as a training ground for new cashiers...They do not accept credit cards nor checks in the line, and the number of items to ring up is limited. New trainees can't get into too much trouble here.)

In terms of priorities in waiting lines. (Or, don't moan too loud...)

In case of a disaster of some sort, how does a hospital decide which patients it will see first in the emergency room? Ask the students.

Students will often say the worst cases first.

After some student guesses, mention that there is what is termed "Triage." There are three groups. The worst patients will probably die even if you help them. The best patients will probably survive even if you don't do anything. The middle set of patients are the ones who need help to survive. This middle group is ranked the highest priority.

Top this off by reminding students that if they are ever in an auto accident with other people and rushed to a hospital, moan and groan a lot to get attention and a high priority, but don't over do it!!!

Cases, Exercises and Spreadsheets (Source)

"Sof-Optics, Inc. (A)" (HBS 9-681-052)

Chapter 7 - Quality Management

Overview

This chapter introduces concepts that are essential for every business student. It is good to point out that employers are seeking prospects that understand and can apply quality principles. There is also a continuing movement towards teamwork in achieving quality improvement. This chapter covers the Malcolm Baldrige National Quality Award, the elements of quality management, ISO 9000 and continuous improvement. The technical note to this chapter covers the important subject of statistical quality control.

Major Points of the Chapter

1. Quality improvement is a management process.

2. The focus of efforts is on the process, not the individual.

3. ISO 9000 is the standard for companies desiring to do business is Europe. However, ISO 9000 registration is not legally required-although most European companies require the certification of suppliers.

4. The MBNQA process provides valuable information concerning a company's quality processes.

5. Firms should be committed over the long term to continually improve. It is interesting to point out that Dr. Deming visited the Japanese in the 1950's and it took over 20 years for Japan to be truly accepted as world class quality manufacturers. In the U.S. recent articles have complained about TQM yielding the right results after only two or three years of implementation.

6. The concept of the service quality (SERVQUAL) survey instrument is introduced in this chapter. This is a popular instrument that can be used to evaluate quality in service companies. The actual forms are included on the Student CD, Website.

Teaching Tips

You may ask the students to evaluate a certain aspect of the university such as the admissions office or the business school using the Baldrige criteria. Often, the students can be very critical. Next, ask the students to use the Baldrige evaluations to formulate recommendations to be presented to someone in authority such as the Dean of the Business School.

Cases, Exercises and Spreadsheets (Source)

"Hank Kolb" (Book)

"Shortening Customers' Telephone Waiting Time" (Book)

"Kristen's Cookie Co. (B)" (HBS 9-686-015)

"Steinway & Sons" (HBS 9-682-025)

Videos/Clips (Source)

"Quality" (Vol. I)

"Improving Operations Methods" (Vol. II)

"Quality Product & Process Design at Detroit Diesel" (Vol. IV)

"Value-Driven Production at Trek" (Vol. IV)

"Valuation of Operations at ATCco (Vol. VI)

"Manufacturing Quality at Honda (Vol. VII)

"A Day in the Life of Quality at Honda (Vol. VII)

"Quality-Defined" (CD-ROM)

"Baldrige Award" (CD-ROM)

"Cost of Quality" (CD-ROM)

"Failsafing" (CD-ROM)

"Quality Tools" (CD-ROM)

<u>WebSites</u>

Baldrige Award (http://www.qulaity.mst.gov)

ISO 9000 (http://www.iso.ch)

Deming Institute (http://www.deming.org)

CASE

Hank Kolb - Director of Quality Assurance – Teaching Note

1. Fishbone diagram

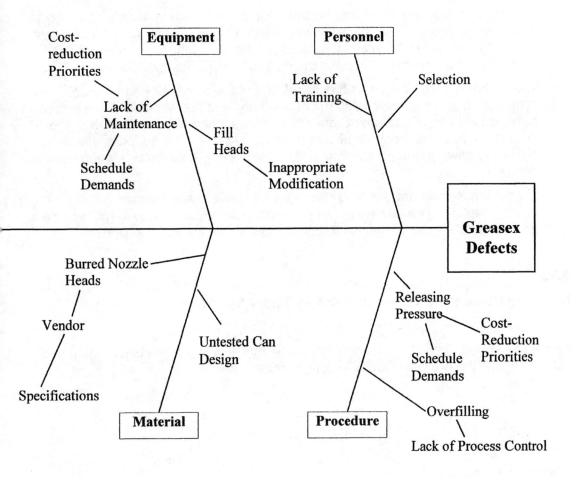

2.   The greatest barrier facing Kolb is the lack of quality awareness at the company. Although Morganthol stresses the importance of quality, he sends the message that cost reduction and reduced delivery time are top priorities. The first step should be to form a quality council headed by Morganthol and comprised of top management. The purpose of this council is to develop the quality mission and objectives for the company.

Kolb can immediately contribute to the council by providing in-depth training in quality practices. Top management must possess both commitment and knowledge in order to lead by example. Next, a limited number of quality improvement teams can be formed to address specific quality problems.

These teams might be cross-functional or from a single functional area. The composition of the team will depend on the nature of the problem. If the process being examined crosses functional boundaries, then the membership should include participants from all affected areas. As with the councils, the teams should receive thorough training before beginning their quality improvement efforts.

Morganthol should not describe the focus on quality as a program. Rather, the quality emphasis is a new way of managing the business. The new management process itself should be subject to periodic quality audits and improvement.

CASE

Shortening Customer's Telephone Waiting Time – Teaching Note

This case is explanatory. The students should be made aware of the use of the basic 7 quality tools and the process used in making improvement.

Technical Note 7 – Process Capability and Statistical Quality Control

Overview

We have introduced quality control early in the book to reflect the fact that product and service quality has become the basis for competition of most major producers. The chapter covers the standard QC concepts of quality costs, and statistical process control. It also touches on Taguchi concepts and service quality measurements.

Major Points of the Chapter

1. High quality results from controlling the production process, not from after-the-fact inspection.

2. Motorola's six-sigma design results in 3.4 defects per million units produced.

3. Preventing defects is cheaper than fixing them.

4. Quality is a corporate-wide responsibility, not just the job of the QC department.

5. The need for SQC continues as all processes exhibit some variability.

Teaching Tips

An easy in-class acceptance sampling exercise can be run using some candy. You can tell the students that you just received this big bag of candy from your supplier, but you are concerned that it may be defective. Ask them to help you inspect it. You can indicate that you do not want to do 100% inspection, since then there would not be any candy left to eat! First set up an acceptance sampling plan. You need to set up an AQL and LTPD so that the sample size is about 6 (you can have 6 people on each team doing the sampling). If you set LTPD to .2 and AQL to .01 you will find that the sample size is 6, and that the lot will be rejected if any defects are found. It is fun to put plenty of defects in the bag. You can do this by breaking or melting some of the pieces. Have each team get their sample and inspect their candy. Tell them that they cannot eat it until the lot is accepted. Poll each team to find out if they accept or reject their lot. Ask for the candy to be returned from each team that rejects their lot! This can lead into a quick discussion the dimensions of quality (see exhibit 6.8 from chapter 6). This is a fun exercise that will wake your students up with a shot of sugar.

Cases, Exercises and Spreadsheets (Source)

"Process Control at Polaroid (A)" (HBS 9-693-047)

Videos/Clips (Source)

"Quality" (Vol. I)

"Quality Production & Process at Detroit Diesel" (Vol. IV)

"Value-Driven Production at Trek" (Vol. IV)

"Manufacturing Quality at Honda" (Vol. VII)

"A Day in the Life of Quality at Honda" (Vol. VII)

"SPC at Honda" (Vol. VII)

"Acceptance Sampling" (CD-ROM)

"Coordinate Measuring Machine" (CD-ROM)

"Motorola Six Sigma" (CD-ROM)

"Statistical Process Control" (CD-ROM)

WebSites

ASQC (http://www.asqc.org)

Managerial Briefing 8 – Electronic Commerce and E-OPS

Overview

Operations management is impacted by the use of the Internet and in an OM course it is important that students understand how companies gain competitive advantage through the use of use of this infrastructure. In this briefing, we survey what companies are doing with electronic commerce and focus on the impact that these activities have on the operations of a firm. We believe that the use of the Internet infrastructure will evolve into a new paradigm for operations management, where the Internet is used to coordinate all participants in the supply chain. We have coined the term *E-Operations* or *E-OPS* for short to refer to the application of the Internet and its related technologies to the field of OM.

Major Points of the Managerial Briefing

1. Definition of Electronic Commerce and the two "laws" that explain the power of E-Commerce.

2. Moore's Law defined – computing power doubles ever 18 to 24 months.

3. Metcalfe's Law defined – the utility of value of a network equals the square of the number of users.

4. E-Ops defined – the application of the Internet to the field of OM.

5. Business Web Models (a way to categorize Internet businesses): Aggregators, Marketplace, Alliance, Value Chain, and Distributive Network.

6. Survey of E-Ops applications.

Teaching Tips

This briefing can be assigned as a reading. At the end of the chapter there is an Internet enrichment exercise called the E-Ops Game. This is a game that can be played by your students where they have opportunity to run their own Internet business. Players run a simulated business that sells generic computers over the Internet. Students need to take on the roles of purchasing, manufacturing and sales in running their company.

The game is played over the Internet using a browser, so no setup is required on the part of the instructor. Students compete within their class and also with students from around the world who are also playing the game. Students will discover that to really score well they need to work in teams where they split up the functions. For example, on player would be responsible for purchasing, a second for manufacturing, and a third working to sell the computers. The game can be played in this way, since multiple players can log into the same account. Instructions for playing the game are given below.

Cases, Exercises and Spreadsheets (Source)

The E-Ops Game (Book)

WebSites

E-Ops Game (http://www.pom.edu/ebus)

The E-Ops Game – Instructions

The goal of the game is to make as much money as possible during the time played. The player must play at least 15 minutes to get a score that qualifies for the "top 100" list. The player needs to manage all roles in the e-business. These roles include purchasing material, scheduling production and selling the product. All of the activities are conducted over the Internet.

The game can be accessed from the http://www.pom.edu/ebus. Each player (representing a separate company) needs to set up an account using the "Create New Account" button. Each account needs a Name, School, Course Number, and Instructor. It is important that all the individual accounts associated with your class use the same Course Number, since this is the field used to distinguish the students in your class from the students in other classes that are playing the game. In addition, each account needs a UserID and a Password. Once the account has been setup it can be quickly logged into using this UserID and Password. Notice that on the login screen there is an option for "initializing" the account. Checking this box reinitializes the account to when it was initially setup, giving the player the ability to completely start over with playing the game. Players do not need to "log-off" the system, rather when all transactions have been executed the player can simply quit playing. The "performance rating", "profit" and other evaluation criteria, will not change unless the player introduces more transactions.

The business involves selling generic computers over the Internet. The company makes two types of computers. A low-end computer called "Computer1" and a high end one called "Computer2". These computers are made in a factory that can make exactly one computer each second. The computers are made in batches and there is no setup time when moving from one batch to another batch. The computers are assembled using parts that need to be purchased. The following are the bills of material for each computer:

Product	Parts needed
Computer1 ($400) 10% late penalty	One Memory Module ($20) One CPU1 ($80) One Disk Drive ($100) Note: Labor is $20/computer
Computer2 ($500) 10% late penalty	Two Memory Modules ($40 for two) One CPU2 ($160) One Disk Drive ($100) Note: Labor is $20/computer

Parts are purchased in batches through an Internet trading company. The player solicits bids for parts by indicating how many units of a particular part would like to be purchased. The market responds with a time when the parts can be delivered and a price. The price for the batch of parts is dependent on the order quantity and the time of delivery.

Similarly, computers are sold over the Internet. The player has the option of offering a batch of computers to the Internet market or "querying" the market to see what buyers currently want. In both cases the sales price for the computers is dependant on the the the quantity purchased and the delivery time. These computers are sold like commodities.

Keep in mind that everything happens in Internet time, that being seconds. Parts arrive at an exact second in the future. The assembly process is scheduled to the second and computer orders are shipped (if they are available) at a specific second.

The following are a few assumptions built into the system that will help in understanding what is going on:

1. The simulation will not allow ordering additional material if your cash balance is less than zero. When ordering material, the accounts payable account is credited. The vendor is paid when the order arrives. Similarly, when computers are sold the order backlog account is credited. Cash is actually received and the backlog cleared when the computers are delivered. Given the timing of material and computer orders it is possible to run some float through these accounts.

2. The assembly process. One computer is made each second. Computers are not scheduled until the parts are actually available. In the list of future events, there are two events that relate to assembly. The first indicates that a particular type of computer is "scheduled". The date on the event is when the computers will actually go into finished goods inventory. When a batch of computers is "scheduled" the parts are allocated to the assembly order and removed from the on-hand balance. The second type of assembly event is marked "Waiting for Material". These are orders that have been entered into the system but parts are not yet "on-hand". The due date on "Waiting for Material" orders is when the order was entered into the system. There may be multiple "Waiting for Material" orders for a computer type in the system. One bit of confusion is in knowing exactly how many parts are needed over and above what have already been ordered (i.e. some kind of time phased run out calculation). The player needs to calculate this from the data provided in the status report.

3. Buying material. Batches of material can be bought on the spot market (i.e. right now) or in the future. The spot market prices are given in the table above. There is a maximum 10% discount given for 600-unit order quantity (the discount starts at 100 units and maxes out at 600). There is a maximum 20% discount for items purchased 5 minutes in the future. These are simple linear functions.

4. Selling computers. The same discounts are in place for the computers as are present for material. The margin on both computers is exactly the same. There is a 10% penalty for late delivery of computers. This is captured as a "delivery

penalty" cost in the operating statement. The cash received from the customer is reduced by this penalty.

The key evaluation criterion is the "performance rating." The program calculates the number of computers that you could produce over the time you have been playing and multiplies this number of units by an expected per computer profit margin (this is $180/computer). Your actual profit margin is then divided by this expected profit margin and multiplied by 100 to get the performance rating.

The elapsed time clock starts running when you start running your factory the first time. It continues until your last transaction is processed. "Idle time" is the time that your factory is idle after it has been used to make computers the first time.

Good luck with the game!

Chapter 8 – Supply Chain Strategy

Overview

This chapter introduces the topic of supply-chain strategy. The chapter defines what supply chain management is and the dynamics that are inherent in the operation of supply chains. Measure of inventory turn and days-of-supply are introduced with an example using Dell Computer, the definitive leader in the use of the concepts discussed in this chapter. Important topics such as the "Bull Whip Effect" are discussed together with Fishers' framework for efficient verses responsive supply chains. Outsourcing is discussed together with the elements of the materials management system, purchasing, intra-plant logistics, and finished goods distribution. It is important to realize that the integrated approach to supply-chain management is an important mechanizing for tying together traditional organization functions.

Major Points of the Chapter

1. Definition of Supply Chain Management
2. Measuring Supply Chain performance – inventory turns and day-of-supply.
3. Understanding the bullwhip effect.
4. Effective verses responsive supply chains and how this relates to the type of product produced.
5. Outsourcing and supply chain logistics.
6. Global sourcing of product.
7. Principles of mass customization and inventory positioning.

Teaching Tips

Play the "Beer Game" if you have the time. It is great fun and is an important lesson distribution system dynamics that the students will not forget. The manual version takes about 2.5 hours to play. A new Internet version can be played in about 75 minutes, but requires a classroom with individual computers for each student.

Cases, Exercises and Spreadsheets (Source)

The Beer Game (http://www.pom.edu/beer/)

Pepe Jeans (Book)

Videos/Clips (Source)

"Supplier Development Outreach Program" (Vol. II)

"International Logistics" (Vol. V)

"A Day in the Life of Quality at Honda" (Vol. VII)

CASE

Pepe Jeans – Teaching Note

This case is designed to illustrate the use of process postponement in the manufacturing of fashion jeans. The case can be done with a marketing instructor very effectively. Pepe Jeans is a real company in the UK, but the data given in the case is fictitious, so you might anticipate some questions that relate to whether Pepe actually made the changes that are developed in the case.

The HP Deskjet case, in Chapter 13 also illustrates postponement, but from the viewpoint of inventory cost saving through pooling synergy. Using Pepe Jeans and HP Deskjet together is a good way to illustrate the types of changes companies are making today as they globalize operations.

The following are the answers to the discussion questions:

1. Acting as an outside consultant, what would you recommend that Pepe do? Given the data in the case, perform a financial analysis to evaluate the alternatives that you have identified. (Assume that the new inventory could be valued at six weeks' worth of the yearly cost of sales. Use a 30 percent inventory carrying cost rate.) Calculate the payback period for each alternative.

   Assume that Sales are 200M

   Cost of Sales @ 40% = 80M
   Operating Expense @ 28% = 56M
   Profit @ 32% = 64M

   If lead-time is cut to 6 weeks then cost of sales go up 30%
   80 + 24 = 104M
   Assuming that operating expenses stay the same, Pepe would only make 40M/yr assuming that sales to not go up.

   Locating the finishing operation in the UK requires the following investment:
   Equipment = 1M
   Renovation = .3M
   Inventory investment cost. First, assume that the cost of the jeans would be reduced by 10% or 80M x .1 = 8M. The basic jeans would then cost about 72M. Inventory investment
   (6 weeks supply of basic jeans) = 72 x (6/52) = 8.31M (Value of inventory)
   Inventory Carrying Cost (yearly) = 8.31M x .3 = 2.49M
   Total cost of the investment = 1M + .3M + 2.49M = 3.79M

   Yearly savings for the option is the cost of sales reduction of 10% accompanied by a yearly increase in UK operating expenses of .5M.

8M + .5M = 7.4M savings per year.

Profit would improve to 71.4M and increase of 11.6%.

The payback on the investment is then
3.79M / 7.4M = .5 years

This looks like a very attractive investment.

2. Are there other options that Pepe should consider?

Pepe may want to consider sourcing the Jeans in Europe, but this would probably not be very attractive, since costs would go up due to the much higher labor costs.

Another option would be to keep with the current supplier arrangement, but carry inventory in the UK. In this case, Pepe could deliver orders from stock, rather than manufacturing everything directly to order. The investment in the inventory and the cost to manage that inventory would need to be offset by increased sales. Some interesting issues can be discussed relating to this option including the need to forecast sales, how unsold (obsolete) inventory would be sold, how would returns be handled, and how the distribution center would be operated.

Playing the Beer Distribution Game Over the Internet – Overview and Instructions[6]

Possibly one of the most widely used classroom exercises for demonstrating the dynamics of a supply chain is the Beer Distribution Game. The System Dynamics Group developed the exercise at the Massachusetts Institute of Technology's Sloan School of Management [Sterman 1989]. Normally the game is played manually on a game board with paper demand and order cards. Pennies are used to track the movement of cases of beer. This note describes a version of the game that can be played over the Internet that has the advantages of quicker setup, quicker game play, and quicker analysis of game results.

The Beer Distribution Game simulates a phenomenon known as the "bullwhip" effect. The classic example of the bullwhip effect was observed at Procter & Gamble (P&G) with the sales of Pampers diaper [Lee 1997]. While the consumers, in this case babies, consumed diapers at a steady rate, the variability of demand grew as it progressed up the supply chain. For instance when P&G looked at demand for raw materials to their suppliers, such as 3M, they saw large swings. Many additional examples of the phenomena have been identified in the literature.

The manual version of the game is played on a board that represents the production and distribution of beer (see Figure 1). Teams of students represent different parts of the supply chain. Players take on the following roles to simulate the supply chain echelons for each brewery:

the **retailer** sells cases of beer to a consumer and orders cases of beer from the wholesaler,

the **wholesaler** sells cases of beer to the retailer and orders cases of beer from the distributor, and

the **distributor** sells cases of beer to the wholesaler and orders beer from the factory.

The **factory** brews the beer.

Pennies represent cases of beer and are moved between the positions on the board. The object of the game is to minimize two inventory related costs: holding cost ($0.50/case/period) and backordering cost ($1.00/case/period). Costs are assessed each period at each echelon as the game is played. During each period the players receive orders, evaluate their inventory position and decide orders and shipments for their echelon. Consumer demand for beer is simulated using a deck of cards according to a predetermined sequence and given to the retailer each period. A fixed shipping delay of two periods between each echelon simulates the time required to receive,

1. ———————————

[6] Adapted from F. Robert Jacobs, "Playing the Beer Distribution Game Over the Internet," *Production and Operations Management* (Special issue on teaching Supply Chain Management), July 2000.

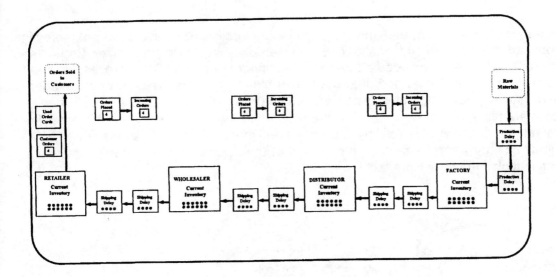

Figure 1: Beer Distribution Game – Manual Board Setup

process, ship and deliver orders. In the case of the factory, a lead-time of two periods is required to produce a new beer order.

The game starts in equilibrium with 12 cases of beer in inventory at each echelon and 4 cases in each of the delay positions (see Figure 1). Normally, the simulation begins with four weeks of steady demand (4 cases per week) and all the players are directed to order and ship four cases each period, to maintain the initial equilibrium. Following the four-period startup, players are then instructed to order any quantity they wish. At this point, there is an increase in customer demand to eight cases per week. This change in demand induces disequilibrium into the system to which the students must react. A complete description of the game including the specific "rules of play" is given in Heineke and Meile [1995].

Note that the increase in demand is introduced at the retailer, who may respond with a change in the size of the order to the wholesaler. The retailer, in deciding what to order, may perceive the increase in demand in a number of ways. The wholesaler does not see the change in the order size until the next period. So the knowledge of this change in demand propagates through the system over the next four to five periods.

Sterman [1989] performed econometric tests to explain player behavior and found that an anchoring and adjustment heuristic for stock management was a good fit to the behavior. As noted by Sterman, players fall victim to several 'misperceptions of feedback.' Specifically, the players failed to account for control actions, which had been initiated but have not yet had their effect (i.e. they were looking at inventory on-hand rather than inventory position). In Sterman's studies, the majority of players attributed the dynamics they experienced to external events, when in fact these dynamics were internally generated by their own actions.

Professor Dan Steele of the University of South Carolina has developed an interesting model of the process that the decision-maker uses in playing the Beer Game (see Figure 2). His model includes a forecast of the future demand. This forecast is used to calculate a stocking level goal that the player thinks is appropriate. An actual order is then placed in an attempt to bring the inventory up to this target level. When the upstream player sees this order, for example when the wholesaler sees the order from the retailer, the player reacts by ordering even more inventory. As we move up the supply chain toward the factory, the impact of the demand spike is further overstated, thus inducing the bullwhip effect.

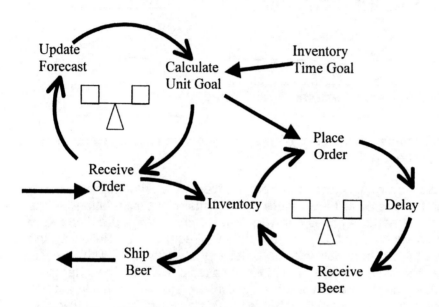

Figure 2: Model of decision process for players of the Beer Game

Major causes for the bullwhip effect in practice have been proposed as: 1. Demand forecast updating, 2. Order batching, 3. Price fluctuation, and 4. Rationing and shortage gaming (see reference 2). Although, in playing the Beer Game, we do not explicitly state what caused the change in demand at the retailer, students likely perceive that some external event has caused this change in demand. If we believe Professor Steele's model, then forecast updating and the processing of this new information relative to the current inventory position, is the major reason for the effect generated in the Beer Game simulation.

Click the button that corresponds to your team and team assignment:	Factory	Distribution	Wholesaler	Retailer
Team 1: Budweiser				
Team 2: Miller				
Team 3: Coors				
Team 4: Heinekin				
Team 5: Samuel Adams				
Team 6: Lennie's				
Team 7: Guiness				
Team 8: Harp				

Figure 3 Initial Team Selection Screen

The Internet version of the game actually is driven by demand supplied in a file, so it is easy to input alternative demand streams that are representative of external factors as mentioned above. Price fluctuations could be reflected in periods of high and low demand that represent buying patterns influenced by the pricing. Placing limits on the maximum capacity of the factory could simulate rationing. There are many scenarios that could be developed to demonstrate various external factors as found in the real world. Performing experiments to study the impact of these proposed causes for the bullwhip effect could be an interesting research project.

Playing the Internet Version of the Game

Playing the manual version of the game can be a great experience, but it consumes a significant amount of time. Typically it takes about an hour to explain the game and get the game board set up. Another hour and half is spent actually playing the game. After playing the game the students must be given time to tabulate results, calculate costs, and construct graphs. A debriefing is then completed that takes another 30 to 45 minutes. In total, a minimum of three hours needs to be devoted to the game. Often the debriefing is complicated by errors in tabulating results that can lead to confusion.

With the Internet version of the game, students work at personal computers in a classroom, using a web browser to play the game. A special program resident on a web server keeps track of the game. Many teams can play the game simultaneously (to date the program has been used with eight teams playing at the same time). The program is designed to take decisions from each position in the distribution system,

101

check that the decisions are valid, compute inventory and backorder levels, and calculate costs. At any point in the simulation, detailed graphs can be requested which show inventory, backorder, and ordering information for each position on a team.To start the game, students are divided into teams, and then each student (or pair of students) is assigned a position on the team (retailer, wholesaler, distributor, or factory). Students log into the system from the beer game starter screen (see Figure 3) by simply clicking into their position. Keep in mind that each team plays the game totally independent of the other teams. The instructor leads the students through each period of playing the game.

Players are presented with the screen shown in Figure 4. This screen has three frames. The frame at the upper left is used to record decisions. Here the player enters the number of cases to ship downstream and the number of cases to order from the upstream position. The program will not allow a player to ship more than the combined current demand plus backlog, nor can the player ship beer that is not currently in inventory.

The instructor determines when each period has passed and manually triggers the update of the system. The server records the decisions and updates the inventory positions using a special instructor form (see Figure 5). Players may change their decisions at any point up to the time when the program is instructed to update the database. The top right panel (Figure 4) shows the current inventory position. This area shows the current demand, backorder position, shipment amount, inventory level, the amount that will be delivered next period, the amount that will be delivered two periods from now, and the current proposed order. The inventory and backorder costs incurred by the player are also displayed in this panel. The player asks for this screen to be updated by clicking on a status update button in the decision panel.

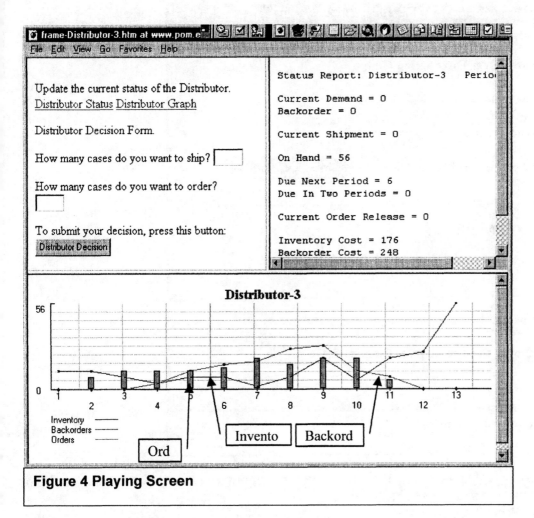

Figure 4 Playing Screen

A graph, in the lower panel, shows the inventory, backorders, and orders (shown with the bars) up to this point in the game. The graph is updated manually by clicking on the graph update button in the decision panel. The graph gives the player data on how the game has gone thus far (the inventory and backorder lines are different colors on the computer screen, but have been annotated for this paper). In looking at the graph, one might be surprised to see that the player has backorders and inventory during some of the periods. The data shows the status at the beginning of the period, so it is possible that a player has just received some inventory and the player is in a backorder position relative to demand. Normally students will ship exactly what was ordered plus the backlog subject to availability but some students may decide to hold back inventory thinking that the request from the downstream position does not seem reasonable.

Normally, the game is played for 35 to 40 periods to fully capture the "bullwhip" effect in the system. The Internet version can be played at a rate of approximately 45 seconds per period allowing the entire game to be played in 35 minutes. Clearly, one of the main advantages of using the Internet version is the speed in being able to complete the

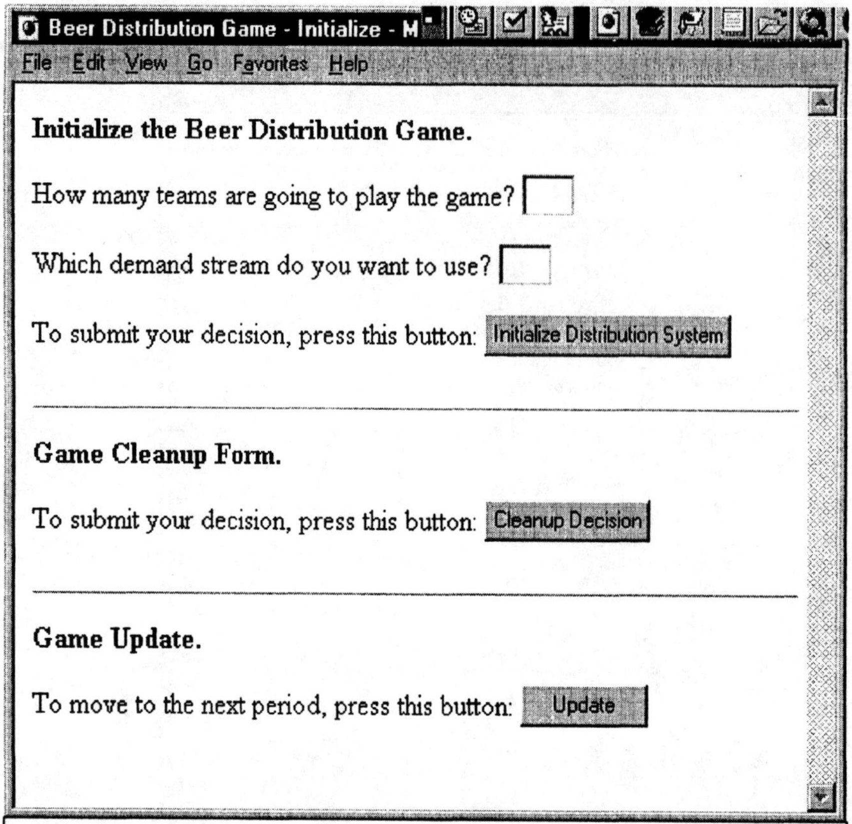

```
┌─────────────────────────────────────────────────────────────┐
│ ◻ Beer Distribution Game - Initialize - M▪  [icons]          │
│ File  Edit  View  Go  Favorites  Help                        │
│ ┌─────────────────────────────────────────────────────────┐ │
│ │ Initialize the Beer Distribution Game.                  │ │
│ │                                                          │ │
│ │ How many teams are going to play the game? [    ]        │ │
│ │                                                          │ │
│ │ Which demand stream do you want to use? [   ]            │ │
│ │                                                          │ │
│ │ To submit your decision, press this button: [Initialize  │ │
│ │                                              Distribution │ │
│ │                                              System]      │ │
│ │ ─────────────────────────────────────────────────────── │ │
│ │                                                          │ │
│ │ Game Cleanup Form.                                       │ │
│ │                                                          │ │
│ │ To submit your decision, press this button: [Cleanup     │ │
│ │                                              Decision]    │ │
│ │ ─────────────────────────────────────────────────────── │ │
│ │                                                          │ │
│ │ Game Update.                                             │ │
│ │                                                          │ │
│ │ To move to the next period, press this button: [Update]  │ │
│ │                                                          │ │
│ └─────────────────────────────────────────────────────────┘ │
│ Figure 5 Instructor Screen                                   │
└─────────────────────────────────────────────────────────────┘
```

Figure 5 Instructor Screen

exercise. Valuable class time need not be spent moving poker chips, recording inventory levels, and calculating costs.

On completion of the game, the debriefing session can start immediately since statistics and graphs documenting the performance of each team are immediately available. Figure 6 shows a debrief graph for a particular team. From this figure, which for clarity only includes 25 simulated periods, we see how significant levels of inventory were built in reaction to the increase in demand in period four. In each panel, a graph showing one of the positions on the team is displayed. In the case of the simulation shown in Figure 6, inventory levels reached a maximum of 339 units at the wholesaler, 465 units at the distributor, and 500 units at the factory. A quick scan of the variation in the size of the orders at the retailer, wholesale, distributor and factory shows how each player reacted differently to the information. On viewing the graphs, team members can easily recall and explain what happened as they played the game. A significant benefit of the Internet version of the game is that it eliminates the confusion during the debriefing due to student errors in tabulating the results.

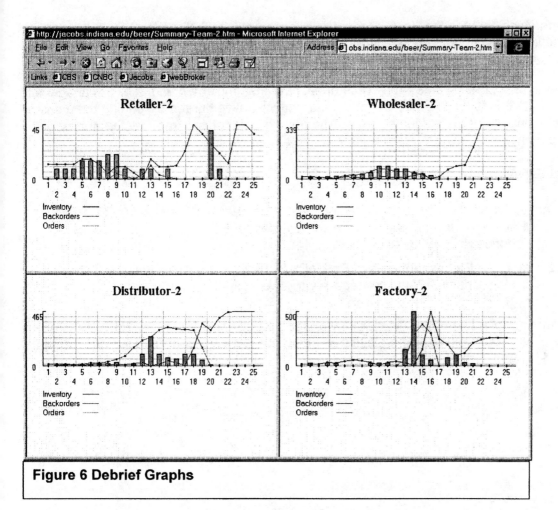

Figure 6 Debrief Graphs

In addition to discussing the performance of each of the teams, the debrief session should also show examples of the bullwhip in actual settings. A few examples are given in [3]. A model that helps to explain the behavior such as Figure 2 can also be used. Finally, a discussion of how companies should design their supply chain and information support systems to avoid the problem is a useful way to conclude the discussion.

Conclusions

The Internet version of the game was developed in August 1996 and has been used at Indiana University and other schools on many occasions. The program can be run off the web site at http://www.pom.edu/beer/, and need not be installed on a local server. In the future, the program may be made available for installation on a local server.

Instructor's can use the "test" account to experiment with the game. The "Public 1" and "Public 2" accounts are available to use with classes. Contact Professor Jacobs (Jacobs@indiana.edu) if you would like a private account set up for your school.

The Internet Beer Game represents one of the first implementations of a management game that uses the Internet. By taking the administrative burden of running the game off the shoulders of the students and instructors the Internet can improve the quality of the experience and leave more time for learning and analysis.

<u>References</u>

Heineke, Janelle N., and Larry C. Meile (1995), *Games and Exercises for Operations Management: Hands-On Learning Activities for Basic Concepts and Tools*, Prentice Hall, 1995, 101-111.

Lee, Hau L., V. Padmanabhan and Seungjim Whang (1997), "The Bullwhip Effect in Supply Chains," *Sloan Management Review* (Spring, 1997), 93-102.

Sterman, John D. (1989), "Modeling Managerial Behavior: Misperceptions of Feedback in a Dynamic Decision Making Experiment," *Management Science*, Vol. 35, No. 3 (March 1989), 3.

Chapter 9 - Strategic Capacity Planning

Overview

As illustrated by the Euro Disney vignette at the beginning of the chapter, capacity planning has become an important strategic variable for many companies. Capacity related decisions could either enhance or worsen competitiveness over the long term. Capacity is discussed in the chapter from both economic and managerial perspectives. The economic concepts of best operating level and economies of scale are discussed. From a managerial perspective, the capacity planning process, decision trees and multi-site service growth concepts are discussed.

Major Points of the Chapter

1. The objective of strategic capacity planning is to specify the overall capacity level of resources - facilities, equipment, and labor force size - that best supports the company's competitive strategy.

2. A firm's available capacity ultimately depends upon what it plans to produce.

3. The need to focus capacity on a fairly limited set of production objectives is key to successful production.

4. When considering adding capacity, key considerations include maintaining system balance, frequency of capacity additions, and use of external capacity.

5. Service capacity is subject to more volatile demand fluctuations and utilization directly impacts service quality.

6. Large plants can benefit from both economies of scale and learning effects. However, emerging literature argues that economy of scope (flexibility) is also an important variable in assessing competitiveness.

Teaching Tips

The Shouldice Hospital case included in the book is a sure winner. This case can be augmented with the web site, a spreadsheet, and a video tape.

The Student CD, Website-ROM includes a demo version of the TreeAge decision tree software shown in exhibits 9.4 and 9.5. The "Hacker's Computer Store Problem" discussed in the book is included as an example with the software.

Cases, Exercises and Spreadsheets (Source)

"Donner" (HBS 9-689-030),

"Shouldice Hospital" (Book) and Spreadsheet (CD-ROM)

"National Cranberry Cooperative (Abridged)" (HBS 9-688-122)

Videos/Clips (Source)

"JIT at Tri State Industries – Part I" (Vol. V)

"Shouldice Hospital" (Vol. III)

"International Logistics" (Vol. V)

WebSites

Shouldice Hospital (http://www.shouldice.com)

TreeAge Software (http://www.treeage.com)

CASE

Shouldice Hospital - A Cut Above – Teaching Note

Mon. - Fri. Operations with 90 beds (30 patients per day)
Beds Required

Check-in	Monday	Tuesday	Wednesday	Thursday	Friday	Saturday	Sunday	
Monday	30	30	30					
Tuesday			30	30				
Wednesday			30	30	30			
Thursday				30	30	30		
Friday								
Saturday								
Sunday	30	30					30	
Total	60	90	90	90	60	30	30	**450**
Utilization	66.7%	100.0%	100.0%	100.0%	66.7%	33.3%	33.3%	**71.4%**

Mon. - Sat. Operations with 90 beds (30 patients per day)
Beds Required

Check-in	Monday	Tuesday	Wednesday	Thursday	Friday	Saturday	Sunday	
Monday	30	30	30					
Tuesday		30	30	30				
Wednesday			30	30	30			
Thursday				30	30	30		
Friday					30	30	30	
Saturday								
Sunday	30	30					30	
Total	60	90	90	90	90	60	60	**540**
Utilization	66.7%	100.0%	100.0%	100.0%	100.0%	66.7%	66.7%	**85.7%**

Mon. - Fri. Operations with 134 beds (minimum)
Beds Required

Check-in		Monday	Tuesday	Wednesday	Thursday	Friday	Saturday	Sunday	
	Monday	44	44	44					
	Tuesday			44	44				
	Wednesday			44	44	44			
	Thursday				44	44	44		
	Friday								
	Saturday								
	Sunday	44	44					44	
	Total	88	132	132	132	88	44	44	**660**
	Utilization	65.7%	98.5%	98.5%	98.5%	65.7%	32.8%	32.8%	**70.4%**

Mon. - Fri. Operations with 134 beds (maximum 158 beds)
Beds Required

Check-in		Monday	Tuesday	Wednesday	Thursday	Friday	Saturday	Sunday	
	Monday	52	52	52					
	Tuesday			52	52				
	Wednesday			52	52	52			
	Thursday				52	52	52		
	Friday								
	Saturday								
	Sunday	52	52					52	
	Total	104	156	156	156	104	52	52	**780**
	Utilization	77.6%	116.4%	116.4%	116.4%	77.6%	38.8%	38.8%	**83.2%**

It is possible to go up to 52 patients a day, but this requires that patients sleep in the hostel rooms on their first night. The minimum value of 44 shows the number assuming these hostel rooms are not used.

Can the capacity of the rest of Shouldice keep up?

One operating room can handle about 1 patient every hour. Since there are five operating rooms, each must be able to handle 52/5 or 10.4 patients per day. This means they must be operated 10.4 hours a day. Even at 44 patients a day, they would still operate 8.8 hours a day. In order to finish operating early enough for all patients to recover by the evening, Shouldice would probably have to add operating room capacity. At 4 patients per day per surgeon, the 44 operations per day could be done with 11 surgeons, leaving one surgeon extra to cover vacations, but 52 patients per day would require at least 13 surgeons.

Using the financial data given in the fourth discussion question it is easy to justify the expansion to 135 beds. The following is the analysis as presented in the spreadsheet included on the CD-ROM.

		Beds Required							
		Mon	Tues	Wed	Thurs	Fri	Sat	Sun	
	Mon	45	45	45					
	Tues		45	45	45				
	Wed			45	45	45			
Check-in day	Thurs				45	45	45		
	Fri								
	Sat								
	Sun	45	45					45	
Total Beds	Total	90	135	135	135	90	45	45	675
135	Utilization	66.7%	100.0%	100.0%	100.0%	66.7%	33.3%	33.3%	71.4%

Operating Rooms	Operations	45
5	Oper/Room	9
Surgeons		
12	Oper/Surg	3.75

Cost of expansion	Beds	45
	Cost/Bed	$100,000
	Total	$4,500,000

Incremental Revenue	Rev/Oper	$1,300
	Surgeon	$600
	Incr Rev	$700

Additional	Oper/Week	75
	Rev/Week	$52,500
	Payback	85.7 Weeks

Technical Note 9 - Facility Location

Overview

Facility location decisions comprise part of the overall strategic plan for many companies. As operations globalize, location decisions become more complex. In the past, operations management courses focused on tools for minimizing costs and distances such as linear programming. This chapter also focuses on qualitative, climatic variables such as political risk, infrastructure and the availability of free trade zones.

Major Points of the Chapter

1. Offices can be "everywhere and nowhere."

2. Communication technology and the "global village" allow greater flexibility in locating operations.

3. A variety of factors are considered in locating an operation.

4. Companies should use location as a means of achieving competitive advantage.

5. Quantitative tools are presented such as the center of gravity transportation method.

Teaching Tips

Center of Gravity or "Drop-The-String" Method

This simple method to find the minimum cost location consists of a board having holes placed appropriately to represent locations of existing facilities. There are *n* strings attached to a common knot, and each string is passed through a hole. A weight corresponding to the number of shipments between the planned facility and existing locations is attached to the end of each string. The knot is then grasped (using an overlapping grip), pulled taut, and then dropped (ideally, to a series of drumrolls). The resting spot of the knot indicates the weighted geographic center of the location space. Bulldozers may then be called in. (Well, almost.)

The Applichem case is a great for discussing the problem associated with sourcing product globally. In addition, the case allows the students to learn about using the Excel Solver to solve transportation problems. There is a tutorial on the Student CD, Website that demonstrates setting up and running transportation problems in Excel. Students may find this tutorial very helpful.

Cases, Exercises and Spreadsheets (Source)

"Applichem – The Transportation Problem" (Book)

"The Plant Location Puzzle" (Book)

"New Balance Athletic Shoes" (HBS 9-680-110)

CASE

The Plant Location Puzzle – Teaching Note

This case appeared in the *Harvard Business Review* (March-April 1994). It was followed by six analyses by eight experts in manufacturing strategy and plant location (*HBR* pp. 23-37). The main points we have gleaned from these are included in the answers to each of the questions posed on text page 393.

1. What is the competitive environment facing EDC?

The U.S. market for bicycles is growing at only 2 percent per year, while the Asian market was nearly doubling. There are also two main competitors (in Taiwan and China) who are already exporting substantial shares of their output. We might expect to see them opening up new factories in the U.S.! The market for EDC bicycles in Asia looks promising, especially if there is a movement towards using bikes for recreation as well as basic transportation. Obviously, competitors whose home is in Asia will have an advantage in understanding how their distribution channels operate, work force capabilities, government bureaucracy, etc.

2. What are EDC's strengths in manufacturing?

Mainly, it's their ability to manufacture innovative, high performance bicycles, can get them to market quickly. This in turn stems from their ability to work together cross-functionally. This is facilitated by co-location of manufacturing, engineering, development, design, marketing, purchasing, and other functions at the Boulder campus. Note that their strength in manufacturing must be considered as inseparable from their capabilities as an enterprise.

3. Should EDC establish a manufacturing division in Asia?

The experts generally agree that EDC should have a presence in Asia, but differ on whether they should joint venture or go it alone, one plant or several, and also on timing.

4. What plan of action would you recommend to Ann Reardon?

Whichever way you go, it's important to develop a long-term strategy, not just a reaction to the market opportunity. As one of the experts points out, none of the functional managers in the case sees product development and product engineering as essential elements of the Asian expansion issue, yet rapid new product introduction is part of their past success.

114

Teaching Strategy

We would suggest going through each of the four questions in the order given. Question 3 lends itself to debate, so the instructor might want to choose up teams and have them go to it. Question 4 also presents a wide range of options that could be debated. We would suggest that the instructor push hard for specifics of the plan of action. Go slow vs. go-fast is the crux of the issue.

The major learning point that we see is that the location decision must be tied to a clear understanding of how a company's current capabilities match (or must be altered) for it to compete in a foreign location in the future. Ann Reardon must do a good deal more homework.

CASE

Applichem – The Transportation Problem – Teaching Note

This case is a good problem that requires the students to use the transportation method of linear programming to solve a facility location problem. There is an interesting dilemma in the case due to the transportation model indicating that a plant in Japan should be closed, when strategically this might not be such a good idea. This makes for good class discussion relating to criteria that cannot be captured in a purely quantitative analysis of a situation.

Another item that might be good to discuss with this case is the impact of exchange rate volatility relative to the plant location problem. Many global companies (such as automobile manufacturers) locate in countries in order to reduce exchange rate risk. Exchange rate risk is not described in any major way in the book, but it is important that students understand how important this can be in making facility location decisions.

A spreadsheet (Applichem.xls) is included on the student CD to help students solve this problem. Additional information about using the Excel solver is included in a Tutorial included on the CD. The following are answers to the discussion questions.

Discussion Questions:

1. Evaluate the cost associated with the way Applichem's plant capacity is currently being used?

Applichem - The Transportation Problem

Product Made and Shipped During Past Year (in 100,000 lb units)

Plant/Country	Mexico	Canada	Venezuela	Europe	United States	Japan
Mexico City	3.0		6.3			7.9
Windsor Ontario, Canada		2.6				
Caracas, Venezuela			4.1			
Frankfort, Germany			5.6	20.0	12.4	
Gary, Indiana					14.0	
Osaka, Japan						4.0
Total	3.0	2.6	16.0	20.0	26.4	11.9

Plant Production Costs and Capacity (per 100,000 lbs)

	Production Cost (per 100 lbs)	Plant Capacity (100,000 lbs units)
Mexico City	92.63	22.0
Windsor Ontario, Canada	93.25	3.7
Caracas, Venezuela	112.31	4.5
Frankfort, Germany	73.31	47.0
Gary, Indiana	89.15	18.5
Osaka, Japan	149.24	5.0

Transportation Cost, Import Duties and Demands for Release-ease

Plant/Country	Mexico	Canada	Venezuela	Europe	United States	Japan
Mexico City	0.00	11.40	7.00	11.00	11.00	14.00
Windsor Ontario, Canada	11.00	0.00	9.00	11.50	6.00	13.00
Caracas, Venezuela	7.00	10.00	0.00	13.00	10.40	14.30
Frankfort, Germany	10.00	11.50	12.50	0.00	11.20	13.30
Gary, Indiana	10.00	6.00	11.00	10.00	0.00	12.50
Osaka, Japan	14.00	13.00	12.50	14.20	13.00	0.00
Total Demand	3.00	2.60	16.00	20.00	26.40	11.90
Import Duty	0.0%	0.0%	50.0%	9.5%	4.5%	6.0%

117

Cost of Each Alternative (per 100,000 lbs shipped)

Plant/Country	Mexico	Canada	Venezuela	Europe	United States	Japan
Mexico City	92.63	104.03	145.95	112.43	107.80	112.19
Windsor Ontario, Canada	104.25	93.25	148.88	113.61	103.45	111.85
Caracas, Venezuela	119.31	122.31	112.31	135.98	127.76	133.35
Frankfort, Germany	83.31	84.81	122.47	73.31	87.81	91.01
Gary, Indiana	99.15	95.15	144.73	107.62	89.15	107.00
Osaka, Japan	163.24	162.24	236.36	177.62	168.96	149.24

Cost of Current Allocation of Capacity

Plant/Country	Mexico	Canada	Venezuela	Europe	United States	Japan
Mexico City	277.89	0.00	919.45	0.00	0.00	886.28
Windsor Ontario, Canada	0.00	242.45	0.00	0.00	0.00	0.00
Caracas, Venezuela	0.00	0.00	460.47	0.00	0.00	0.00
Frankfort, Germany	0.00	0.00	685.80	1466.20	1088.83	0.00
Gary, Indiana	0.00	0.00	0.00	0.00	1248.10	0.00
Osaka, Japan	0.00	0.00	0.00	0.00	0.00	596.96

Total Cost $7,872.44

2. Determine the optimal use of Applichem's plant capacity using the Solver in Excel.

Optimal Solution

Plant/Country	Mexico	Canada	Venezuela	Europe	United States	Japan	Capacity Used	Idle Capacity
Mexico City	3.0	0.0	0.0	0.0	3.2	0.0	6.2	15.80
Windsor Ontario, Canada	0.0	2.6	0.0	0.0	1.1	0.0	3.7	0.00
Caracas, Venezuela	0.0	0.0	4.5	0.0	0.0	0.0	4.5	0.00
Frankfort, Germany	0.0	0.0	11.5	20.0	3.6	11.9	47.0	0.00
Gary, Indiana	0.0	0.0	0.0	0.0	18.5	0.0	18.5	0.00
Osaka, Japan	0.0	0.0	0.0	0.0	0.0	0.0	0.0	5.00
Demand Met	3.0	2.6	16.0	20.0	26.4	11.9		

Cost of Optimal Solution

Plant/Country	Mexico	Canada	Venezuela	Europe	United States	Japan
Mexico City	277.89	0.00	0.00	0.00	344.95	0.00
Windsor Ontario, Canada	0.00	242.45	0.00	0.00	113.79	0.00
Caracas, Venezuela	0.00	0.00	505.40	0.00	0.00	0.00
Frankfort, Germany	0.00	0.00	1408.35	1466.20	316.11	1083.00
Gary, Indiana	0.00	0.00	0.00	0.00	1649.28	0.00
Osaka, Japan	0.00	0.00	0.00	0.00	0.00	0.00

Total Cost $7,407.42

3. What would you recommend that Applichem management do? Why?

A major issue is rather the Japan plant should be closed. Of course, if it is closed Applichem will probably lose the Japanese market totally. The students should be asked to evaluate the cost of keeping the plant open. To evaluate this alternative a constraint can be added that forces the Japanese plant to operate at capacity. The following is a spreadsheet solution with the Japan plant forced open. Notice that the increase is cost is only about $200,000.

Optimal Solution

Plant/Country	Mexico	Canada	Venezuela	Europe	United States	Japan	Capacity Used	Idle Capacity
Mexico City	2.3	0.0	0.0	0.0	0.0	0.0	2.3	19.70
Windsor Ontario, Canada	0.0	2.6	0.0	0.0	0.0	0.0	2.6	1.10
Caracas, Venezuela	0.0	0.0	4.5	0.0	0.0	0.0	4.5	0.00
Frankfort, Germany	0.7	0.0	11.5	20.0	7.9	6.9	47.0	0.00
Gary, Indiana	0.0	0.0	0.0	0.0	18.5	0.0	18.5	0.00
Osaka, Japan	0.0	0.0	0.0	0.0	0.0	5.0	5.0	0.00
Demand Met	3.0	2.6	16.0	20.0	26.4	11.9		

Cost of Optimal Solution

Plant/Country	Mexico	Canada	Venezuela	Europe	United States	Japan
Mexico City	213.05	0.00	0.00	0.00	0.00	0.00
Windsor Ontario, Canada	0.00	242.45	0.00	0.00	0.00	0.00
Caracas, Venezuela	0.00	0.00	505.40	0.00	0.00	0.00
Frankfort, Germany	58.32	0.00	1408.35	1466.20	693.69	627.96
Gary, Indiana	0.00	0.00	0.00	0.00	1649.28	0.00
Osaka, Japan	0.00	0.00	0.00	0.00	0.00	746.20

Total Cost $7,610.88

Chapter 10 - Just-in-Time and Lean Systems

Overview

Chapter 10 presents just-in-time (JIT) production from philosophical, systems, and historical perspectives. The philosophical view was contained in the "seven wastes" identified by Shigeo Shingo and Taichi Ohno at Toyota. Continual attention to reduction of the seven wastes is at the core of the manufacturing application of JIT. The systems view of JIT is centered on the design elements of the JIT system such as focused factory networks, group technology, quality at the source, JIT production, uniform plant loading, Kanban, and setup-time reduction. From a historical perspective, many of the JIT concepts resulted from the modern application of the teachings of Henry Ford. JIT approaches have been widely adopted around the world and help define world-class practice. JIT concepts are also applicable to services.

Major Points of the Chapter

1. The Japanese approach to productivity has led to lower costs and higher production.

2. The improvements in Japanese productivity are a result of implementing the Japanese philosophy of avoiding waste and respecting people.

3. A major source of improvement has been the adoption of JIT systems that combine the elements of total quality control, demand pull, and inventory reduction.

4. Kanban is very similar to fixed-order quantity/order-point systems. Kanban has been more successful because the Japanese have controlled the total manufacturing environment.

5. Kanban is a manual system that is most appropriate for repetitive production. MRP II is a computer-based system and is appropriate for non-repetitive production

6. JIT should be studied because it has been very successful. However, not all aspects of it are appropriate for adoption by United States firms.

7. JIT techniques that are applicable in manufacturing environments also apply in service organizations.

Teaching Tips

Hewlett-Packard's Greeley division has made a videotape that demonstrates the advantages of pull systems relative to push systems. We can't tell you whom to contact to obtain a copy of the tape, but it seems that many of the large computer companies and APICS chapter members have bootleg copies of it, which you might be able to borrow. (The tape is 40 minutes long and shows HP managers clumsily assembling Styrofoam boxes. It's corny but effective.)

The segments on "Lean Production" and "Improving Operations Methods" cover many of the topics discussed.

Cases, Exercises and Spreadsheets (Source)

"Quick response Apparel" (Book)

"Toyota Work Contracts" (Book)

Quality Parts Company" (Book)

"Sunwind" (European Case Clearing)

"Johnson Control, Automotive Systems Group: The Georgetown, Kentucky Plant" (HBS 9-693-086)

"Toyota Motor Manufacturing, U.S.A., Inc." (HBS 9-693-019)

Videos/Clips (Source)

"JIT at Federal Signal" (Vol. IV)

"Tri-State Converting to JIT" (Volume V)

"Lean Production" (Vol. I)

"Supplier Development Outreach Program" (Vol. II)

"Stockless Production" (Hewlett-Packard)

"Improving Operations Methods" (Vol. II)

"Just-In-Time Defined" (CD-ROM)

"Big JIT" (CD-ROM)

"Little JIT" (CD-ROM)

"Kanban – Container System (CD-ROM)

"Kanban – Visual System" (CD-ROM)

"Andon Board" (CD-ROM)

"Jidoka" (CD-ROM)

"Waste – Defined" (CD-ROM)

CASE

Toyota, Ford, GM and Volkswagen – Some Differing Opinions about Working with Suppliers – Teaching Note

Questions

1. GM and Ford have quickly pushed the development of large Internet sites to create an environment where suppliers must compete for business. Ford and GM argue that these Internet sites should reduce cost since the negotiations are streamlined. How do you think the suppliers view these sites?

The opinions of suppliers probably vary depending on how competitive they feel they can be. Actually, opening up these trading sites offers many new opportunities to new companies to expand their business. Those companies that are most efficient can really clean up, whereas those not efficient will die very quickly.

2. Rather than having vendors compete against one another, Toyota is interested in treating suppliers as partners. Is Toyota just being "old fashioned" in their views?

Toyota being "old fashioned".. I doubt it. Actually, let there be no doubt that Toyota wants to reduce cost as much as possible. The philosophy is just different. Toyota thinks that it can be done by working closely with its vendors, whereas Ford and GM just focus on pitting the companies against each other. This difference in approach may be cultural to a large extent. Clearly there is more than one way to do this, and these are both highly successful approaches.

3. A major reason of the differences in opinions may be the difference in what Toyota considers "competitive" components. These are the components that would mostly be bought using the Internet trading sites. Who is right? Are steering wheels and wire connectors competitive components?

Defining "competitive" components is a tough one. There are a lot of vendors in the world that specialize in steering wheels and even more that make wire connectors. The issue here is largely one of the design of the product. Including more parts as "competitive" sure makes the product more unique, which may create value in the marketplace. On the other hand it may increase cost.

CASE

Quality Parts Company – Teaching Note

QUESTIONS:

1. Which of the changes being considered by the manager of Quality Parts Company go counter to the JIT philosophy?

Almost all of the recommended changes run counter JIT principles: Using MRP to "keep the skids filled" implies the use of inventory as a motivator to push production. Adding external inspectors is counter the JIT practice of in-process inspection. Setting up a rework line only institutionalizes the acceptance of rework. Labor and machine utilization are not objectives of JIT. The focus should be more on flexibility and reducing the waste of overproduction. The installation of high rise shelving indicates an acceptance of wasteful inventory.

2. Make recommendations for JIT improvements in such areas as scheduling, layout, Kanban, task groupings, and inventory. Use quantitative data as much as possible; state necessary assumptions.

Answers will vary. The students might be encouraged to use the Lotfi and Pegels software to develop layouts. Machines and operations might be located in U-shaped layouts according to the assembly line balance.

3. Sketch the operation of a pull system for quality for Quality Parts Company's current system.

Answers will vary. The U-shaped layout is a useful tool. Machining cells might also be utilized.

4. Outline a plan for the introduction of JIT at Quality Parts Company.

The plan will depend on the specific recommendations. Likely steps include acceptance of recommendations, development of an implementation schedule, training, team development, waste reduction, retooling, reallocation of workspace, and implementation of workflows. Top down direction in the change should be emphasized. Shigeo Shingo estimates that most companies will need five years to implement JIT.

Managerial Briefing 11 – Enterprise Resource Planning Systems

Overview

There is widespread agreement that the SAP has set new standards in the information technology market with R/3. The system was introduced in 1992, and leading companies around the world have implemented it. The purpose of this chapter is to provide an overview of the software package, showing how the program developed over time and describing the comprehensive set of applications that are included. Our purpose is not to endorse the R/3, but rather to present it as an example of a significant new class of enterprise resource planning (ERP) software.

Key Points

1. R/3 is built around a comprehensive set of application modules. The modules are used to support different functional areas in the firm.

2. R/3 has existed since 1992.

3. A significant feature of R/3 is its use of a data warehouse. This allows data to be easily aggregated and disaggregated by the user.

4. The major components are as follows: financial accounting, human resources, manufacturing and logistics, and sales and distribution.

5. Many companies have found R/3 difficult to implement.

Teaching Tips

This Managerial Briefing can be augmented with a video tape which can be obtained from SAP-America. Their offices are located in Boston, MA. Phone numbers and additional information can be obtained form the SAP website at http://www.sap.com.

A unique book titled *Why ERP?* is available from McGraw-Hill. This book is written as a novel, similar to the style used in *The Goal* for quick and fun reading. This book is designed to introduce the basic capabilities that are included in ERP systems and the reason why ERP systems are attractive investments. In addition, issues that can make the installation of the software a challenge, particularly in a multi-site firm are discussed. The website for the book with additional information is http://www.pom.edu/erp/.

Cases, Exercises and Spreadsheets (Source)

"Vandelay Industries, Inc." (HBS 9-697-037)

Videos/Clips (Source)

"SAP R/3" (Video tapes are available from SAP)

Chapter 11 - Forecasting

Overview

Forecasting is a prerequisite to any type of planning, and is an integral part of production planning and inventory control. In order to create a forecast, several techniques are possible such as qualitative, time series analysis, causal relationships, and simulation models. This chapter concentrates on time series analysis first taking the student through the simple moving average, weighted average, single exponential smoothing, and regression analysis. Since these techniques lag in following changes in the real system being forecasted, the student is then taken through two models which add in trend factors and seasonal effects. Lastly, the very simple almost naïve technique called "focused forecasting" is presented. This is included to show that the effectiveness of a forecasting model is not necessarily related to its sophistication. A very simple technique, which is easily understood, can often outperform a more mathematically complicated model. It is important to recognize that managers need the ability to interpret and question the assumptions of forecasts they receive from forecasting analysts. This chapter aids in providing such expertise.

Major Points of the Chapter

1. Forecasting is the basis for production planning, budgeting, and most other business activities.

2. Perfect forecast accuracy is unattainable but nevertheless desirable goal.

3. Maintaining flexibility in the system compensates for errors in forecasting.

4. Often, the simpler forecasting models provide results as good or better than the more sophisticated models.

5. The performance records of forecasting models should be tracked for evaluation purposes.

Teaching Tips

Microsoft Excel has some extensive forecasting procedures built into the "Data Analysis Tool Pack". Students find it interesting if you demonstrate some of these tools (exponential smoothing, moving averages, and regression are available).

Cases, Exercises and Spreadsheets (Source)

"Forecasting Spreadsheet" (CD-ROM)
"L. L. Bean, Inc.: Item Forecasting and Inventory Management" (HBS 9-893-003)

Videos/Clips (Source)

None

Chapter 12 - Aggregate Planning

Overview

In this chapter, aggregate planning is introduced in the context of a hierarchy of planning steps resulting in a sequential disaggregation of high-level requirements to periodic production schedule. Aggregate planning problems are closely related to capacity decisions and involve sensitive personnel issues such as staffing levels. Aggregate planning is introduced through the use of a manufacturing case and a services case. The manufacturing case is entitled CA&J Company and the services example is Tucson Parks and Recreation. Remember that aggregate planning is performed at a high, strategic level and does not involve detailed resource planning. Aggregate planning systems must be flexible enough to handle variations in demand. Also, once planning rules are established, they must be followed. The important topic of yield management is also discussed in the chapter.

Major Points of the Chapter

1. Aggregate planning translates annual business and marketing plans into a production plan for all products.

2. Aggregate planning is medium range planning (generally to 18 months into the future).

3. Setting production rates, work force levels, and inventory balances is the main purpose of aggregate planning.

4. The complexity of the real world often makes aggregate planning more of an art than a science.

5. The concept of yield management is used to allocate capacity to the right type of customer at the right price and time to maximize revenue.

Teaching Tips

This is a good chapter to do a spreadsheet exercise. The example given in the chapter is included on the CD-ROM. In addition, a case titled "Bradford Manufacturing" has been developed. This case used the Excel Solver and as an option the instructor can conduct an in-class simulation using the results from the first part of the exercise.

Cases, Exercises and Spreadsheets (Source)

"Aggregate_Planning Spreadsheet" (CD-ROM)

"Aggregate_Planning_Solved_Problem Spreadsheet" (CD-ROM)

"Bradford Manufacturing Spreadsheet" (CD-ROM)

Videos/Clips (Source)

"Schedule Services - the United Solution" (Vol. IV)

CASE

Bradford Manufacturing – Planning Plant Production - Teaching Note

This is a case that is designed to give the student experience with developing an aggregate plan. A follow up in-class simulation exercise can also be done with the students. The simulation involves the operation of the plant over the first 13 to 20 weeks of the year. The simulation allows students to experience the problems associated with implementing an aggregate plan.

Assign the case as a homework assignment. The student should be instructed to develop an aggregate plan. Remind them to use the spreadsheet named "Bradford Manufacturing" from the CD. You might want to take 10 minutes in the class prior to the day when you plan to do the simulation exercise to quickly familiarize students with the spreadsheet.

Remind students to bring a printout of their aggregate plan to class and to bring their notebook computer, if they have one.

Start the class by asking about their aggregate plans. Generate a range of costs that students obtained on the board.

Next, ask students to describe how they obtained their solution to the problem. Try to characterize the different approaches. Some likely categories would be "Trial and Error", "A simple heuristic", and "Excel Solver".

Following this, the spreadsheet can be brought up and some of the better solutions displayed. You can also run the Solver if you like at this time. You will need to "unprotect" the spreadsheet to run the Solver (Tools > Protection > Unprotect). Finish this section by putting a solution in the Aggregate Plan portion of the spreadsheet that seems to be a good one.

Now move to the Simulation Worksheet part of the spreadsheet. Here the plan has been reorganized into a weekly master schedule with the data from the Aggregate Plan initially seeding the schedule. The idea is to now work through the weekly schedule by putting in what actually happened in terms of sales and production rates. After seeing the data each week, students should be given the opportunity to change next weeks schedule. You should do this for at least the first 13 weeks. Then you can click on the Actual Costs worksheet and compare the budgeted cost to the actual cost of running the plant.

To make the simulation interesting use actual demand that demonstrates the old "hockey stick" phenomenon. Sales should be real slow at the beginning of the quarter and then surge at the end. Remember there is a sale at the end of the 1st quarter. Try to be real straight when you go from week to week and don't hint at the fact that demand will take off at the end. This can be a good lesson for the student.

The following are a set of production rates and demand that work well:

Week	Production Rate	Demand	Week	Production Rate	Demand
1	423	140	11	465	112
2	455	120	12	450	200
3	430	100	13	455	450
4	435	125	14	450	160
5	435	125	15	430	165
6	460	105	16	450	160
7	465	115	17	455	145
8	470	120	18	470	150
9	455	105	19	460	155
10	460	110	20	455	160

You can complete the exercise by discussing the following items:

Why did demand vary the way it did during the first quarter?

Why is it important for manufacturing and marketing to coordinate plans?

What types of things can marketing do to make it easier on manufacturing? (Separate the deals from the deliveries. Everyday low pricing, etc.)

Do you think that management should change their inventory target?

Teaching Plan for a class using Bradford Manufacturing

Explain how Aggregate Planning fits into the overall process of Planning and Control – show chart.

What is Aggregate Planning ?
- Setting workforce levels
- Aggregate inventory levels
- Production rate
- 6-18 month horizon
- Product groups – rather than individual products

A strategy for how demand will be met, given current resource constraints.

Why is Aggregate Planning important?
- Key interface to the capital budgeting process

10 minutes into the class

Bradford Manufacturing
- What are the key drivers of this plan?
Forecast -> Marketing/market Research
Ending Inventory Target -> Management
Technical Parameters – define current resource constraints and costs.
- Evaluate the costs associated with the current plan.

Develop a solver plan. Rationalize the plan. – Integerize

30 minutes into class

- Two basic strategies – chase demand or level demand (use inventory)

- Put a high hiring and firing cost into the solution and generate a level plan. Use hiring and training cost of $15,000 and layoff cost of $5,000.

35 Minutes into class

- Explain the relationship between the Aggregate Plan and the Master Schedule

Run the simulation (takes about 40 minutes)
Conditions
    Inventory target – 1 week
    Hiring/training = $5,000
    Layoff cost = $3,000

    Initial inventory = 200(000) units

    Offer prize!

    First, each student (or pair of students) need to finalize an Aggregate Plan, then move to the simulation worksheet. Make sure initial inventory is set correctly. Show actual cost worksheet. Run simulation per the previous instructions.

Chapter 13 - Inventory Control

Overview

Firms invest 30-35 percent of assets in inventory. Yet, they continue to manage inventory haphazardly. This chapter focuses on inventory control for conditions of independent demand, where each inventory item is analyzed as an individual item, considering its own demand and various costs.

This chapter presents basic concepts and definitions. Several simple models of the periodic and fixed quantity type are included. Also in this chapter, inventory control through marginal analysis (the newspaper boy problem), and ABC classification is covered. Additionally, examples of inventory policy in several service areas are included.

As a word of caution on this chapter: The chapter covers a great deal of material and a number of different inventory models. The instructor should select those portions he or she wishes to emphasize and advise the students to scan the remaining material (unless adequate time has been scheduled, of course).

Major Points of the Chapter

1. There are two basic inventory model types—those that are based on ordering at set time intervals and those that are based on ordering set amounts as the need arises.

2. Relevant inventory costs consist of holding, setup, ordering, and shortage costs.

3. A key issue in inventory analysis is in determining how to provide for various service levels, i.e., what should the order quantities and reorder points be to meet demand directly from stock on hand.

4. The ABC technique of inventory analysis focuses management attention on the important items.

5. EOQ models have been controversial. When the appropriate assumptions are satisfied, these models can be very useful.

Teaching Tips

Reorder points can be made more tangible in students' minds if you point out consumer products that have built in ROPs. Examples are cough syrup bottles, gas gauges, and checkbooks. We often sketch these on transparencies along with the following reorder signal.

Asking students to name a business where absolute accuracy is a must can convey the importance of inventory accuracy. Answer: Banks.

There is a tutorial on EOQ included on the CD-ROM. This tutorial shows with an Excel spreadsheet the trade-off between ordering and carrying costs as the order quantity varies.

The HP DeskJet case is good for tying this material to Supply Chain Strategy. The case demonstrates the potential saving from pooling inventory. The pooling comes by making generic printers in the Vancouver plant and then localizing the printers in Europe. This is a pretty advanced case, so it is important to make sure students understand the basic equal order period model before assigning the case.

Cases, Exercises and Spreadsheets (Source)

"Inventory_Control Spreadsheet" (CD-ROM)

"Hewlett-Packard – Supply the DeskJet Printer in Europe" (Book)

"HP DeskJet Spreadsheet" (CD-ROM)

"Finish Line" (IRM)

Videos/Clips (Source)

"Tutorial EOQ" (CD-ROM)

"Manufacturing Inventory" (Vol. II)

"Washburn Guitars" (Vol. III)

"Inventory Defined" (CD-ROM)

"Inventory Costs" (CD-ROM)

"Inventory Service Parts" (CD-ROM)

CASE

Hewlett-Packard – Supplying the DeskJet Printer in Europe – Teaching Note

First review the Reorder Point model and the Equal Order Period model (this could be done on the day prior to when the DeskJet case is being discussed. It's important that the average inventory calculations are covered, since this is no covered in the book.)

Let's use some different numbers, just for another problem example.

d = 20 units/day, std. dev. = 4 unit/day

L = 10 days

96% confidence

Q = 600 units

ROP (min level) = D(lead time) + SS

D(lead time) = 10 * 20 = 200

SS = 1.75 * Std dev(lead time) ---- sqrt(10*4^2) = 12.65

SS = 1.75 * 12.65 = 22.14

ROP = 222 unit

What is average inventory?   Q/2 + SS = 600/2 + 22 = 322

Equal Order Period model

Max Level = D(lead time + review period) + SS

Review period is 30 days

D (T+L) = (30+10) * 20 = 800

SS = 1.75 * Std dev (lead time + review period) -- sqrt (40*4^2) = 25.3

SS = 1.75 * 25.3 = 44.271 –> 44

Max Level = 20 * (30+10) + 44 = 800 + 44 = 844

If we have 200 on hand (and nothing on order) then q = 844 – 200 = 644

What is average inventory? D(T)/2 + SS = (20 *30)/2 + 44 = 344

To begin the discussion of the HP case, ask the following question:

If HP did not produce a generic computer, what would our model suggest the average inventory to be?

Let's consider model AB

Monthly mean 15,830.1, Std Dev = 5,624.6

Review Cycle = 1 week

Lead Time = 6 weeks

Average Weekly Demand = 15,830.1/4 = 3,957.525

Std. Dev. = sqrt (5624.6^2/4) = 2,812.3

Average inventory = 3957.525/2 + 2.1 * sqrt(7 * 2,812.6^2)

= 17,260 units

These are worth $250 each = 4,315,000 total value of inventory

Inventory carrying cost = 4,315,000 * .25 = $1, 078,950

This is compared to HP's current policy of carrying 1 month's worth of inventory for the model AB. This cost is (15,830.1 * 250 * .25) = $989,381.25. In this case the model would suggest that additional inventory be kept.

Next bring up the spreadsheet (from the Student CD, Website-ROM) and do the calculations for the rest of the items. The calculations are then done for the pooled demand. The savings are pretty dramatic as can be seen from the following completed spreadsheet.

Exhibit 13.17: DeskJet Demand Data from Europe

Europe Options	NOV	DEC	JAN	FEB	MAR	APR	MAY	JUN	JUL	AUG	SEP	OCT	Mean	Std Dev	Std Dev (1 week)
A	80	-	60	90	21	48	-	9	20	54	84	42	42	31	16
AB	20,572	20,895	19,252	11,052	19,864	20,316	13,336	10,578	6,096	14,496	23,712	9,792	15,830	5,385	2,693
AU	4,564	3,207	7,485	4,908	5,295	90	-	5,004	4,385	5,103	4,302	6,153	4,208	2,111	1,055
AA	400	255	408	645	210	87	432	816	430	630	456	273	420	195	98
AQ	4,008	2,196	4,761	1,953	1,008	2,358	1,676	540	2,310	2,046	1,797	2,961	2,301	1,119	559
AY	248	450	378	306	219	204	248	484	164	363	384	234	307	99	49
TOTAL	29,872	27,003	32,344	18,954	26,617	23,103	15,692	17,431	13,405	22,692	30,735	19,455	23,109	5,978	2,989

	Target	Std Dev (6 weeks)	SS - Statistical Demand	Exp.	Max Level	Expected Inventory - cycle stock + safety stock
A	42.33	38.01	78.06	63.50	141.56	83
AB	15830.08	6595.40	13545.30	23745.13	37290.42	15,524
AU	4208.00	2585.10	5309.15	6312.00	11621.15	5,835
AA	420.17	239.13	491.10	630.25	1121.35	544
AQ	2301.17	1370.18	2814.00	3451.75	6265.75	3,102
AY	306.83	120.92	248.34	460.25	708.59	287
Total	23108.58		22485.96			25,375

	Std Dev (6 weeks)	SS	Exp.	Max Level	Expected Inventory
Pooled Demand	7,322	15,037	34,663	49,700	17,925

EXTRA CASE

Finish Line

F. Robert Jacobs – Indiana University

Introduction

Finish Line runs retail athletic shoe stores in more than 200 locations. The company is based in Indianapolis, Indiana where its corporate warehouse is located. Don Courtney, Vice President, in charge of Management Information Systems, Materials Movement and Distribution, assessed the impact of a new Finish Line megastore located in the Circle Center Mall in Indianapolis.

> "One of the things we noticed early on was that we started having lots of products come in specifically for the Circle Center store. We were doing business with vendors we had not done business with before. A lot of products were just unique to that store and didn't go to any other stores."

The distribution center was set up to handle the mass distribution of products that would be sent to all of the stores. The special products for the Circle Center store would be ordered in small quantities. These products would take up just as much space to process as the normal products.

> "..so we developed a predistributed purchase order so that the product was distributed immediately on receipt. This eliminated having to give it an assigned location and having to create pick lists just for that one store. So we did smooth out that process early in the phase of product coming in for that store. We did it by experience. We didn't guess that one early. We did it when we saw it coming in, recognizing it was taking just as much effort for one store as it was for 200 stores."

Many aspects of the operation of the new store were different. The new store, with 15,000 square feet of retail space, compared to the normal 5,000 square foot stores, presented new operations challenges for Don and his team. Don wondered what other surprises were waiting as he prepared for the new store's first week of operation and the upcoming Christmas buying season.

Logistics at the Finish Line

The efficient flow of material through the Finish Line distribution system is important to the success of the company. Buyers who anticipate the needs of the many stores order the product. Vendors, such as Nike and Reebok, send the product to the warehouse in Indianapolis. On receipt, the product is stored in a location determined by a computer program designed to maximize the use of space in the warehouse.

A complete inventory of items in the stores, in transit between the stores and the warehouse, and in the warehouse, is maintained by a computer located at corporate headquarters. Each night, the computer calculates lists of items that are needed by each store. This list is specially sorted so that the items can be quickly picked in the warehouse. Once picked, a conveyor moves the items to an area where they are sorted by store.

The Finish Line has contracted with a few trucking companies which deliver product using large semi-trailers. The normal stores each receive a delivery every three-week days. This three-day schedule allows stores to be replenished two times per week in two out of three weeks. In a three-week period, they get five shipments. The new Circle Center store receives shipments every day of the week. Products can also be transshipped between stores when necessary.

Product Buyers

Products sold at the Finish Line stores are divided into about 40 departments. Examples of these departments include basketball shoes, running shoes, cross trainers, tennis shoes, and football shoes. Apparel, such as jackets, are also organized by department. Buyers specialize in departments, allowing them to become familiar with the products and the particular characteristics of customer demand and supplier manufacturing practice.

Shoes generally make up about 70 percent of the business. This varies, though, according to the time of the year. In August, 85 percent of the business might be Fall back-to-school shoes. This drops to 50 percent in December, when it is easier to buy a sweatshirt or baseball cap as a gift.

The buyers see the Finish Line business as highly fashion oriented. Seventy-five percent of the product that comes into the distribution center is new. Often the product is very similar to one ordered last year. Customers expect the latest style and color. The buyers can look at how a similar product sold last year when all of it was available. Looking at how it sold in total may be misleading, since they are normally going to sell what they bought.

The product is normally not replenished. Rather, the item is purchased, pushed out to the retail stores and sold. There are exceptions to this, particularly with staple items, such as socks. Determining the amount to be purchased can be difficult.

Even though it only takes two to three months for the company to actually produce the product, the normal lead-time quoted by a company like Nike or Reebok is six months. From the many choices presented, the buyer is faced with the difficult problem of anticipating what will be hot six to twelve months into the future. Imagine how difficult it is to anticipate the success of a Jordan or O'Neil during the next basketball season! The life of a new style is less than six months.

The order quantity is built up from forecasts of demand done at the store level. The actual distribution of sizes sold at each store is part of the calculation. These forecasts are then adjusted based on projected store department sales figures.

The supplier collects orders from buyers at all the major retail outlets using strict deadlines. Missing the forecast for an item can be disastrous, since there is normally no second chance to reorder. Ordering too many results in having to discount the item at one of the outlet stores where discontinued styles are sold.

Once the order arrives from the supplier, approximately 60 percent is immediately distributed to the stores. The allocation to the stores is calculated from the forecasts used to determine the original order, adjusted for store closings and new stores. The rest of the order is stored in the warehouse, and used to replenish store inventory.

Retail Store Inventory Replenishment

The central computer keeps a perpetual inventory of every stock keeping unit (SKU) at every store and in the warehouse. An SKU is a unique item in inventory. In the case of shoes, for example, an SKU is a specific style, color, and size pair of shoes. A typical store has approximately 5,000 SKUs and the Circle Center store has more than 10,000 SKUs.

Each night, the computer calls each store and downloads information concerning each sale to a customer, returns from a customer, receipts from the warehouse, and transfers to another store. The computer knows the exact location of each unit of each SKU sold by the Finish Line. If a store needs, for example, a size 10 mens, black, Michael Jordan, basketball shoe, the system can be queried for the current location of a pair. The system keeps detailed sales history information to aid the buyers in their purchasing decisions.

Associated with each SKU at each location, a minimum and maximum quantity target is defined. These values are used to control the replenishment of inventory at each location. The system generates a replenishment order for a location whenever the on hand balance plus the amount in transit to that location is less than the minimum level. The size of the order is the quantity needed to bring the level up to the maximum amount.

For a typical style at a store there might only be 24 to 30 pairs, and that can be spread over 12 or 13 sizes. For the largest and smallest sizes the minimum and maximum quantity typically would be set to one. The minimum and maximums might be two for the sizes other than the 9's to 11's, which might be set at a minimum of three and maximum of four.

Don Courtney commented on the first Friday of sales at the Circle Center store:

> "...the first Friday we sold 286 pairs of men's shoes and those represented 276 different SKUs. So it was all one of this, one of that, and one of this. And without having that broad range of offerings, obviously we wouldn't be able to do that. So it's very important when you have that kind of business, it's very important that when you sell one, you can replace it."

At some point, replenishment is no longer possible from the distribution center. At this time the buyers have to decide which stores will receive the remaining inventory. The buyers run what is called a *grid sheet* that shows store by store the recent sales and the sizes available for a style. From this they can see where the sizes are broken up and make transfers to stores where the style is selling well. Other factors the buyer must consider when making the transfers are the total number of shoes that a store can hold, the minimum number of shoes a store needs to have on hand to do business, the number of different styles on hand at the store, and the number of display locations at the store.

The Finish Line has a few stores that they refer to as close out or outlet stores. In these stores, shoes are displayed in large racks by size. So ultimately, when styles are broken to a point where all the sizes cannot be maintained in inventory, the style is closed out in these special stores.

The Layout of the Circle Center Store

The layout of the new store is typical of the other stores, just much larger. Along each wall are display ranks where a single shoe of each style is shown. These display racks are organized by men's shoes, women's shoes, hiking shoes, and golf shoes. There is a large display area for sports apparel in the rear of the store.

Other than for a few sale items, the inventory for each style is kept in a stock room that is adjacent to the store. Similar to the display racks, the stock room is organized by shoe style and by size within the style.

When a customer indicates an interest in a shoe, the salesperson goes to the stockroom to retrieve a pair. The shoes are brought back to the customer and fitted. If the customer wants the shoes, they are then purchased at the centralized cash register kiosk.

Don had some concerns with the organization of the Circle Center store:

> "When we opened that store, we had plenty of everything in that first weekend, every time a salesperson left the shoe wall to go to the back room, you knew he or she was going to come back with the size that was requested. There's going to come a day, even in the first weeks, when like everybody else, you'd never have everything. We're always in the process of some styles fazing out.

141

Why that's such a concern to me with Circle Center is that it's a long walk, a walk all the way across the store. We keep our back room in an order. You put all the basketball shoes together so that if you go back for a particular basketball shoe, because that's what the customer wanted, and we don't have it in their size, you can find another basketball style in the same look, same price range, to come back and say, 'Well, I don't have that, but I have this. Would you like this other shoe?'

In fact, we have wired the columns in that store so that we could install a couple of touch screen terminals that could be used to quickly check store stock. We've even talked about doing headsets and having somebody in the back room checking, retrieving, and running the shoes to the shoe wall."

Inventory Accuracy

Accuracy in the inventory system is extremely important to the successful operation of the Finish Line system. Each item that is picked from the distribution center is scanned to verify what was obtained. It is easy for mistakes to be made, though. For example, if the quantity asks for seven of a particular item, the picker can scan the item and quickly enter the quantity seven. If they are picking T-shirts, it is easy for an extra one to be there that they did not see. Even though they have the right item, the right size, the right SKU, the quantity is incorrect.

The orders for each store are batched and sent in cartons. The system knows what should be in each carton. Sometimes, though, items get sent to the wrong store due to sorting errors in the warehouse. On receipt, the store must verify that what the system thought was in the carton is actually in the carton. Mistakes can even be made at this point in the process. Stores only get credited with what they verify as having been received.

Don commented on the problem:

> "But I'll tell ya', the times that we send 'em the biggest shipments are the times when they are the most crowded, and the most busy, and we don't give them space in the back room to check it well. I mean, they're lucky sometimes that they don't have to take those cartons, they're strung out along the hallway for a couple of hours, as they're working out sorting it and they can make as many mistakes checking it in as we make sending it to them."

Finish Line takes a complete physical of the entire inventory, including the stores and the distribution center, twice a year. Generally, 15 to 20 stores are checked each week. These store counts are done either by visiting store managers or by an outside firm. The distribution center is shut down for a few days over a weekend to count inventory.

Performance Measures

The two primary performance measures used to evaluate the logistics system, are inventory turns and stockouts. Inventory turns is calculated as the cost of goods sold during a year divided by average inventory value. Both the cost of goods and the inventory value are calculated using the amount paid the vendor for each item. Currently, Finish Line turns their inventory a little more than two times per year.

It is difficult to get a true measure of lost sales due to not having inventory available. Stockouts are measured by an audit every night of each SKU at each store location. A stockout is recorded where the inventory level is zero. Average stockouts currently only run at about 3 percent of the SKU/location combinations.

Discussion Points

1. How important is it to have a mix of products? When shoes slack off during the winter, the apparel business picks up. What are the implications of seasonal products? What problems does this create for The Finish Line?

2. Spread of risk. Given the way the buying takes place for the shoe products, who is taking the most risk? Is it the manufacturer or the buyer?

3. Differences between stores. A particular store might be an A store for ethnic basketball, a B store for outdoor wear, and a C store for running. The buyer has the ability to assign the A, B, C ranking by department. They can even get down to a style-by-style ranking. How does this impact the management of inventory?

4. How should the minimum and maximum levels be set? How important is it to have all the sizes for a particular style in stock?

5. What changes would you suggest to the performance measures currently used?

6. Given the way inventory is currently managed, does the current inventory turns performance make sense? Review Exhibit I to help evaluate this question.

Exhibit I - Nike X6-03 Running Shoe - Sales Summary

Date	Distribution Center (units on-hand)	Retail Stores (on-hand and in-transit)	Outlet Stores (on-hand and in-transit)	Lost (units)	Period Sales (units)	Period Revenue
Jan. 22	10,000	0	0		0	($600,000)
Feb. 19	3,754	5,492	0	2	752	$67,642[7]
March 18	3,052	4,542	0	20	1,632	$146,798
April 15	410	3,862	0	3	3,319	$298,544
May 13	0	617	0	1	3,654	$292,137
June 10	0	137	62	6	412	$30,699[8]
July 8	0	28	88	11	72	$5,615

[1]Initial price set at $89.95

[2]Retail price reduced to $79.95. Outlet store price $59.95.

1. ─────────────────

CASE

Finish Line – Teaching Note

1. How important is it to have a mix of products? When shoes slack off during the winter, the apparel business picks up. What are the implications of seasonal products? What problems does this create for The Finish Line?

This relates well to Aggregate Planning. The stores need products that compliment one another to maintain the profitability of the business. Purchasing so that seasonal products sell out each year is very important to minimize the cost associate with obsolete (out of fashion) goods.

2. Spread of risk. Given the way the buying takes place for the shoe products, who is taking the most risk? Is it the manufacturer or the buyer?

It looks like the buyer (Finish Line) is taking much of the risk. The situation with Nike is unique, in many other cases the opposite is true.

3. Differences between stores. A particular store might be an A store for ethnic basketball, a B store for outdoor wear, and a C store for running. The buyer has the ability to assign the A, B, C ranking by department. They can even get down to a style-by-style ranking. How does this impact the management of inventory?

Stocking levels would be very different for the same item in each store.

4. How should the minimum and maximum levels be set? How important is it to have all the sizes for a particular style in stock?

Actually, the minimum and maximum levels can both be set to one for many items. This is due to the frequent replenishment. Of course, this would not be true for the high demand styles and sizes.

5. What changes would you suggest to the performance measures currently used?

They should track how often they go to get a shoe for a customer and come back with a substitute or no shoe at all.

6. Given the way inventory is currently managed, does the current inventory turns performance make sense? Review Exhibit I to help evaluate this question.

For items similar to the Nike shoe, you would expect the inventory turn to be about 4 times per year (assuming they order about a 6 months supply with each order, and that the shoes sell out evenly over that period). Since in the case, they say that their inventory turn is about 2, they much have many items that do not sell this quickly. The data in the table seems to agree with the scenario presented in the case for the Nike shoe.

Chapter 14 – Material Requirements Planning

Overview

Material Requirements Planning is important to the practice of inventory planning and control. Because MRP would not be possible in any significant application without a computer, this chapter strongly stresses computer files and methodology. At the same time, attempts were made to keep the chapter relatively simple so as to not become overpowering. The instructor, if he or she wishes, may supplement this chapter by adding more depth on some of the finer points. Additional information may be obtained by referring to any of the requirements planning program manuals such as those from IBM & Hewlett Packard or by referring students to various journals, particularly APICS journals and Conference Proceedings starting from 1980.

Among advanced MRP topics discussed are MRPII, MRP and JIT, lot sizing in MRP, and Enterprise Resource Planning (ERP). SAP is introduced as a state-of-the-art ERP system. This chapter also recognizes the importance of EDI and the networking of suppliers and customers.

Major Points of the Chapter

1. Materials requirements planning (MRP) refers to the calculation of the quantity and timing of materials, parts, and components needed to create an end item.

2. A product structure tree identifies the elements of a product and shows the order in which the product is created.

3. A bill of materials is a standard method to list the quantities of materials that make up a product.

4. This chapter discusses new advances such as Flow Manufacturing/JIT logic combined with MRP.

5. MRP is a tool to improve firm competitiveness.

Teaching Tips

Most POM specialists have collected war stories from the MRP crusade. Many of these focus on how the guys on the shop floor resort to informal methods of inventory control (e.g., little black books which tell the true status of jobs in contrast to fancy computer printouts which are inaccurate or out of date). MRP zealots often criticize the EOQ formula's inaccuracy—"The only thing right about it is the 2, but even this is based on a constant usage rate, and therefore is suspect too."

To relate the MRP concept to something everybody in class is familiar with, we show a transparency of a shopper preparing a shopping list and tie this into Exhibit 14.6. The transparency master is provided on the next page.

HOMEMAKER PREPARING WEEKLY SHOPPING LIST FOR PANTRY

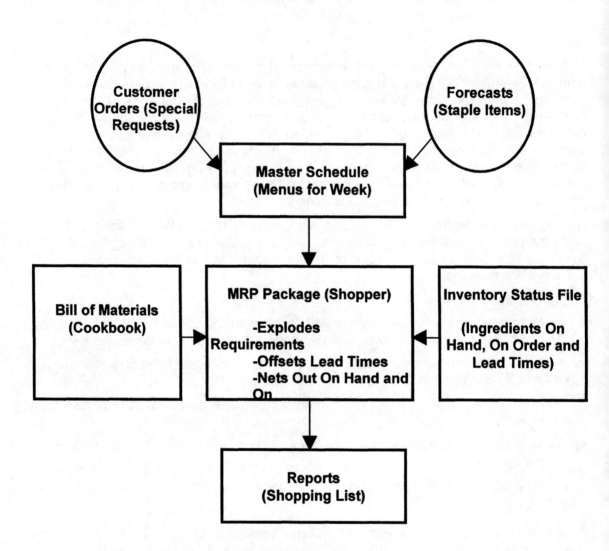

Note: MRP just prepares the shopping list; it does not do the shopping!

Cases, Exercises and Spreadsheets (Source)

"Nichols Company" (Book)

"Nichols_Case Spreadsheet – 2 parts" (CD-ROM)

"Brunswick Motors" (IRM)

"Digital Equipment Corp.: The Endpoint Model" (HBS 9-688-059)

Videos/Clips (Source)

"Production Tour of the Vision Light System at Federal Signal" (Vol. IV)

"Lean Production" (Vol. I)

"Manufacturing Inventory" (Vol. I)

"MRP II" (CD-ROM)

CASE

Nichols Company – Teaching note

Purpose of the case: To show the interdependency of the forecast, MPS, MRP, capacity limitations, backorder costs, shortage costs, and lot sizing.

The Nichols case does an excellent job of teaching not only the production/operation aspects, but also in teaching spreadsheets. To help the students, we have included two sample spreadsheets on the CD-ROM included with the book. These spreadsheets are "stripped down" versions of what is needed to completely solve the case. The basic logic is included in the samples, but they only cover 10 weeks, and they can use much improvement.

If you just want to do a quick exercise, limit the time horizon to 10 weeks and specify that backordering cannot be used. The first spreadsheet (Nichols_Case.xls) as given can be easily modified to answer questions 1 and 2. Question 3 can be answered with the second spreadsheet (Nichols_part3.xls).

The followings outlines a more comprehensive exercise that can be used as a class project.

Student Teams. Teams of 2-3 students each.

Time for students to complete case. Allow 3-4 weeks.

Response from Students. Students really like the experience and view it as very beneficial.

Using Nichols Case repeatedly.   For repeated usage in subsequent quarters, semesters, or seminars, simply change the data using different forecasts, different capacities, different processing requirements, etc. If you wish to experiment first, you can expand the case, for example, to include another product or work center.

On the first day of class, completely discuss the case and what is involved. Be clear, but yet do not give out the actual formulas that are to be used. Students need to figure these out themselves (the simplified spreadsheets help).

Either bring in overhead transparencies to show what the output looks like, or if possible, bring in a computer to demonstrate a completed program. Showing what the end product would look like gives the students a sense of direction. The computer demonstration can include changing the forecast or gross requirements and noting the effect on capacity by bringing up the tables of the machine center capacities. When transparencies or a computer is used, the entire class period will be needed.

Each class period until the case is due, five or ten minutes should be allocated so that students can contribute their progress reports, ask questions, and bring up peculiar experiences.

Note: The trickiest part of this project is in determining backorder and shortage costs. For the sample spreadsheets, no backordering is included, requirements not met are shown as net requirements. It is important to point this "problem" with the spreadsheet out, if the student's are going to allow backordering in the MRP.

The entire output consumes quite a few pages. The submitted case by a student team can be 40-50 pages, depending on print and paper size. The written report can be very short—3 or 4 pages as an overview and presenting summarized results.

Because of the lengthy output, this write up shows only a sample of output using screen captures. When trying to bring capacity within limits, it is very helpful to construct graphs of the workcenter hours. Working back and forth, the workcenter loads can be brought within capacity.

The following is a narrative for how the case can be solved. This takes about 2-3 hours to develop in full. This is just one solution and many other solutions are valid. This solution does not allow backordering.

A solution to the case

The following are a set of specific steps that can be used to complete the case using the spreadsheet (Nichols_Case.xls) supplied on the Student CD, Website as a starting point.

1. The student must expand the horizon to 27 weeks.

2. Enter demand for A, B, C for weeks 1-27.

3. Copy on-hand, net requirements, and planned order release formulas for A, B and C.

Note: with the way the spreadsheet is set up, it is easiest to show your master schedule for items A, B and C in the planned order receipt row. Changing entries in this row, totally updates the spreadsheet. You may want to show how an actual Master Schedule can be set up to feed data to the scheduled receipt rows for items A, B and C.

4. Fill in planned order receipts for A, B, C - use lot-for-lot. Point out to students how net requirements are generated when demand is not met and how on hand increases when excess material is scheduled.

J27 = =+ J7*4

		J	K	L	M	N	O	P	Q	R	S
1	Product A										
2		8	9	10	11	12	13	14	15	16	17
2		8	9	10	11	12	13	14	15	16	17
3	Gross requirements	1000	1100	1400	1400	1700	1700	1800	1900	2200	2000
4	On-Hand	0	0	0	0	0	0	0	0	0	0
5	Net requirements	0	0	0	0	0	0	0	0	0	0
6	Planned order receipt	1000	1100	1400	1400	1700	1700	1800	1900	2200	2000
7	Planned order release	1100	1400	1400	1700	1700	1800	1900	2200	2000	1700
8											
9	Product B										
10		8	9	10	11	12	13	14	15	16	17
11	Gross requirements	1800	1600	1600	1700	1700	1700	1700	1900	2300	2300
12	On-Hand	0	0	0	0	0	0	0	0	0	0
13	Net requirements	0	0	0	0	0	0	0	0	0	0
14	Planned order receipt	1800	1600	1600	1700	1700	1700	1700	1900	2300	2300
15	Planned order release	1600	1600	1700	1700	1700	1700	1900	2300	2300	2100
16											
17	Product C										
18		8	9	10	11	12	13	14	15	16	17
19	Gross requirements	1400	1100	1800	1700	1300	1700	1700	1500	2300	2300
20	On-Hand	0	0	0	0	0	0	0	0	0	0
21	Net requirements	0	0	0	0	0	0	0	0	0	0
22	Planned order receipt	1400	1100	1800	1700	1300	1700	1700	1500	2300	2300
23	Planned order release	1100	1800	1700	1300	1700	1700	1500	2300	2300	2000
24											
25	Component D										
26		8	9	10	11	12	13	14	15	16	17
27	Gross requirements	4400	5600	5600							
28	On-Hand	0	0	0							
29	Net requirements	0	0	5600							
	Nichols	4400	5600	0							

5. Update the components D, E, F, G, H. Do this by copying gross requirements, on hand, net requirements, planned order receipts, and planned order releases. Point out how the gross requirements for these items are linked through the formulas in the gross requirements row for each item.

File Edit View Insert Format Tools Data Window Help										_|&|x|
L30		= 0								

	A	K	L	M	N	O	P	Q	R	S	T
1	Product A										
2		9	10	11	12	13	14	15	16	17	18
18		9	10	11	12	13	14	15	16	17	18
19	Gross requirements	1100	1800	1700	1300	1700	1700	1500	2300	2300	2000
20	On-Hand	0	0	0	0	0	0	0	0	0	0
21	Net requirements	0	0	0	0	0	0	0	0	0	0
22	Planned order receipt	1100	1800	1700	1300	1700	1700	1500	2300	2300	2000
23	Planned order release	1800	1700	1300	1700	1700	1500	2300	2300	2000	1700
24											
25	Component D										
26		9	10	11	12	13	14	15	16	17	18
27	Gross requirements	5600	5600	6800	6800	7200	7600	8800	8000	6800	6400
28	On-Hand	0	0	0	0	0	0	0	0	0	0
29	Net requirements	0	5600	6800	6800	7200	7600	8800	8000	6800	6400
30	Planned order receipt	5600	0	0	0	0	0	0	0	0	0
31	Planned order release	0	0	0	0	0	0	0	0	0	0
32											
33	Component E										
34		9	10	11	12	13	14	15	16	17	18
35	Gross requirements	1400	1400	1700	1700	1800	1900	2200	2000	1700	1600
36	On-Hand	0	0	0	0	0	0	0	0	0	0
37	Net requirements	0	1400	1700	1700	1800	1900	2200	2000	1700	1600
38	Planned order receipt	1400	0	0	0	0	0	0	0	0	0
39	Planned order release	0	0	0	0	0	0	0	0	0	0
40											
41	Component F										
42		9	10	11	12	13	14	15	16	17	18
43	Gross requirements	8800	9000	10200	10200	10600	11400	13400	12600	11000	10200
44	On-Hand	0	0	0	0	0	0	0	0	0	0
45	Net requirements	0	9000	10200	10200	10600	11400	13400	12600	11000	10200

6. Fill in the planned order receipts for D, E, F, G. Use lot-for-lot to start.

L74   =0.2*L7

	A	I	J	K	L	M	N	O	P	Q	R	S
1	Product A											
2		7	8	9	10	11	12	13	14	15	16	
56												
57	Component H											
58		7	8	9	10	11	12	13	14	15	16	
59	Gross requirements	1400	1100	1800	1700	1300	1700	1700	1500	2300	2300	
60	On-Hand	0	0	0	0	0	0	0	0	0	0	
61	Net requirements	0	0	0	0	0	0	0	0	0	0	
62	Planned order receipt	1400	1100	1800	1700	1300	1700	1700	1500	2300	2300	
63	Planned order release	1100	1800	1700	1300	1700	1700	1500	2300	2300	2000	
64												
65	Raw Material I											
66		7	8	9	10	11	12	13	14	15	16	
67	Gross requirements	27200	33600	33800	35800	37400	38600	40200	49400	47000	41000	3
68	On-Hand	0	0	0	0	0	0	0	0	45500	45500	4
69	Net requirements	0	0	0	0	0	0	0	0	0	0	
70	Planned order receipt	27200	33600	33800	35800	37400	38600	40200	94900	47000	41000	3
71	Planned order release	33600	33800	35800	37400	38600	40200	94900	47000	41000	37400	3
72												
73	Work Center 1											
74	Product A	200	220	280	280							
75	Component D	660	840	840	1020							
76	Component G	2100	2520	2550	2310							
77	Component H	55	90	85	65							
78	Total Load	3015	3670	3755	3675							
79	Work Center 2											
80	Product B	540	480	480	510							
81	Component E	165	210	210	255							
82	Component F	1140	1320	1350	1530							
83	Component G	700	840	850	770							

Nichols

8. Copy work center 1, 2, 3, 4 cells for period 11-27. This can all be done in one copy.

9. Check for capacity problems -

      Work center 1 - 6,000

      Work center 2 - 4,500

      Work center 3 - 2,400   (Problems in periods 3, 12-17, 24)

      Work center 4 - 1,200   (Problems in periods 12-16)

	A	I	J	K	L	M	N	O	P	Q	R	S
1	Product A											
2		7	8	9	10	11	12	13	14	15	16	
71	Planned order release	33600	33800	35800	37400	38600	40200	94900	47000	41000	37400	3
72												
73	Work Center 1											
74	Product A	200	220	280	280	340	340	360	380	440	400	
75	Component D	660	840	840	1020	1020	1080	1140	1320	1200	1020	
76	Component G	2100	2520	2550	2310	2550	2550	2610	3450	3450	3090	
77	Component H	55	90	85	65	85	85	75	115	115	100	
78	Total Load	3015	3670	3755	3675	3995	4055	4185	5265	5205	4610	
79	Work Center 2											
80	Product B	540	480	480	510	510	510	510	570	690	690	
81	Component E	165	210	210	255	255	270	285	330	300	255	
82	Component F	1140	1320	1350	1530	1530	1590	1710	2010	1890	1650	
83	Component G	700	840	850	770	850	850	870	1150	1150	1030	
84	Total Load	2545	2850	2890	3065	3145	3220	3375	4060	4030	3625	
85	Work Center 3											
86	Product C	140	110	180	170	130	170	170	150	230	230	
87	Component F	1520	1760	1800	2040	2040	2120	2280	2680	2520	2200	
88	Component H	110	180	170	130	170	170	150	230	230	200	
89	Total Load	1770	2050	2150	2340	2340	2460	2600	3060	2980	2630	
90	Work Center 4											
91	Product A	100	110	140	140	170	170	180	190	220	200	
92	Product B	144	128	128	136	136	136	136	152	184	184	
93	Product C	70	55	90	85	65	85	85	75	115	115	
94	Component D	440	560	560	680	680	720	760	880	800	680	
95	Component E	55	70	70	85	85	90	95	110	100	85	
96	Total Load	809	923	988	1126	1136	1201	1256	1407	1419	1264	
97												
98												

Nichols

10. For workcenter 3 notice that the most of the capacity is used by component F (which uses .2 hrs/unit.

Note component F total demand is 231,800 units. Over 25 periods this is 9,272/period.

11. One solution is to prebuild. For periods 1-15 build 10,000 cases and in periods 16-26 make 8,000 cases.

12. For workcenter 4, component D is the big user. Total gross requirements is 143,000-200. Over 25 periods this is 5,720/period. One strategy is to run 5,900 in periods 2-20 and drop to 5,800 in periods 21-26. This works pretty well with just a small overload in period 15.

	12	13	14	15	16	17	18	19	20	21
Product A										
Work Center 1										
Product A	340	360	380	440	400	340	320	280	220	200
Component D	885	885	885	885	885	885	885	885	870	870
Component G	2550	2610	3450	3450	3090	2730	2700	2940	2850	2970
Component H	85	75	115	115	100	85	90	110	95	120
Total Load	3860	3930	4830	4890	4475	4040	3995	4215	4035	4160
Work Center 2										
Product B	510	510	570	690	690	630	570	540	540	570
Component E	270	285	330	300	255	240	210	165	150	210
Component F	1500	1500	1500	1200	1200	1200	1200	1200	1200	1200
Component G	850	870	1150	1150	1030	910	900	980	950	990
Total Load	3130	3165	3550	3340	3175	2980	2880	2885	2840	2970
Work Center 3										
Product C	170	170	150	230	230	200	170	180	220	190
Component F	2000	2000	2000	1600	1600	1600	1600	1600	1600	1600
Component H	170	150	230	230	200	170	180	220	190	240
Total Load	2340	2320	2380	2060	2030	1970	1950	2000	2010	2030
Work Center 4										
Product A	170	180	190	220	200	170	160	140	110	100
Product B	136	136	152	184	184	168	152	144	144	152
Product C	85	85	75	115	115	100	85	90	110	95
Component D	590	590	590	590	590	590	590	590	580	580
Component E	90	95	110	100	85	80	70	55	50	70
Total Load	1071	1086	1117	1209	1174	1108	1057	1019	994	997

Next change the raw materials planned releases to meet demand.

13. Calculate costs associated with this schedule. This cost is $8,515,956.

AC94 = =0.1*AC31

	A	V	W	X	Y	Z	AA	AB	AC	AD	AE
1	Product A										
2		20	21	22	23	24	25	26	27		
74	Product A	220	200	280	280	300	320	300	0		
75	Component D	870	870	870	870	870	870	0	0		
76	Component G	2850	2970	2970	3090	3060	3210	0	0		
77	Component H	95	120	120	130	120	125	0	0		
78	Total Load	4035	4160	4240	4370	4350	4525	300	0	1948625	
79	Work Center 2										
80	Product B	540	570	510	510	510	540	570	0		
81	Component E	150	210	210	225	240	225	0	0		
82	Component F	1200	1200	1200	1200	1200	1200	0	0		
83	Component G	950	990	990	1030	1020	1070	0	0		
84	Total Load	2840	2970	2910	2965	2970	3035	570	0	1909456.3	
85	Work Center 3										
86	Product C	220	190	240	240	260	240	250	0		
87	Component F	1600	1600	1600	1600	1600	1600	0	0		
88	Component H	190	240	240	260	240	250	0	0		
89	Total Load	2010	2030	2080	2100	2100	2090	250	0	1970675	
90	Work Center 4										
91	Product A	110	100	140	140	150	160	150	0		
92	Product B	144	152	136	136	136	144	152	0		
93	Product C	110	95	120	120	130	120	125	0		
94	Component D	580	580	580	580	580	580	0	0		
95	Component E	50	70	70	75	80	75	0	0		
96	Total Load	994	997	1046	1051	1076	1079	427	0	1675440	
97											
98								Inventory Carrying		$1,011,760	
99								Labor		$7,504,196	
100								Total		$8,515,956	
101											

Nichols

14. Finally consider multiples of 100 for end items, 50 for components and 1,000 for materials.

Products are ok with the initial values, except for product A, period 6.

Companents need to be revised. On hand levels should be less than 500.

The raw material needs to be revised. On hand levels should be less than 1,000.

A	V	W	X	Y	Z	AA	AB	AC	AD	AE
1 Product A										
2	20	21	22	23	24	25	26	27		
75 Component D	900	900	900	825	825	825	0	0		
76 Component G	2850	3000	3000	3000	3150	3150	0	0		
77 Component H	100	125	100	125	125	125	0	0		
78 Total Load	4070	4225	4280	4230	4400	4420	300	0	1951900	
79 Work Center 2										
80 Product B	540	570	510	510	510	540	570	0		
81 Component E	225	150	150	150	150	150	0	0		
82 Component F	1200	1200	1200	1200	1200	1200	0	0		
83 Component G	950	1000	1000	1000	1050	1050	0	0		
84 Total Load	2915	2920	2860	2860	2910	2940	570	0	1909875	
85 Work Center 3										
86 Product C	220	190	240	240	260	240	250	0		
87 Component F	1600	1600	1600	1600	1600	1600	0	0		
88 Component H	200	250	200	250	250	250	0	0		
89 Total Load	2020	2040	2040	2090	2110	2090	250	0	1970587.5	
90 Work Center 4										
91 Product A	110	100	140	140	150	160	150	0		
92 Product B	144	152	136	136	136	144	152	0		
93 Product C	110	95	120	120	130	120	125	0		
94 Component D	600	600	600	550	550	550	0	0		
95 Component E	75	50	50	50	50	50	0	0		
96 Total Load	1039	997	1046	996	1016	1024	427	0	1679161.3	
97										
98								Inventory Carrying	$1,056,388	
99								Labor	$7,511,524	
100								Total	$8,567,911	
101										
102										

Nichols

Notice the cost went up to $8,567,911 from $8,515,956, an increase of $51,955.

Inventory costs increased $44,672 (1,056,388-1,011,716)

Labor went up $7,328 (7,511,524-7,504,196)

Why are the inventory costs so much higher? Due to the remnant inventory. Still this is not too significant considering the magnitude of these costs

EXTRA CASE

Brunswick Motors, Inc. - An Introductory Case for MRP

Recently, Phil Harris, the Production Control Manager at Brunswick, read an article on Time-Phased Requirements Planning. He was curious about how this technique might work in scheduling Brunswick's engine assembly operations, and decided to prepare an example to illustrate the use to Time-Phased Requirements Planning.

Phil's first step was to prepare a master schedule for one of the engine types produced by Brunswick - the Model 1000 engine. This schedule indicates the number of units of the Model 1000 engine to be assembled each week during the past twelve weeks, and is shown below. Next, Phil decided to simplify his requirements planning example by considering only two of the many components that are needed to complete the assembly of the Model 1000 engine. These two components, the Gear Box and the Input Shaft, are shown in the Product Structure Diagram shown below. Phil noted that the Gear Box is assembled by the Sub-Assembly Department, and is subsequently sent to the main engine assembly line. The Input Shaft is one of several component parts manufactured by Brunswick that are needed to produce a Gear Box sub-assembly. Thus, levels 0, 1, and 2 are included in the Product Structure Diagram to indicate the three manufacturing stages that are involved in producing an engine: the Engine Assembly Department, the Sub-Assembly Department, and the Machine Shop.

The manufacturing lead times required to produce the Gear Box and Input Shaft components are also indicated in the Product Structure Diagram. Note that two weeks are required to produce a batch of Gear Boxes, and that all of the Gear Boxes must be delivered to the assembly line parts stockroom before Monday morning of the week in which they are to be used. Likewise, it takes three weeks to produce a lot of Input Shafts, and all of the shafts that are needed for the production of Gear Boxes in a given week must be delivered to the Sub-Assembly Department stockroom before Monday morning of the week.

In preparing the MRP example Phil planned to use the attached worksheets, and to make the following assumptions:

1. *Seventeen Gear Boxes are on hand at the beginning of week 1 and five Gear Boxes are currently on order to be delivered at the start of week 2.*

2. *Forty Input Shafts are on hand at the start of week 1 and twenty-two are scheduled for delivery at the beginning of week 2.*

ASSIGNMENT:

1. Initially, assume that Phil wants to minimize his inventory requirements. Assume that each order will be only for what is required for a single period.

2. Phil would like to consider the costs that his accountants are currently using for inventory carrying and setup for the gear box and input shafts. These costs are as follows:

Part	Cost
Gear Box	Setup = $90/order
	Inventory Carrying Cost = $2/unit/period
Input Shaft	Setup = $45/order
	Inventory Carrying Cost = $1/unit/period

3. Given the cost structure, determine a schedule that minimizes cost.

Model 1000 Master Schedule

Weeks	1	2	3	4	5	6	7	8	9	10	11	12
Demand	15	5	7	10		15	20	10		8	2	16

Model 1000 Product Structure

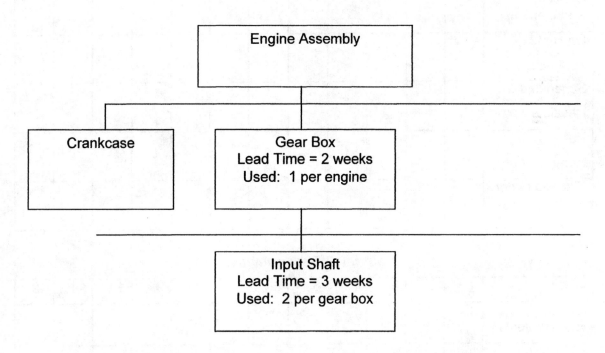

161

Engine Assembly Master Schedule

Weeks	1	2	3	4	5	6	7	8	9	10	11	12
Quantity												

Gear Box Requirements

Weeks	1	2	3	4	5	6	7	8	9	10	11	12
Gross Requirements												
On Hand												
Scheduled Receipts												
Net Requirements												
Planned Order Release												

Input Shaft Requirements

Weeks	1	2	3	4	5	6	7	8	9	10	11	12
Gross Requirements												
On Hand												
Scheduled Receipts												
Net Requirements												
Planned Order Release												

Engine Assembly Master Schedule

Weeks	1	2	3	4	5	6	7	8	9	10	11	12
Quantity												

Gear Box Requirements

Weeks	1	2	3	4	5	6	7	8	9	10	11	12
Gross Requirements												
On Hand												
Scheduled Receipts												
Net Requirements												
Planned Order Release												

Input Shaft Requirements

Weeks	1	2	3	4	5	6	7	8	9	10	11	12
Gross Requirements												
On Hand												
Scheduled Receipts												
Net Requirements												
Planned Order Release												

Engine Assembly Master Schedule

Weeks	1	2	3	4	5	6	7	8	9	10	11	12
Quantity												

Gear Box Requirements

Weeks	1	2	3	4	5	6	7	8	9	10	11	12
Gross Requirements												
On Hand												
Scheduled Receipts												
Net Requirements												
Planned Order Release												

Input Shaft Requirements

Weeks	1	2	3	4	5	6	7	8	9	10	11	12
Gross Requirements												
On Hand												
Scheduled Receipts												
Net Requirements												
Planned Order Release												

Brunswick Motors, Inc. - An Introductory Case for MRP – Teaching Note

This is a simple case that can be used as an in-class exercise. To start the class, quickly explain the basics of calculating net requirements. Then, distribute this case, have the students read the case, and give a brief explanation or what they are expected to do. It is probably best to have students work in pairs for this exercise.

1. Initially, assume that Phil wants to minimize his inventory requirements. Assume that each order will be only for what is required for a single period.

Engine Assembly Master Schedule

Weeks	1	2	3	4	5	6	7	8	9	10	11	12
Quantity	15	5	7	10		15	20	10		8	2	16

Gear Box Requirements

Weeks	1	2	3	4	5	6	7	8	9	10	11	12
Gross Requirements	15	5	7	10		15	20	10		8	2	16
On Hand 17	2	2										
Scheduled Receipts		5										
Net Requirements			5	10		15	20	10		8	2	16
Planned Order Release	5	10		15	20	10		8	2	16		

Input Shaft Requirements

Weeks	1	2	3	4	5	6	7	8	9	10	11	12
Gross Requirements	10	20		30	40	20		16	4	32		
On Hand 40	30	32	32	2								
Scheduled Receipts		22										
Net Requirements					38	20		16	4	32		
Planned Order Release		38	20		16	4	32					

2.   Phil would like to consider the costs that his accountants are currently using for inventory carrying and setup for the gearbox and input shafts. These costs are as follows:

Part	Cost
Gear Box	Setup = $90/order
	Inventory Carrying Cost = $2/unit/period
Input Shaft	Setup = $45/order
	Inventory Carrying Cost = $1/unit/period

Gear Box
        Setup Cost = 8 x 90 = $720
        Inventory = 4 x 2 = $8
        Total = $728
Input Shaft
        Setup Cost = 5 x 45 = $225
        Inventory = 96 x 1 = $96
        Total = $321
        Total Cost = $1,049

Note: The inventory carrying costs are based on beginning of week balances. When doing lot sizi in the book, end of week balances are used in the inventory holding cost calculations.

3. Given the cost structure, determine a schedule that minimizes cost.

Engine Assembly Master Schedule

Weeks	1	2	3	4	5	6	7	8	9	10	11	12
Quantity	15	5	7	10		15	20	10		8	2	16

Gear Box Requirements

Weeks	1	2	3	4	5	6	7	8	9	10	11	12
Gross Requirements	15	5	7	10		15	20	10		8	2	16
On Hand 17	2	2	_10_			_30_	_10_			_18_	_16_	
Scheduled Receipts		5				45				26		
Net Requirements			5	10		15	20	10		8	2	16
Planned Order Release	15			45				26				

Input Shaft Requirements

Weeks	1	2	3	4	5	6	7	8	9	10	11	12
Gross Requirements	30			90				52				
On Hand 40	10	32	32									
Scheduled Receipts		22										
Net Requirements				58				52				
Planned Order Release	58				52							

Gear Box

     Setup Cost = 3 x 90 = $270

     Inventory = 88 x 2 = $176

     Total = $446

Input Shaft

     Setup Cost = 2 x 45 = $90

     Inventory = 74 x 1 = $74

     Total = $164

     Total Cost = $610

Chapter 15 - Operations Scheduling

Overview

As mentioned in the opening vignette in the chapter, cash flow is related to work flow. Therefore, scheduling concepts are of interest to the entire firm. This chapter surveys general approaches to short term scheduling in manufacturing and service industries, with major emphasis placed on job shop situations. Approaches include basic priority rules, input-output control, shop floor control, capacity planning, and Johnson's Method for manufacturing. In the service area, personnel scheduling is covered.

Major Points of Chapter

1. Job-shop scheduling cannot be effective without priority control, capacity planning, and shop-floor control.

2. Most of the approaches to job-shop scheduling have focused on priority rules to decide which job to do next. The current trend is to focus on scheduling in light of bottleneck processes using the philosophy.

3. Simulation is the standard way to evaluate priority rules in complex job shops.

4. Work force scheduling is the primary scheduling concern in most services.

5. Hewlett Packard's shop floor control system is discussed in the chapter.

Teaching Tip

Having students think of WIP as dollar bills floating through a shop can emphasize the importance of work throughput as opposed to capacity utilization in a job shop. The faster they float through, the greater the cash flow and receivables. A backlog in front of a workstation then can be visualized as idle dollars. (Finance majors like this analogy.)

Cases, Exercises and Spreadsheets (Source)

"Keep Patients Waiting? Not in My Office" (Book)

"Manzana Insurance: Fruitvale Branch" (HBS 9-692-015)

Videos/Clips (Source)

"Washburn Guitars" (Vol. III)

"Service" (Vol. I)

"Project Management – Building the Alton Super Bridge" (Vol. VI)

"Scheduling Services - the United Solution" (Vol. IV)

"Airline Scheduling" (CD-ROM)

"Priority Rules" (CD-ROM)

"Sequencing" (CD-ROM)

CASE

Keep Patients Waiting? Not in my office! – Teaching Note

Answers to Questions

1. The features of the appointment scheduling system crucial in capturing "many grateful patients" were:

    I.   A careful allotment of proper time to each patient according to the individual's needs.

    II. Giving each patient a specific time such as 10:30 as opposed to ambiguous timings such as "come in a half-hour."

    III. Keeping openings in the time slot for emergency patients.

    IV. Dealing efficiently with latecomers and with telephone calls from patients in a way so as to minimize the interference with the schedules of regular patients.

2. The assistants in charge of scheduling are instructed to keep openings in the time slot for emergency cases. The number of such openings varies according to different times of the week and different seasons. These cases are usually taken care of after the initial visits are over, which are allowed a time of 30 minutes, but often last for less time. If the interruption due to an emergency case is a short one, the doctor can catch up with regular appointments. If it is a long one, the patients scheduled for the next one or two hours are given the choice of making new appointments or waiting. In case the patients choose to wait, they are tried to fit into the slots for the emergency cases. In this way it is ensured that the appointments for the whole day are not messed up.

3. The case of latecomers is handled efficiently to make sure that the other appointments do not lag behind due to them. If a patient is late by 10 minutes or less, he is treated right away but is reminded of the original appointment time. If a patient is late by more than 10 minutes the other schedules are followed. The late patient is either given another appointment or squeezed in as soon as possible.

    No-shows are recorded in the patient chart for up to a maximum of three times, after which the patient is sent a letter saying that time was allotted for him and he failed to keep the appointments for three times. He is also told that if the same case is repeated in the future, then he will be billed for the wasted time.

Technical Note 15 - Simulation

Overview

This supplement covers the mechanics of Monte Carlo simulation and the general simulation methodology. The essence of this tutorial is how empirical and normal distributions can be used in the simulation process. Spreadsheets and simulations are discussed to provide information to aid in solving real-world (and end-of-chapter) problems.

Major Points of the Chapter

1. In simulation, a real system is reduced to a model, and this model is manipulated to react in the same manner as the real system.

2. *Using a simulation model* allows study and experimentation without interrupting the real system.

3. Simulation is widely used in all process fields, not just in operations management.

4. Business-type simulations are usually done on a digital computer, and random numbers are generally used to simulate probable occurrences.

5. The cost and time to build a simulation model can range from "little cost and very soon" to "extremely expensive and many years."

6. Remember that simulation model validity rests on the assumptions and limitations of the models. Simulation models should be externally validated.

Teaching Tips

Students readily catch on to simulation if you relate it to a child's game such as All-Star Baseball. In this game, cardboard disks represent real ballplayers and the proportion of times they get singles, doubles, triples, strikeouts, etc. The disk is placed over the spinner which when spun points to a number representing one at-bat for that player. If it lands on 1, it's a home run, 2 a strikeout, etc. No doubt someone in class has played it and can act as a resource person on its fine points.

The spreadsheets donate by John McClain are very good. LineSim is great for doing quick simulations of assembly lines and CellSim can be used to analyze simple job shops. These spreadsheets are included on the Student CD, Website. Instructions for using them are part of the spreadsheet.

Cases, Exercises and Spreadsheets (Source)

"Two-Stage_Assembly_Line Spreadsheet" (CD-ROM)

"LineSim" (CD-ROM)

"CellSim" (CD-ROM)

ADVANCED CASE

Understanding the Impact of Variability on the Capacity of a Production System – Teaching Note

This is an exercise that is very successful at allowing students to discover the impact that variability in processing times and buffering has on the production rate of a serial system. It is good to quickly show students how the spreadsheet works in class, before making this assignment.

Discussion Questions

1. Start with the spreadsheet just as Professor McClain configures it initially. Click on the "Design" tab and note that we have a three-station assembly line. The stations are named "Joe", "Next's", and "M2". There is a buffer area downstream from "Joe" with a capacity of 1 unit, and another downstream from "Next's" with a capacity of 1 unit. The way this simulation is designed, "Joe" will always have something to work on and "M2" can always deposit finished work in a storage area.

   Notice that the processing time distribution is Shifted Exponential with a mean of 5 and a standard deviation of 5. The shape of this distribution is described in the "Instructions" tab. Suffice it to say, that there is much process time variation when using this distribution. Answer the following question before going on to the next part of the exercise.

   Question 1: How many units would you expect to be able to produce over 100 time periods?

   Pretty obvious, students should expect 20 units to be produced. Some might say 18 recognizing that the system starts out with no work-in-process.

2. Click on the "Run" tab and using the default values for "Run-In Time", "Run Length" and "Repetitions", run the simulation. Tabulate the average utilization at each machine based on the five repetitions and tabulate the mean and standard deviation of the output of the system (this data is in the "Machine" worksheet).

Question 2: How many units did you actually produce per 100 time periods? Explain any difference between your simulation result and your estimate made in question 1.

Most answers are between 11 and 15 - this is due to blocking and starving of the various process stages since the variability of processing times was relatively.

3. In the next part, we would like you to map out the impact that increased buffer inventory has on the output of the system. You can change the buffer behind "Joe" and "Next" by changing the inventory cell designated "Joe's Inventory" (this is on the "Design" worksheet) and then clicking on "Make Storage Areas Like #1".

Question 3: Create a graph that shows the impact that changing the buffer stock has on the output of the system. Consider buffer levels that vary from 0 to a maximum of 20 units. What can you conclude from your experiment?

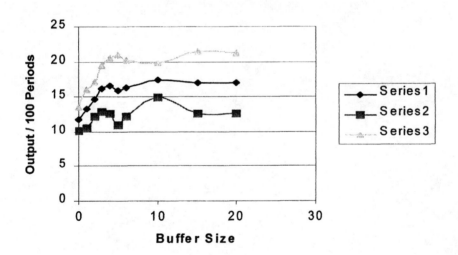

This is a graph of the output at the 1st, 2nd and 3rd workstation – the conclusion should be that "a small amount of buffer gives you some increase in output, but after 4 or 5 units, not much incremental improvement.

4. Finally, we would like you to experiment with the impact of a bottleneck in the system.

Question 4: What would be the impact on the performance of our system if "M2" had a processing time that averaged 6 time units (assume that "Joe" and "Next" still run at an average of 5)? What happens to the inventory after "Joe" and "Next"? Does varying the size of these inventories have any impact?

The inventory buffers behind the bottleneck fill up, but due to the decreased impact of the bottleneck stations, the output should be higher than in Q2.

Question 5: What happens if instead of "M2" being the bottleneck, "Joe" is the bottleneck? Do the buffers at "Joe" and "Next" have any impact?

No, in this case the buffers have no impact since the bottleneck is at the first station.

Chapter 16 - Operations Consulting and Reengineering

Overview

Since many operations students take jobs in consulting firms or in consulting roles in a company, this chapter has been included in the text. Operations consulting deals with assisting clients in developing operations strategies and improving production and service processes. The operations consultant must be able to assist management in selecting the most appropriate technologies and systems. This chapter provides an overview of what operations consults do, the economics of consulting businesses, and the types of tools operations consults use to carry out their work.

In addition, the chapter describes Business Process Reengineering, a major activity of many consulting firms.

Major Points of the Chapter

1. Fredrick Taylor is credited as the "father of management consulting."

2. Consulting firms are often characterized as specializing in either strategic planning or tactical analysis and implementation.

3. Individuals working in consulting firms can be categorized as "finders", "minders", or "grinders".

4. Consulting firms must leverage the skills of partners to be profitable.

5. Consulting firms use very structured methodologies to ensure consistency in the completion of their projects. These methodologies employ many of the techniques described in this book.

6. Reengineering is the fundamental rethinking and radical redesign of business processes to achieve dramatic improvements.

7. The focus of reengineering efforts is towards inter-functional and inter-organizational, customer based processes.

8. The five principles of reengineering are compress linear processes, relocate work, parallel process work, compress vertical processes, and avoid repetition.

9. The six-step approach for reengineering is to state a case for action, identify process to be reengineered, evaluate enablers of reengineering, understand the current process, create a new process design, and implement the new reengineered process.

10. Reengineering and continuous process improvement are compatible ideas.

Teaching Tips

Share some of your consulting experiences with the class.

A good project for this chapter is to ask student teams to study the structure of some process they all must deal with at the university. A good example is the class registration and scheduling process. Students are then asked to reengineer the process. Final reports are given with organization charts and process flow sheets outlining the reengineered activity. Students should address difficulties in implementation of the new process.

Cases, Exercises and Spreadsheets (Source)

"Deloitte & Touche Consulting Group" (HBS 9-696-096)

"A California Auto Club Reengineers Customer Service" (Book)

Videos/Clips (Source)

"Reengineering at Catepillar" (Vol. III)

"Reengineering Defined" (CD-ROM)

CASE

A California Auto Club Reengineers Customer Service – Teaching Note

1. Describe the customer service process at CSAA and discuss the different phases of the reengineering effort.

   The customer service process is fragmented. A customer has to stand in different lines to buy insurance, get maps, or do anything else. The phases of the reengineering effort included the three "quickies." These quick hits provided immediate results. A comprehensive survey was performed to see what the perceptions of members and employees were. The survey revealed dissatisfaction with the functional silos of the existing organization. Next, reengineering teams were formed to address customer and employee concerns.

2. Discuss the role of process enablers in the development of the new design.

   The following enablers existed:

   Organizational: frustration with current processes, belief in need to improve, reaction to quick results.

   Technological: availability of computer systems to simplify and integrate work in a cross-functional manner.

Chapter 17 - Synchronous Manufacturing and Theory of Constraints

Overview

This is an integrating chapter. To appreciate its implications the most, the reader should have read the previous chapters on scheduling, inventory control, MRP, and JIT.

This chapter is based on the teachings of Dr. Eli Goldratt, who for the past decade or so has been accusing our industrial firms of not operating correctly. He points out problems throughout the entire organization, extending from the objectives of the firm at one end through to the control of the system at the other. Some of these points are more specific in the "Major Points of the Chapter" below.

Major Points of Chapter

1. THE GOAL OF THE FIRM IS TO MAKE MONEY.

2. The operational goals of the firm should be to increase throughput, decrease inventory and decrease operating expenses.

3. Unbalanced capacity is preferable to balanced capacity. Instead, the flow of product through the system should be balanced.

4. A bottleneck is a resource whose capacity is less than its demand. A nonbottleneck has excess capacity. A capacity constrained resource (CCR) is one whose utilization is near capacity.

5. An hour saved at a bottleneck adds an extra hour to the entire productive system. An hour saved at a nonbottleneck is a mirage and adds an hour to idle time.

6. The drum is the bottleneck. The buffer is inventory that is placed in front of a bottleneck to make sure that it is constantly being utilized. The rope is a communication link from the bottleneck to stations upstream from the bottleneck to assure that the drum receives only as much material as it needs.

Teaching Tips

An interesting opening into this chapter focuses on the hockey stick phenomenon. Why do people in industry start the month off smoothly and end it by working frantically on weekends? While this is discussed in the chapter, students do not fully grasp that this actually is the commonplace happening. During the month, the system performance is measured in terms of "efficiencies," "utilizations," "labor ratios," etc. However, as the month draws to a close, there is the realization that product must be shipped to meet some target or budgeted level.

Having the students compare Goldratt's definitions to definitions commonly used in business can develop interesting discussion. The following overhead can be used to lead the discussion.

Goldratt's Definitions

THE GOAL OF THE FIRM IS TO MAKE MONEY

PERFORMANCE MEASURES

<u>Financial Measurements (Conventional)</u>

Net profit – an absolute measurement in dollars

Return on investment – a relative measure based on investment

Cash flow – a survival measurement

<u>Operational Measurements</u>

Inventory – all the money that the system has invested in purchasing things it intends to sale

Operating expenses – all the money that the system spends to turn inventory into throughput.

INCREASE THROUGHPUT WHILE SIMULTANEOUSLY REDUCING INVENTORY AND REDUCING OPERATING EXPENSE

PRODUCTIVITY IS ALL THE ACTION THAT BRING A COMPNAY CLOSER TO ITS GOALS

Cases, Exercises and Spreadsheets (Source)

"The Great Manufacturing Crapshoot" (IRM)

"Solve the OPT Quiz – A Challenge in Scheduling" (Book)

EXTRA CASE

Manufacturing - The Great Crapshoot

Introduction

Those individuals who have been involved with manufacturing every day know it can be a very tough, but potentially rewarding activity. *The Great Crapshoot* gives you the chance to delve beyond the obvious and get a fresh perspective on how the game of manufacturing really works.

Objective of the game

Just like a real manufacturing facility, the goal of this game is to maximize the goods shipped out of the door and to minimize inventory[9]. The game is played over a 20-toss period, which represents 20 days of manufacturing, or roughly a month's work. At the end of 20 tosses, each team of 6 players (1 player for each Workstation) calculates the total number of shipped chips, and the total of all work-in-process inventory. The Team having the best score (highest number shipped, lowest inventory) of all the teams playing the game wins.

Rules of play

All those playing *The Great Crapshoot* are operating a production plant whose product is chips. The chips arrive at your plant (handed out at the game's start) as raw material. It is your job to process these chips through the 6 Workstations in the plant so they may become finished chips and be shipped out as sold goods. Chips in between workstations are work-in-process (WIP) inventory.

There are two important phenomena existing in a real manufacturing plant that also exist here:

(1) Dependent Events: chips cannot move on to Work Station 2 without first passing through Workstation 1. Likewise all chips must move from 1 to 2 to 3, etc., and can be shipped only after passing through Workstation 6.

(2) Statistical Fluctuations: the number of chips that can be processed by Work Station 1 and moved to Workstation 2 is controlled by Workstation 1's die toss. In a real plant, average output is made up of good days and bad days. On good days with perfect attendance and no breakdowns or distractions, output is high. On bad days, with breakdowns, process and quality problems, accidents, excessive

1. ───────────────

[9]Only work-in-process inventory in this game. Finished chips are immediately shipped; consequently, there is no finished goods inventory.

absenteeism, material shortages, etc., output is low. In any case, output will vary around an average according to the latter factors.

Each Workstation foreman takes his die and tosses at the same time as the others. One such round of tosses constitutes a day of production in the plant. After the toss, each foreman moves the number of chips forward indicated by the die. If the die toss exceeds the total number of chips available in WIP, only the existing number of chips is moved forward.

Questions to consider prior to start of game

(1) How many chips do you expect to complete during the 20-day period?

(2) How much work-in-process should you have at the end of the 20-day period?

(3) How much time should it take to process a chip from Raw Materials to completion at Work Station 6?

Questions to consider after playing the game

(1) How many chips did you actually complete during the 20 day period?

(2) How did work-in-process inventory vary during the game? How much did you have at the beginning of the game? How much at the end?

(3) Explain what is going on?

(4) How did the time is takes to process a chip vary from the beginning of the game to the end?

Work Station #_____

Day	1	2	3	4	5	6	7	8	9	10	Halftime
WIP											
Die Toss											
Lost Production											

Day	11	12	13	14	15	16	17	18	19	20	Totals
WIP											
Die Toss											
Lost Production											

181

Manufacturing – The Great Crapshoot – Teaching Note

This is a great little exercise and it really makes your student think. It takes about 60 minutes to complete the entire exercise. You will need 1 die for each student and approximately 100 chips per six-person team. Explain how the game will be played at the beginning, and that everyone will move from one period to the next at the same time (this is very important). In other words, you will pace the entire system. Start out with four chips between each workstation and a pile of chips in front of the first workstation.

Go through the "Questions to consider prior to start of game" first. Then, start playing the game.

Start slowly at first, making sure that your students are all making their moves at the same time, and that they are all recording their results. Stop at the end of the first 10 periods and collect intermediate data from each team.

Complete the last 10 periods and then go through the "questions to consider after playing the game."

Questions to consider prior to start of game

(1) How many chips do you expect to complete during the 20-day period?

The students should calculate that 70 chips should be produced (20 x 3.5).

(2) How much work-in-process should you have at the end of the 20-day period?

You may get some different ideas from the teams. Most will probably agree that if we start with 20, we should end with 20. Tell them that they should not count the inventory before the first workstation, nor should they count the finished goods.

(3) How much time should it take to process a chip from Raw Materials to completion at Work Station 6?

Most will probably say six periods.

Questions to consider after playing the game

(1) How many chips did you actually complete during the 20 day period?

They should have completed much less than the 70 that was expected. This is due to the loss of throughput caused by the starving that sometimes occurs at workstations 2 though 6.

(2) How did work-in-process inventory vary during the game? How much did you have at the beginning of the game? How much at the end?

They should all have more work-in-process inventory. This is due to the fact that the first workstation is never starved and the others are starved. More work is going into the system than is coming out. The WIP should theoretically build to infinity!

(3) Explain what is going on?

You should try to get them to realize how the bottleneck moves depending on the amount of WIP in front of a workstation.

(3) How did the time is takes to process a chip vary from the beginning of the game to the end?

It goes up depending on the amount of WIP.

It is good to end by asking them what could be done to fix the system. There are many ideas such as the following:
- Reduce the variance in the processes.
- Pace the line in some way.
- Add more capacity at workstations 2 through 6.

Irwin Operations Management Video Series

The video series includes professionally developed videotapes showing students real applications of essential manufacturing and service topics. Each tape contains "plant tours" to help students see how companies are using operations management concepts and techniques to be productive and competitive.

In addition to the videotapes, short clips from each tape have been created. Each clip depicts such items as a concept described by a manager, an example from a company or the illustration of an idea described using professional animation. These clips have been digitized and are useful for presentation during a class session or to augment an online exercise.

The videotapes are available free of charge from McGraw-Hill and can be ordered through your McGraw-Hill representative. The digitized video clips can be obtained from three different sources: the Student CD, the Instructor CD, and from the author supported book website at http://www.pom.edu/pom/.

The following series of tables contain descriptions of the videotapes and references to each video clip that has been taken from each tape.

Volume I (Tapes 1 and 2) (ISBN 0-256-12349-7)

Tape 1

Lean Production (13 minutes) This segment shows and discusses how Lean Production is used at Caterpillar, Cummins Engine, and Navistar. Interviews with upper management at the three companies bring out the importance of customer-driven "pull" systems and how the companies employ JIT, Kanban, Jidoka, and MRP II to perform better.

Suggested Classroom Use: This tape can be used with Chapter 1 Introduction, Chapter 2 Operations Strategy & Competitiveness, Chapter 10 JIT, and Chapter 14 MRP.

FILE NAME	CONCEPT	DESCRIPTION	AVAILABLE FROM	TIME IN	TIME OUT
LP1.avi	Lean Production	Definition	Student CD, Website	2:20	2:40
LP2.avi	Lean Production	Other definitions	Website	3:42	3:55
LP3.avi	Lead Time	Reduction Example	Instructor CD, Website	5:00	5:38
LP4.avi	Flexibility Multimodels	Caterpillar	Student CD, Website	6:10	7:06
LP5.avi	Group Technology	Example Cummins	Instructor CD, Website	7:50	8:31
LP6.avi	Jidoka	Example/Definition Quality as the source	Student CD, Website	8:32	9:21
LP7.avi	Inventory turns	Example	Website	9:40	10:31
LP8.avi	MRPII	Description/Example - Navistar	Student CD, Website	11:43	13:13

186

Volume I, Tape 1 (0-256-12349-7)

Quality (13 minutes) George Bush at the Baldrige Award ceremony opens this segment, which goes on to list the seven basic tools. Then Zytec, Motorola, and Hewlett Packard are used as examples.

Suggested Classroom Use: This tape can be used with Chapter 7 Quality Management and Technical Note 7 Process Capability and Statistical Quality Control.

FILE NAME	CONCEPT	DESCRIPTION	AVAILABLE FROM	TIME IN	TIME OUT
QC1.avi	Quality Imperative	President Bush speaking	Website	15:26	15:55
QC2.avi	Baldrige Award	Description	Student CD, Website	16:39	17:15
QC3.avi	Baldrige Criteria	Listing	Website	17:15	17:44
QC4.avi	Quality Management	Motorola Example Six-Sigma/Galvin	Student CD, Website	17:45	18:46
QC5.avi	Quality/Customer Focus	Zytec Ex./SPC	Website	18:49	19:28
QC6.avi	Quality/Tracking	Zytec Andon example	Instructor CD, Website	19:52	20:27
QC7.avi	Quality/costs	H-P example	Website	20:30	21:06
QC8.avi	Quality Tools	Statistical tools (Cause/effect; check sheet pareto; run chart; histogram control chart; scattergram)	Student CD, Website	21:26	22:45
QC9.avi	Flow Charts	H-P example Process Improvement	Instructor CD, Website	23:57	24:56
QC10.avi	Pareto diagram	H-P example	Instructor CD, Website	24:56	25:38

Volume I, Tape 1 (0-256-12349-7)

The Manufacturing Process (10 minutes) This segment presents the Hayes-*Wheelright* continuum, from customized, low-volume to mechanized, high-volume manufacturing. Most of the segment is on-site footage from a tool and die shop, Caterpillar, Ford, and Nucor Steel.

Suggested Classroom Use: This tape can be used with Chapter 4 Process Analysis, Chapter 5 Product Design & Process Selection – Manufacturing, and Technical Note 5 Facility Layout.

FILE NAME	CONCEPT	DESCRIPTION	AVAILABLE FROM	TIME IN	TIME OUT
MP1.avi	Product/Process Matrix	Description	Student CD, Website	28:38	30:00
MP2.avi	Product/Process Types	Three examples	Instructor CD, Website	30:01	30:18
MP3.avi	PPM/Job Shop	Machine tools	Student CD, Website	30:24	32:06
MP4.avi	PPM/Batch	Caterpillar	Student CD, Website	32:09	33:17
MP5.avi	PPM/Assembly line Ford		Student CD, Website	33:26	34:25
MP6.avi	PPM/Continous	Nucor Steel	Student CD, Website	34:28	35:42

188

Volume I, Tape 2 (0-256-12349-7)

Computer-Integrated Manufacturing (12 minutes) This segment presents an on-site tour of the Nucor Steel mini-mill, focusing on the automation system. Included are interviews with the plant manager, controller, and caster supervisor. This segment includes good illustrations of controls, process manufacturing, automation, and productivity.

Suggested Classroom Use: This tape can be used with Chapter 2 Operations Strategy & Competitiveness and Supplement C Operations Technology.

FILE NAME	CONCEPT	DESCRIPTION	AVAILABLE FROM	TIME IN	TIME OUT
NU1.avi	Computer Integrated Manufacturing	System explanation	Website	1:28:45	29:14
NU2.avi	Productivity	Improvement example	Website	29:14	29:40
NU3.avi	Incentives/teamwork	Overview, Nucor	Website	29:45	30:15
NU4.avi	CIM System	Graphic Illustration	Student CD, Website	30:18	31:02
NU5.avi	CIM/Financials	Description	Website	31:51	32:47
NU6.avi	Sequencing	Nucor Steel example	Website	35:28	35:51

Volume I, Tape 2 (0-256-12349-7)

Manufacturing Inventory (11 minutes) This segment contrasts Navistar's high turnover-low inventory heavy truck manufacturing system with the high inventory-service parts business at Caterpillar. Interviews bring out Navistar's reduction efforts as well as Caterpillar's responsiveness and the corresponding effects on inventory and costs.

Suggested Classroom Use: This tape can be used with Chapter 13 Inventory Control and Chapter 14 MRP.

FILE NAME	CONCEPT	DESCRIPTION	AVAILABLE FROM	TIME IN	TIME OUT
MI1.avi	Inventory Cost		Instructor CD, Website	1:00:36	1:09:20
MI2.avi	Inventory Definition		Student CD, Website	1:32	2:03
MI3.avi	Inventory Costs		Instructor CD, Website	2:10	2:28
MI4.avi	Inventory Part Numbers	Navistar example	Website	2:47	4:14
MI5.avi	Inventory Service Parts	Caterpillar example	Student CD, Website	6:21	7:56
MI6.avi	Inventory Service		Instructor CD, Website	9:10	9:35

190

Volume I, Tape 2 (0-256-12349-7)

Service (11 minutes) This segment features First National Bank of Chicago and particularly the operations aspect of its check-clearing system. Interviews are included, which help reiterate the point that service businesses use "operations" principles to deliver quality "products." ("This segment could be used as a "launch" vehicle for a service section in the course, or as a "surprise" to illustrate services in the scheduling, or control segment of the course.)

Suggested Classroom Use: This tape can be used with Chapter 1 Introduction, Chapter 6 Product Design & Process Selection-Services, and Chapter 15 Operations Scheduling.

FILE NAME	CONCEPT	DESCRIPTION	AVAILABLE FROM	TIME IN	TIME OUT
SE1.avi	Service/Overview	Example First National Bank of Chicago, customer base	Website	2:51	2:55
SE2.avi	Service/ location	First National Bank of Chicago	Website	2:56	3:17
SE3.avi	Service/process	Example check clearing at First National Bank of Chicago	Student CD, Website	3:30	4:12
SE4.avi	Service/ demand, capacity	Example First National Bank of Chicago	Student CD, Website	3:57	4:54
SE5.avi	Service/scheduling	Example First National Bank of Chicago forecasting workload	Instructor CD, Website	5:00	5:30
SE6.avi	Service/automation	Example, check processing at First National Bank of Chicago	Website	5:31	6:03
SE7.avi	Service/quality	Example First National Bank of Chicago	Instructor CD, Website	7:50	8:03
SE8.avi	Service/inventory	Interview First National Bank of Chicago services inventory compared to manufacturing	Instructor CD, Website	8:18	8:55
SE9.avi	Service/quality, performance	Example First National Bank of Chicago - performance measurements, graphic	Instructor CD, Website	8:56	10:05
SE10.avi	Quality team	Example First National Bank of Chicago with vendors	Website	10:17	10:53
SE11.avi	Service/manufacturing	Comparison, overview	Website	11:28	12:06

Volume II (ISBN 0-256-15967-X)

Service Systems and the Service-System Design Matrix (12 minutes) First National Bank of Chicago is again highlighted with a survey of their customer services. This segment highlights the distinctions between automated low contact services and highly customized face-to-face encounters. It also relates these examples to other service companies and includes interview segments with managers.

Suggested Classroom Use: This tape can be used with Chapter 1 Introduction, Chapter 4 Process Analysis, Chapter 6 Product Design & Process Selection-Services.

FILE NAME	CONCEPT	DESCRIPTION	AVAILABLE FROM	TIME IN	TIME OUT
SS1.avi.	Service Processes	Description/overview	Instructor CD, Website	2:26	3:04
SS2.avi	Service Design Matrix	Overview and graphic	Student CD, Website	3:25	5:04
SS3.avi	Service, location	First National Bank center	Website	5:14	5:29
SS4.avi	Service, high volume	Example First National Bank - Mail contact	Website	5:40	6:36
SS5.avi	Service/technology	Example " " "	Website	6:57	7:35
SS6.avi	Service/phone contact	Example	Website	7:38	8:16
SS7.avi	Service, face-to-face tight specs	Example	Website	8:21	9:06
SS8.avi	Service, face-to-face loose specs	Example,	Website	9:24	10:20
SS9.avi	Service, total customization	Example, loan	Instructor CD, Website	10:34	11:37
SS10.avi	Service, Management	Example	Website	11:55	12:14

Volume II (0-256-15967-X)

Improving Operations Methods (12 minutes) This segment illustrates how Bernard Welding Equipment Company reduced set-up time and changed from a push to pull system to better serve their customers. The tape illustrates how a high variety of products (3,000 different configurations) can be custom assembled for quick response to customer orders. Topics touched on are Kanban, TQM, team approach, and JIT.

Suggested Classroom Use: This tape can be used with Chapter 2 Operations Strategy & Competitiveness, Chapter 7 Quality Management, and Chapter 10 JIT.

FILE NAME	CONCEPT	DESCRIPTION	AVAILABLE FROM	TIME IN	TIME OUT
OM1.avi	Continuous improvement	TQM interview	Instructor CD, Website	2:57	3:50
OM2.avi	Continuous Improvement	example, Bernard Welding	Website	4:05	4:58
OM3.avi	Redesign	improvement cable process change Bernard Welding	Website	5:00	5:45
OM4.avi	Setup time reduction	example, cost and quality improvement, quicker delivery	Website	6:37	7:25
OM5.avi	Scheduling and Control	Schedule board on assembly line	Website	7:44	8:44
OM6.avi	Assembly / Kanban	Pull system	Website	8:46	9:24
OM7.avi	Containerization	quality control	Website	9:36	10:13
OM8.avi	Employee involvement	In continuous improvement	Website	10:14	11:37

Volume II (0-256-15967-X)

Layout Improvements and Equipment Strategies (10 minutes) This segment features Bernard Welding this time illustrating a reconfigured layout based on process flow as opposed to process type. The segment also shows other improvements such as reducing the distance between related operations, renovating old equipment, upgrading to new technology, failsafing, and use of Kanban.

Suggested Classroom Use: This tape can be used with Chapter 5 Product Design & Process Selection-Manufacturing, and Technical Note 5 Facility Layout.

FILE NAME	CONCEPT	DESCRIPTION	AVAILABLE FROM	TIME IN	TIME OUT
LA1.avi	Layout	example, Bernard Welding graphic	Student CD, Website	3:03	3:30
LA2.avi	Process flow	shop floor redesign	Student CD, Website	3:31	4:05
LA3.avi	PLC, reuse	Reuse example	Website	4:50	5:30
LA4.avi	Flexibility, PLC	Example	Website	5:30	5:52
LA5.avi	Failsafing	quality at the source, Bernard Welding	Instructor CD, Website	5:54	7:10
LA6.avi	Order picking	Example Bernard, u-shape order	Website	7:30	8:28
LA7.avi	FIFO	Example	Website	8:30	8:44
LA8.avi	Employee Teams	Quality team interview	Website	9:40	10:23

194

Volume II (0-256-15967-X)

Supplier Development Outreach Program (16 minutes) From Toyota, this tape describes changes and improvements made at Flex-n-Gate, a manufacturer in Danville, Illinois that supplies Toyota with pickup truck bumpers. Toyota Supplier Development Institute engineers consulted with Flex-n-Gate in the process. It includes factory footage and inter-views with the purchasing manager, project manager, development engineers and plant manager.

Suggested Classroom Use: This tape can be used with Chapter 8 Supply Chain Strategy and Chapter 10 JIT.

FILE NAME	CONCEPT	DESCRIPTION	AVAILABLE FROM	TIME IN	TIME OUT
SU1.avi	Supplier Relationship	Toyota and Flex-n-gate	Instructor CD, Website	1:05:47	6:36
SU2.avi	Kaizen/JIT	Toyota example; production before and after	Website	6:41	7:35
SU3.avi	Setup reduction	Example, dies time reduction	Website	8:22	9:05
SU4.avi	Setups	Example	Website	9:05	9:29
SU5.avi	Kanban	Kanban board, visual example and explanation	Student CD, Website	10:38	11:30
SU6.avi	Process Flow Improvement	Redesign of layout	Website	11:41	12:14
SU7.avi	Warehouse	Inventory and visual techniques for improvement	Website	13:53	14:46
SU8.avi	Continuous Improvement Team	Example Toyota	Website	15:13	15:46
SU9.avi	Continuous Improvement	Interview with supplier operations manager	Instructor CD, Website	16:17	16:40

Volume III (ISBN 0-256-19528-5)

Reengineering at Caterpillar (11 minutes) This segment describes a real program undertaken at Caterpillar's Mossville Engine Center to reengineer the "drawing" process for engines. The five-step procedure this cross-functional group followed streamlined the process while improving customer satisfaction and quality. It also reduced the time required to produce drawings and costs. Interviews with team members are included.

Suggested Classroom Use: This tape can be used with Chapter 2 Operations Strategy & Competitiveness, Chapter 4 Process Analysis, Chapter 5 Product Design & Process Selection-Manufacturing, and Chapter 16 Consulting and Reengineering.

FILE NAME	CONCEPT	DESCRIPTION	AVAILABLE FROM	TIME IN	TIME OUT
RE1.avi	Reengineering, goals	Overview	Instructor CD, Website	1:50	2:45
RE2.avi	Reengineering	Definition	Instructor CD, Website	2:46	3:21
RE3.avi	Reengineering/mission	Team mission statement	Website	3:22	4:14
RE4.avi	Reengineering/process selection	Example - Caterpillar	Student CD, Website	5:47	6:20
RE5.avi	Reengineering/process mapping	Example - Caterpillar	Student CD, Website	6:20	6:45
RE6.avi	Reengineering/process improvement	Example - Caterpillar	Instructor CD, Website	7:57	8:30
RE7.avi	Reengineering/process verification	Example - Caterpillar	Website	8:31	8:53
RE8.avi	Reengineering/process implementation	Example - Caterpillar	Website	8:53	9:44
RE9.avi	Reengineering/results	Example - Caterpillar	Website	10:18	10:44

Volume III (0-256-19528-5)

Washburn Guitars (12 minutes) Washburn manufactures and sells over 150,000 guitars annually. This program provides an on-site overview of their job shop production system, with special emphasis on production scheduling priorities and their use of a flexible numerically controlled machine.

Suggested Classroom Use: This tape can be used with Chapter 5 Product Design & Process Selection-Manufacturing, Chapter 13 Inventory Control, and Chapter 15 Operations Scheduling.

FILE NAME	CONCEPT	DESCRIPTION	AVAILABLE FROM	TIME IN	TIME OUT
PS1.avi	Job shop	Example - Guitar	Website	1:27	1:45
PS2.avi	Schedules, intermittent	Example - Washburn guitar	Instructor CD, Website	2:42	3:10
PS3.avi	Priority rules	Description	Student CD, Website	3:13	4:10
PS4.avi	CNC machine, set up	Scheduling around use of CNC machine	Website	4:24	4:40
PS5.avi	CNC machine, flexibility	Use in flexible manufacturing guitars	Website	4:54	5:29
PS6.avi	Job shop/crafting	Example guitars	Website	5:37	6:10
PS7.avi	Materials	Example guitars	Website	6:11	6:50
PS8.avi	Schedule /painting	Longest time, schedule backward from due date	Instructor CD, Website	7:30	7:54
PS9.avi	Inspection/testing	Job shop, guitars example	Website	8:17	9:07
PS10.avi	Parts/inventory	Example, guitars	Instructor CD, Website	9:08	9:38
PS11.avi	Location selection criteria	guitar site location	Website	9:40	10:20

Volume IV (Tapes I and 2) (ISBN 0-256-21570-7)

Tape I

Value-Driven Production at Trek (9 minutes) This segment describes the distinctive approach Trek uses to manufacture high quality, mass-customized bikes for their customers. The organizing framework is the "value" approach to designing and manufacturing products to match customer needs. On-site footage features interviews and examples of unique uses of materials, testing, and assembly.

Suggested Classroom Use: This tape can be used with Chapter 2 Operations Strategy & Competitiveness, Technical Note 5 Facility Layout, Chapter 7 Quality Management, and Technical Note 7 Process Capability & Statistical Quality Control.

FILE NAME	CONCEPT	DESCRIPTION	AVAILABLE FROM	TIME IN	TIME OUT
VD1.avi	Value/definition	Example, Trek Bike	Instructor CD, Website	0.55	1:16
VD2.avi	Value/dimensions	Performance = speed x quality x flexibility	Website	1:17	1:39
VD3.avi	Value/production	Market wants	Website	1:55	2:45
VD4.avi	R&D/Testing	Example Trek bike	Website	3:15	3:54
VD5.avi	Materials testing	Example Trek bike	Website	3:54	5:15
VD6.avi	Materials/quality	Example Trek bike	Website	5:43	6:06
VD7.avi	Flexible Manufacturing	Process at Trek bike	Instructor CD, Website	6:41	7:15
VD8.avi	Technology	Example Trek bike	Instructor CD, Website	7:16	7:40

Volume IV, Tape 1 (0-256-21570-7)

Scheduling Services - The United Solution (9 minutes) This segment presents an overview of the scheduling system used by United Airlines in planning and delivering over 2,200 trips with 500 planes per day. Interviews with the developers of the 'PEGASYS' computer system which starts the process, along with discussions with key flight scheduling, equipment scheduling, and maintenance scheduling personnel lay out the procedures and issues United must deal with to efficiently deliver service in the travel industry

Suggested Classroom Use: This tape can be used with Chapter 12 Aggregate Planning, Chapter 15 Operations Scheduling, and Supplement A Linear Programming with the Excel Solver.

FILE NAME	CONCEPT	DESCRIPTION	AVAILABLE FROM	TIME IN	TIME OUT
SSU1.avi	Service scheduling	Overview	Website	:55	1:20
SSU2.avi	Service scheduling	Example airlines, MPS	Student CD, Website	1:31	2:17
SSU3.avi	Scheduling/computer system	Example United Airlines flight schedule	Website	2:18	2:45
SSU4.avi	Scheduling/aircraft	Example United airlines	Website	3:19	3:52
SSU5.avi	Scheduling/maintenance	Example United airlines	Website	3:53	4:25
SSU6.avi	Scheduling/flight crew	Example United airlines	Website	4:26	4:49
SSU7.avi	Scheduling/manpower	Example United airlines ground crew, baggage handlers, gate agents, etc.	Website	5:26	5:51
SSU8.avi	Scheduling/computer system	Example United Pegasus	Student CD, Website	5:52	6:45
SSU9.avi	Workload/scheduling	Example United airlines peaks	Instructor CD, Website	6:57	7:39
SSU10.avi	Scheduling/shift bids	Example United airlines	Website	8:18	8:39

Volume IV, Tape 1 (0-256-21570-7)

Quality Product and Process Design at Detroit Diesel (11 minutes) This segment describes the focus Detroit Diesel has on quality, from design of products though the actual manufacturing of engines, including the highly successful "series 60" engine. Interviews with owner Roger Penske, the production manager and assembly workers are included. Also included are on-site examples of the use of technology and talent to increase quality through product and process design.

Suggested Classroom Use: This tape can be used with Chapter 5 Product Design & Process Selection-Manufacturing, Chapter 7 Quality Management, Technical Note 7 Process Capability and Statistical Quality Control, and Supplement C Operations Technology.

FILE NAME	CONCEPT	DESCRIPTION	AVAILABLE FROM	TIME IN	TIME OUT
QD1.avi	Quality/overview	Graphic	Website	:57	1:36
QD2.avi	Quality Function Deployment	Overview	Student CD, Website	1:59	2:46
QD3.avi	Design/testing	Example, Detroit Diesel	Website	4:07	4:27
QD4.avi	In process inspection	Example Detroit Diesel	Website	4:43	5:28
QD5.avi	AGV	Example Detroit Diesel	Website	6:05	6:15
QD6.avi	Automation/tolerances	Example Detroit Diesel, batch inspection	Website	6:48	7:51
QD7.avi	SPC	Example Detroit Diesel	Instructor CD, Website	7:53	8:44
QD8.avi	Design	Example Detroit Diesel	Website	9:20	9:42

200

Volume IV, Tape 2 (0-256-21570-7)

Production Tour of the Vision Light System at Federal Signal (12 minutes) This segment follows the production and assembly process for vision lights at Federal Signal Corporation. This begins with the original bill of materials schedule through incoming parts and kit inspections, and several assembly and sub-assembly processes. Interviews with the master scheduler, operations manager, and supervisors in purchasing are included and all footage is on-site.

Suggested Classroom Use: This tape can be used with Chapter 5 Product Design & Process Selection-Manufacturing, Technical Note 5 Facility Layout, Chapter 12 Aggregate Planning, and Chapter 14 MRP.

FILE NAME	CONCEPT	DESCRIPTION	AVAILABLE FROM	TIME IN	TIME OUT
PT1.avi	Product design	Example at Federal Signal	Website	1:28	1:48
PT2.avi	Production process/steps	Overview of scheduling, planning, subassembly, packing & shipping at Federal Signal	Instructor CD, Website	2:20	2:47
PT3.avi	Bills of Materials	Example Federal Signal	Student CD, Website	2:50	3:49
PT4.avi	Capacity/daily	Example Federal Signal/planning	Instructor CD, Website	3:50	4:29
PT5.avi	Parts/subassembly	Example Federal Signal	Website	4:30	4:56
PT6.avi	Material flow	Example Federal Signal, work cell	Instructor CD, Website	5:05	5:34
PT7.avi	Cellular work stations/flexibility	Example Federal Signal	Student CD, Website	5:39	6:14
PT8.avi	Inspection/incoming	Example Federal Signal in-process, suppliers	Website	6:19	6:55
PT9.avi	Subassembly	Example Federal Signal	Website	7:38	8:11
PT10.avi	Testing/in process	Example Federal Signal	Website	8:39	8:50
PT11.avi	Product design/lights	Example Federal Signal	Website	9:08	9:17

Volume IV, Tape 2 (0-256-21570-7)

JIT at Federal Signal (12 minutes) This segment presents the use of both 'big' and 'little' JIT concepts at Federal Signal to reduce waste, improve quality, and closely meet customer demand in manufacturing a variety of products. On-site examples of Kanban, work cells, and supplier relations are featured as well as short interviews with engineers and employees.

Suggested Classroom Use: This tape can be used with Chapter 10 JIT.

FILE NAME	CONCEPT	DESCRIPTION	AVAILABLE FROM	TIME IN	TIME OUT
JI1.avi	JIT/overview	Graphic pull system	Website	1:18	2:05
JI2.avi	Big JIT	Definition	Student CD, Website	2:12	2:19
JI3.avi	Little JIT	Definition	Student CD, Website	2:19	2:29
JI4.avi	Safety Stock	Example Federal Signal, surplus	Website	2:47	2:57
JI5.avi	Waste	Suzaki waste of inventory, motion and from overproduction	Instructor CD, Website	2:59	3:12
JI6.avi	Group Technology	Work cell, circuit boards example	Instructor CD, Website	3:38	4:17
JI7.avi	Kanban	Visual example, container at Federal Signal	Website	4:55	5:24
JI8.avi	Barcodes/suppliers	Example Federal Signal	Student CD, Website	6:29	6:59
JI9.avi	Changeover/automatic	Example Federal Signal	Website	8:20	9:01
JI10.avi	JIT/Customization	Example Federal Signal	Instructor CD, Website	9:24	9:50

Volume V (ISBN 007-366182-1)

TriState-Converting to JIT -Part 1- Assessment (10 minutes) This video describes and shows the assessment and planning steps taken by Tristate Industries, a small Midwestern supplier of metal products for the construction industry, as it ramps up to deliver a new product and double it's output based on a new contract. Tristate president Don Keller and consultant Jim Therrien analyze the operation and plan the conversion to a just-in-time manufacturing system.

Suggested Classroom Use: This tape can be used with Chapter 5 Product Design & Process Selection-Manufacturing, Technical Note 5 Facility Layout, and Chapter 9 Strategic Capacity Management.

FILE NAME	CONCEPT	DESCRIPTION	AVAILABLE FROM	TIME IN	TIME OUT
BP1.avi	Capacity - Assessment	Capacity process planning at Tri-State Industries	Instructor CD, Website	3:20	4:26
BP2.avi	Batch Process Overview	Example Tri State Industries - traditional batch process	Website	4:27	5:32
BP3.avi	Flow charts – Assessment	Example Tri State Industries	Website	6:26	6:42
BP4.avi	World Class Manufacturing	Small company example-Tri State Industries	Website	6:50	7:10
BP5.avi	Employee involvement/teams	Example Tri-State Industries	Website	8:20	9:09

Volume V (007-366182-1)

TriState-Converting to JIT--Part 2- Implementation (9:50 minutes) This segment shows how TriState implemented the new cells, eliminated a large percentage, of WIP and instituted a Kanban control system. Overviews of the old and new systems are shown along with on-site interviews with employees and managers.

Suggested Classroom Use: This tape can be used with Technical Note 5 Facility Layout and Chapter 10 JIT.

FILE NAME	CONCEPT	DESCRIPTION	AVAILABLE FROM	TIME IN	TIME OUT
TS1.avi	Goals	Example Tri State Industries	Website	2:20	2:36
TS2.avi	Work Cells	Example Tri State Industries of work cells/group technology	Student CD, Website	4:24	5:16
TS3.avi	Kanban	Example Tri State Industries	Instructor CD, Website	5:17	6:17
TS4.avi	Lot Sizes - Kanban	Example Tri State Industries	Website	6:18	7:03
TS5.avi	Teamwork – Innovation	Example Tri State Industries	Website	7:41	8:12
TS6.avi	Poka-yoke - setup time reduction	Example Tri State Industries	Website	9:28	10:39

Volume V (007-366182-1)

International Logistics featuring American President Lines (11 minutes) This segment tours the new Los Angeles harbor operated by American President Lines (APL) and describes the state of the art terminal operations. The use of GPS, and electronic tracking from point of origin to final destination through the harbor and electronic loading maps and schedules are illustrated. Capacity and speed issues are described along with the whole range of services provided by APL to global manufacturers and suppliers.

Suggested Classroom Use: This tape can be used with Chapter 8 Supply Chain Strategy, Chapter 9 Strategic Capacity Management, and Supplement C Operations Technology.

FILE NAME	CONCEPT	DESCRIPTION	AVAILABLE FROM	TIME IN	TIME OUT
LO1.avi	Intermodal transportation	Cargo transfer, trucking example APL	Website	2:57	3:27
LO2.avi	Technology – Logistics	Container Shipping and Tracking at APL	Student CD, Website	3:36	3:49
LO3.avi	Technology – Capacity / logistics	Capacity issues APL terminal	Student CD, Website	4:02	5:13
LO4.avi	Technology – Tracking /GPS	Routing of goods example APL	Student CD, Website	5:50	6:36

Volume VI (ISBN 007-366193-7)

Product Design and Manufacturing at -TriState Industries (10 minutes) This video provides an overview of several key design issues considered during the development and manufacturing process setup for new trailers made by TriState Industries in Indiana. Designer Don Keller discusses tools and methods he used as well as how customer preferences were taken into account. Illustrations of the manufacturing specifications in the plant are included.

Suggested Classroom Use: This tape can be used with Chapter 4 Process Analysis and Chapter 5 Product Design & Process Selection-Manufacturing.

FILE NAME	CONCEPT	DESCRIPTION	AVAILABLE FROM	TIME IN	TIME OUT
TPD 1.AVI	Product Design	General Discussion	Instructor CD, Website	0:59	2:01
TPD 2.AVI	CAD	Description/Example TriState Industries Trailer	Instructor CD, Website	2:02	3:19
TPD 3.AVI	Product Design for Manufacturing	Example TriState Industries	Website	3:20	3:50
TPD 4.AVI	Product Design Prototype	Materials Example TriState Industries	Website	3:51	5:31
TPD 5.AVI	Design Process	Example TriState Industries- New product manufacturing process	Instructor CD, Website	6:07	7:10
TPD 6.AVI	Process Selection	Example TriState Industries	Instructor CD, Website	7:11	7:34

Volume VI (007-366193-7)

Project Management-Building the Alton 'Super Bridge (10 minutes) This segment follows the story of the building of the Alton, Illinois, super bridge across the Mississippi River and is based on a two-hour PBS documentary on the same subject. Highlights include descriptions of design, construction process, and even weather-related issues that project managers had to deal with in completing the project. Interviews with managers and contractors are included.

Suggested Classroom Use: This tape can be used with Chapter 3 Project Management and Chapter 15 Operations Scheduling.

FILE NAME	CONCEPT	DESCRIPTION	TEXT CHAPTER	TIME IN	TIME OUT
PM1.AVI	Projects- Concept	Definition/ Example Alton Bridge	Student CD, Website	:40	1:20
PM2.AVI	Work Breakdown Structure	Example Alton Bridge-Tasks	Student CD, Website	1:35	2:31
PM3.AVI	Project Management Scheduling	GANTT Charts	Student CD, Website	2:58	3:35
PM4.AVI	Project Materials/Delays	Example Alton Bridge-	Website	5:00	6:24
PM5.AVI	PERT/ CPM	Definitions- Scheduling complex projects	Instructor CD, Website	6:30	7:15
PM6.AVI	Project Cost/ Completion	Example Alton Bridge	Website	8:52	9:32
PM7.AVI	Project Crashing	Definition/ Example Alton Bridge	Website	9:40	10:40

Volume VI (007-366193-7)

Valuation of Operations at ABTco (11 minutes) This video describes manufacturing product and process changes made at ABTco, a U.S. and Canadian building products producer which led to a 300 percent increase in overall corporate value in just one year. Besides 'rightsizing,' ABT reallocated and expanded capacity, invested in new and improved technology, reduced inventory, and developed and added 50 new products to their offerings. Interviews with key managers and footage from plants in North Carolina and Michigan are included.

Suggested Classroom Use: This tape can be used with Chapter 2 Operations Strategy & Competitiveness, Chapter 5 Product Design & Process Selection-Manufacturing, Chapter 7 Quality Management, and Supplement B Financial Analysis.

File Name	Concept	Description	Text Chapter	Time In	Time Out
VO1.AVI	Operations Strategy and Goals	Definition and Discussion	Student CD, Website	:30	1:10
VO2.AVI	Rightsizing/Goals	Example ABTco	Instructor CD, Website	2:01	3:05
VO3.AVI	Rightsizing	Example ABTco	Website	3:10	4:26
VO4.AVI	Incentives/Asset Management	Example ABTco- inventory	Instructor CD, Website	4:27	5:10
VO5.AVI	Plant/Process Investment	Example ABTco – equipment/process	Instructor CD, Website	5:11	5:51
VO6.AVI	Improvements in Operations	Example ABTco	Website	5:52	7:10
VO7.AVI	New Product Cycle/ Quality	Example ABTco	Website	7:48	8:56
VO8.AVI	Quality	Example ABTco- types of checks	Website	8:57	9:46
VO9.AVI	Incentives-Employee	Example ABTco- self-directed work teams, gainsharing, etc.	Website	9:53	10:13
VO10.AVI	Value	Example ABTco	Student CD, Website	10:15	10:48

Volume VII (ISBN 007-243781-2)

Manufacturing Quality at Honda (12 minutes) This segment takes viewers inside Honda American Manufacturing Inc. in Ohio where the company's very successful emphasis on quality through continuous improvement is showcased. The steps Honda takes to ensure quality in all stages of production and development of products is outlined and on site footage of team meetings, interviews, and examples are included.

Suggested Classroom Use: This tape can be used with Chapter 7 Quality Management and Technical Note 7 Process Capability & Statistical Quality Control.

File Name	Concept	Description	AVAILABLE FROM	Time In	Time Out
MQ1.avi	Quality – General	Overview Honda America	Website	0:23	2:09
MQ2.avi	Quality - Planning	PDCA at Honda	Website	2:10	4:10
MQ3.avi	Quality – Training	Continuous training/changeovers at Honda	Website	4:24	5:40
MQ4.avi	Quality – Training	Job rotation/quality fatigue at Honda	Instructor CD, Website	5:45	6:47
MQ5.avi	Quality – Standards	Example Honda, photos and tasks	Instructor CD, Website	6:50	7:05
MQ6.avi	Quality – Circle Meetings	Example Honda	Website	7:05	7:55
MQ7.avi	Quality – Suppliers	Example Honda, zero defects	Website	7:56	9:14
MQ8.avi	Quality – Associates	Example Honda, authority to stop the line	Student CD, Website	10:38	11:49

Volume VII (007-243781-2)

A Day in the Life of Quality at Honda (9 minutes) This segment highlights the proactive approach to quality Honda takes in their Ohio plant producing Civics and Accords. A behind the scenes look into a daily quality meeting is shown and several examples of proactive quality problem prevention are illustrated.

Suggested Classroom Use: This tape can be used with Chapter 7 Quality Management, Technical Note 7 Process Capability & Statistical Quality Control, and Chapter 8 Supply Chain Strategy.

File Name	Concept	Description	AVAILABLE FROM	Time In	Time Out
DQ1.avi	Quality Control Meetings	Problem solving/prevention examples	Student CD, Website	0.45	1:28
DQ2.avi	Quality – Defect prevention	Examples Honda, trunk flange	Student CD, Website	1:29	2:28
DQ3.avi	Quality – Proactive prevention	Examples Honda, door film, doors off, material use	Website	2:29	4:15
DQ4.avi	Quality – Automation	Example Honda, robotics	Student CD, Website	4:47	5:54
DQ5.avi	Quality – Teaching/suppliers	Example Honda	Instructor CD, Website	5:58	7:17

Volume VII (007-243781-2)

Statistical Process Control at Honda (6 minutes) This segment illustrates Honda's use of statistical process control to monitor consistency and repeatability of processes. Control charts and reporting for a case study example are shown and described.

Suggested Classroom Use: This tape can be used with Technical Note 7 Process Capability & Statistical Quality Control.

File Name	Concept	Description	AVAILABLE FROM	Time In	Time Out
SPC1.avi	Statistical Process Control	Overview at Honda	Student CD, Website	0.25	1:34
SPC2.avi	SPC – Data collection	Example Honda of door closing test	Website	1:35	3:12
SPC3.avi	SPC – Control charts	Examples of x charts and c_{pk} at Honda	Student CD, Website	3:14	4:50
SPC4.avi	SPC – Out of control	Example Honda	Instructor CD, Website	5:00	6:14

CHASE ○ AQUILANO ○ JACOBS

Operations Management
For Competitive Advantage

Chapter 1

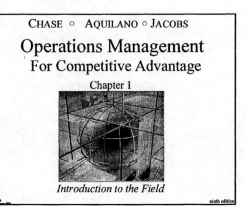

Introduction to the Field

ninth edition

Chapter 1
Overview: Introduction to the Field

- Operations Management
- Why Study Operations Management?
- Production System Defined
- Operations as a Service
- Plan of This Book
- Historical Development of OM
- Current Issues in OM

What is Operations Management?
Defined

Operations management (OM) is defined as the design, operation, and improvement of the systems that create and deliver the firm's primary products and services.

Why Study Operations Management?

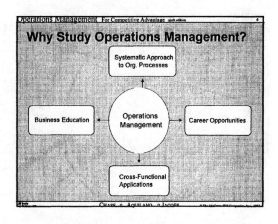

What is a Production System?
Defined

A **production system** is defined as a user of resources to transform inputs into some desired outputs.

Transformations

- Physical--manufacturing
- Locational--transportation
- Exchange--retailing
- Storage--warehousing
- Physiological--health care
- Informational--telecommunications

What is a Service and What is a Good?

- "If you drop it on your foot, it won't hurt you." (Good or service?)

- "Services never include goods and goods never include services." (True or false?)

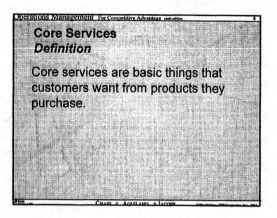

Core Services
Definition

Core services are basic things that customers want from products they purchase.

Core Services Performance Objectives

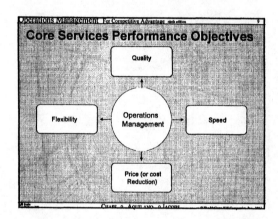

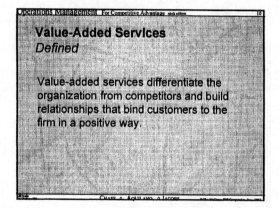

Value-Added Services
Defined

Value-added services differentiate the organization from competitors and build relationships that bind customers to the firm in a positive way.

Value-Added Service Categories

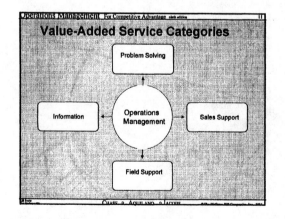

Plan of This Book

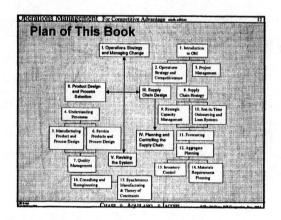

Historical Development of OM

- JIT and TQC.

- Manufacturing Strategy Paradigm.

- Service Quality and Productivity.

- Total Quality Management and Quality Certification.

Historical Development of OM (cont'd)

- Business Process Reengineering.

- Supply Chain Management.

- Electronic Commerce.

Current Issues in OM

- Effectively consolidating the operations resulting from mergers.

- Developing flexible supply chains to enable mass customization of products and services.

- Managing global supplier, production and distribution networks.

Current Issues in OM (cont'd)

- Increased "commiditization" of suppliers.

- Achieving the "Service Factory".

- Achieving good service from service firms.

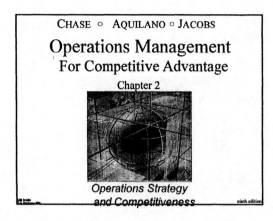

CHASE ○ AQUILANO ○ JACOBS

Operations Management
For Competitive Advantage
Chapter 2

*Operations Strategy
and Competitiveness*

ninth edition

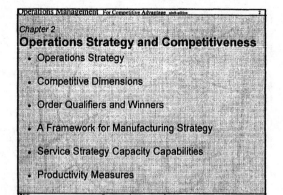

Chapter 2
Operations Strategy and Competitiveness

- Operations Strategy
- Competitive Dimensions
- Order Qualifiers and Winners
- A Framework for Manufacturing Strategy
- Service Strategy Capacity Capabilities
- Productivity Measures

CHASE ○ AQUILANO ○ JACOBS

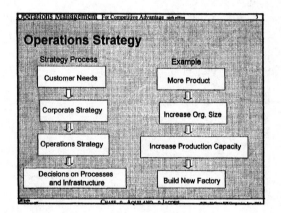

Operations Strategy

Strategy Process	Example
Customer Needs	More Product
Corporate Strategy	Increase Org. Size
Operations Strategy	Increase Production Capacity
Decisions on Processes and Infrastructure	Build New Factory

CHASE ○ AQUILANO ○ JACOBS

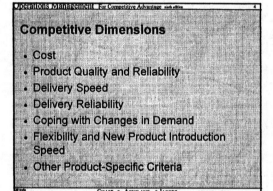

Competitive Dimensions

- Cost
- Product Quality and Reliability
- Delivery Speed
- Delivery Reliability
- Coping with Changes in Demand
- Flexibility and New Product Introduction Speed
- Other Product-Specific Criteria

CHASE ○ AQUILANO ○ JACOBS

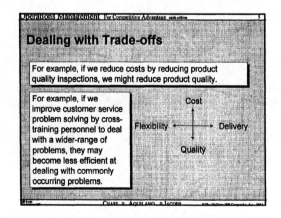

Dealing with Trade-offs

For example, if we reduce costs by reducing product quality inspections, we might reduce product quality.

For example, if we improve customer service problem solving by cross-training personnel to deal with a wider-range of problems, they may become less efficient at dealing with commonly occurring problems.

Cost

Flexibility ← → Delivery

Quality

CHASE ○ AQUILANO ○ JACOBS

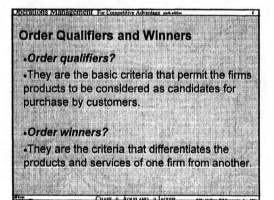

Order Qualifiers and Winners

- **Order qualifiers?**
- They are the basic criteria that permit the firms products to be considered as candidates for purchase by customers.

- **Order winners?**
- They are the criteria that differentiates the products and services of one firm from another.

CHASE ○ AQUILANO ○ JACOBS

Service Breakthroughs

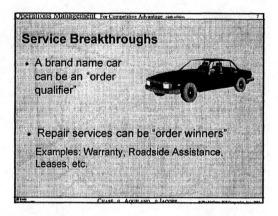

- A brand name car can be an "order qualifier"

- Repair services can be "order winners"

  Examples: Warranty, Roadside Assistance, Leases, etc.

Operations Strategy Framework

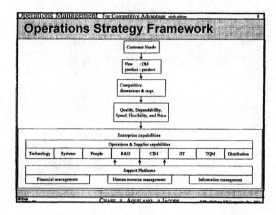

Steps in Developing a Manufacturing Strategy

- 1. Segment the market according to the product group.
- 2. Identify product requirements, demand patterns, and profit margins of each group.
- 3. Determine order qualifiers and winners for each group.
- 4. Convert order winners into specific performance requirements.

Service Strategy Capacity Capabilities

- Process-based
  - Capacities that transforms material or information and provide advantages on dimensions of cost and quality.
- Systems-based
  - Capacities that are broad-based involving the entire operating system and provide advantages of short lead times and customize on demand.
- Organization-based
  - Capacities that are difficult to replicate and provide abilities to master new technologies.

Total Measure Productivity

- Total measure Productivity = $\dfrac{\text{Outputs}}{\text{Inputs}}$

  or

- $= \dfrac{\text{Goods and services produced}}{\text{All resources used}}$

Partial Measure Productivity

- Partial measures of productivity =

- $\dfrac{\text{Output}}{\text{Labor}}$ or $\dfrac{\text{Output}}{\text{Capital}}$ or $\dfrac{\text{Output}}{\text{Materials}}$ or $\dfrac{\text{Output}}{\text{Energy}}$

Multifactor Measure Productivity

- Multifactor measures of productivity =

-
$$\frac{Output}{Labor + Capital + Energy}$$

or

-
$$\frac{Output}{Labor + Capital + Materials}$$

Example of Productivity Measurement

- You have just determined that your service employees have used a total of 2400 hours of labor this week to process 560 insurance forms. Last week the same crew used only 2000 hours of labor to process 480 forms.
- Which productivity measure should be used?
- Answer: Could be classified as a Total Measure or Partial Measure.
- Is productivity increasing or decreasing?
- Answer: Last week's productivity = 480/2000 = 0.24, and this week's productivity is = 560/2400 = 0.23. So, productivity is decreasing slightly.

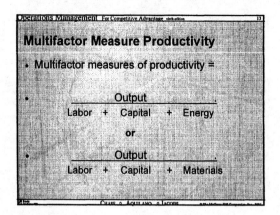

CHASE ○ AQUILANO ○ JACOBS

Operations Management
For Competitive Advantage
Technical Note 2

Learning Curves

ninth edition

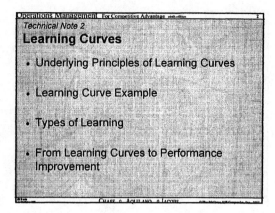

Technical Note 2

Learning Curves

- Underlying Principles of Learning Curves

- Learning Curve Example

- Types of Learning

- From Learning Curves to Performance Improvement

CHASE ○ AQUILANO ○ JACOBS

Underlying Principles of Learning Curves

1. Each time you perform a task it takes less time than the last time you performed the same task.

2. The extent of task time decreases over time.

3. The reduction in time will follow a predictable pattern.

CHASE ○ AQUILANO ○ JACOBS

Example of a Learning Curve

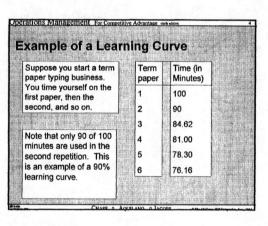

Suppose you start a term paper typing business. You time yourself on the first paper, then the second, and so on.

Note that only 90 of 100 minutes are used in the second repetition. This is an example of a 90% learning curve.

Term paper	Time (in Minutes)
1	100
2	90
3	84.62
4	81.00
5	78.30
6	76.16

CHASE ○ AQUILANO ○ JACOBS

Plotting the Learning Curve

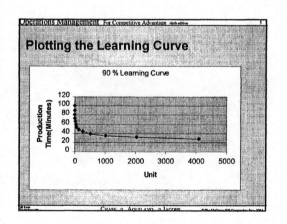

CHASE ○ AQUILANO ○ JACOBS

Types of Learning

- *Individual Learning*
  Improvement when individuals gain a skill or efficiency by repetition of a job.

- *Organizational Learning*
  Improvement from the groups of individuals from repetition and changes in administration, equipment, and product design.

CHASE ○ AQUILANO ○ JACOBS

From Learning Curves to Performance Improvement (Part 1)

- Proper selection of workers.
- Proper training.
- Motivation.
- Work specialization.
- Do one or very few jobs at a time.

From Learning Curves to Performance Improvement (Part 2)

- Use tools or equipment that assists or supports performance.
- Provide quick and easy access for help.
- Allow workers to help redesign their tasks.

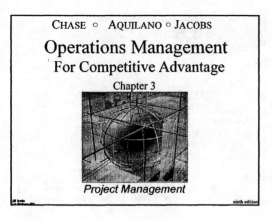

CHASE ○ AQUILANO ○ JACOBS

Operations Management
For Competitive Advantage
Chapter 3

Project Management

ninth edition

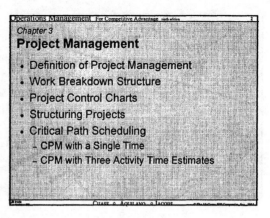

Chapter 3
Project Management

- Definition of Project Management
- Work Breakdown Structure
- Project Control Charts
- Structuring Projects
- Critical Path Scheduling
  - CPM with a Single Time
  - CPM with Three Activity Time Estimates

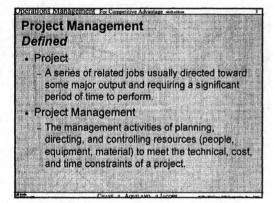

Project Management
Defined

- Project
  - A series of related jobs usually directed toward some major output and requiring a significant period of time to perform.
- Project Management
  - The management activities of planning, directing, and controlling resources (people, equipment, material) to meet the technical, cost, and time constraints of a project.

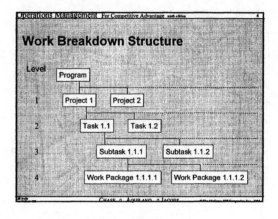

Work Breakdown Structure

Level

Program

1 — Project 1 — Project 2

2 — Task 1.1 — Task 1.2

3 — Subtask 1.1.1 — Subtask 1.1.2

4 — Work Package 1.1.1.1 — Work Package 1.1.1.2

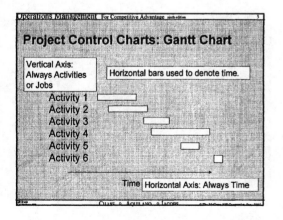

Project Control Charts: Gantt Chart

Vertical Axis: Always Activities or Jobs

Horizontal bars used to denote time.

Activity 1
Activity 2
Activity 3
Activity 4
Activity 5
Activity 6

Time | Horizontal Axis: Always Time

Structuring Projects
Pure Project: *Advantages*

- The project manager has full authority over the project.

- Team members report to one boss.

- Shortened communication lines.

- Team pride, motivation, and commitment are high.

Structuring Projects
Pure Project: *Disadvantages*

• Duplication of resources.

• Organizational goals and policies are ignored.

• Lack of technology transfer.

• Team members have no functional area "home."

Structuring Projects Functional Project: Organization Structure

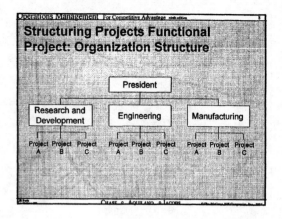

Structuring Projects
Functional Project: *Advantages*

• A team member can work on several projects.

• Technical expertise is maintained within the functional area.

• The functional area is a "home" after the project is completed.

• Critical mass of specialized knowledge.

Structuring Projects
Functional Project: *Disadvantages*

• Aspects of the project that are not directly related to the functional area get short-changed.

• Motivation of team members is often weak.

• Needs of the client are secondary and are responded to slowly.

Structuring Projects Matrix Project: Organization Structure

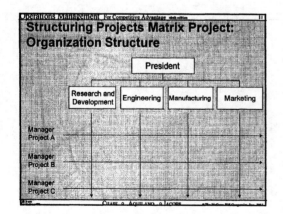

Structuring Projects
Matrix: *Advantages*

• Enhanced interfunctional communications.

• Pinpointed responsibility.

• Duplication of resources is minimized.

• Functional "home" for team members.

• Policies of the parent organization are followed.

Structuring Projects
Matrix: *Disadvantages*

- Too many bosses.

- Depends on project manager's negotiating skills.

- Potential for suboptimization.

Network-Planning Models

- A project is made up of a sequence of activities that form a network representing a project.
- The path taking longest time through this network of activities is called the "critical path."
- The critical path provides a wide range of scheduling information useful in managing a project.
- Critical Path Method (CPM) helps to identify the critical path(s) in the project networks.

Prerequisites for Critical Path Methodology

A project must have:

well-defined jobs or tasks whose completion marks the end of the project;

independent jobs or tasks;

and tasks that follow a given sequence.

Types of Critical Path Methods

- CPM with a Single Time Estimate
  - Used when activity times are known with certainty.
  - Used to determine timing estimates for the project, each activity in the project, and slack time for activities.
- CPM with Three Activity Time Estimates
  - Used when activity times are uncertain.
  - Used to obtain the same information as the Single Time Estimate model and probability information.
- Time-Cost Models
  - Used when cost trade-off information is a major consideration in planning.
  - Used to determine the least cost in reducing total project time.

Steps in the CPM with Single Time Estimate

- 1. Activity Identification.
- 2. Activity Sequencing and Network Construction.
- 3. Determine the critical path.
  - From the critical path all of the project and activity timing information can be obtained.

Example 1. CPM with Single Time Estimate

Consider the following consulting project:

Activity	Designation	Immed. Pred.	Time (Weeks)
Assess customer's needs	A	None	2
Write and submit proposal	B	A	1
Obtain approval	C	B	1
Develop service vision and goals	D	C	2
Train employees	E	C	5
Quality improvement pilot groups	F	D, E	5
Write assessment report	G	F	1

Develop a critical path diagram and determine the duration of the critical path and slack times for all activities

Example 1: First draw the network

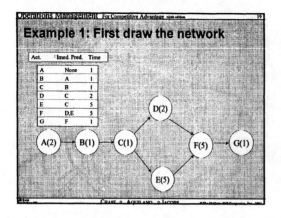

Act.	Imed. Pred.	Time
A	None	1
B	A	1
C	B	1
D	C	2
E	C	5
F	D,E	5
G	F	1

Example 1: Determine early starts and early finish times

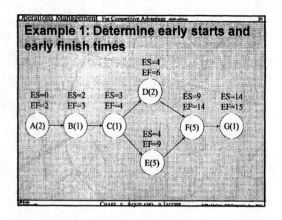

Example 1: Determine late starts and late finish times

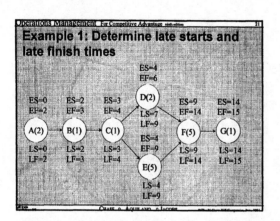

Example 1: Critical Path & Slack

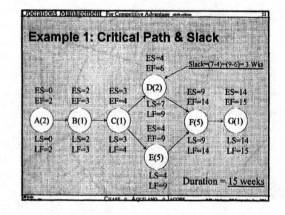

Slack = (7-4) = (9-6) = 3 Wks

Duration = 15 weeks

Example 2. CPM with Three Activity Time Estimates

Task	Immediate Predecesors	Optimistic	Most Likely	Pessimistic
A	None	3	6	15
B	None	2	4	14
C	A	6	12	30
D	A	2	5	8
E	C	5	11	17
F	D	3	6	15
G	B	3	9	27
H	E,F	1	4	7
I	G,H	4	19	28

Example 2. Expected Time Calculations

Task	Immediate Predecessors	Expected Time
A	None	7
B	None	5.333
C	A	14
D	A	5
E	C	11
F	D	7
G	B	11
H	E,F	4
I	G,H	18

$$ET(A) = \frac{3+4(6)+15}{6}$$

$$ET(A) = 42/6 = 7$$

Expected Time = $\dfrac{\text{Opt. Time} + 4(\text{Most Likely Time}) + \text{Pess. Time}}{}$

Example 2. Network

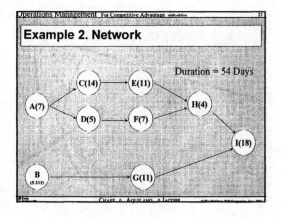

Duration = 54 Days

A(7), C(14), E(11), D(5), F(7), H(4), I(18), B (5.333), G(11)

Example 2. Probability Exercise

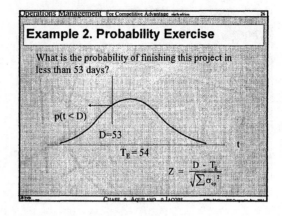

What is the probability of finishing this project in less than 53 days?

$p(t < D)$

D=53

$T_E = 54$

$$Z = \frac{D - T_E}{\sqrt{\sum \sigma_{cp}^2}}$$

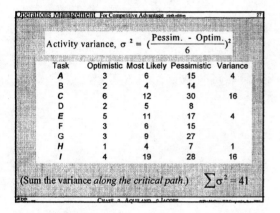

$$\text{Activity variance, } \sigma^2 = \left(\frac{\text{Pessim.} - \text{Optim.}}{6}\right)^2$$

Task	Optimistic	Most Likely	Pessimistic	Variance
A	3	6	15	4
B	2	4	14	
C	6	12	30	16
D	2	5	8	
E	5	11	17	4
F	3	6	15	
G	3	9	27	
H	1	4	7	1
I	4	19	28	16

(Sum the variance *along the critical path*.) $\sum \sigma^2 = 41$

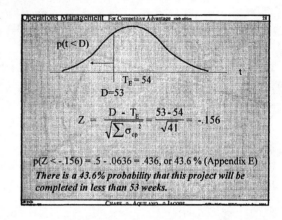

$p(t < D)$

$T_E = 54$

D=53

$$Z = \frac{D - T_E}{\sqrt{\sum \sigma_{cp}^2}} = \frac{53 - 54}{\sqrt{41}} = -.156$$

$p(Z < -.156) = .5 - .0636 = .436$, or 43.6 % (Appendix E)

There is a 43.6% probability that this project will be completed in less than 53 weeks.

Example 2. Additional Probability Exercise

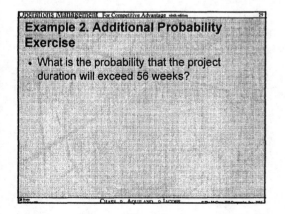

- What is the probability that the project duration will exceed 56 weeks?

Example 2. Additional Exercise Solution

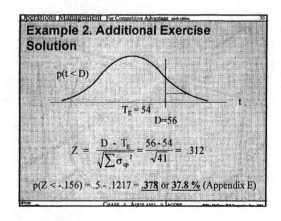

$p(t < D)$

$T_E = 54$

D=56

$$Z = \frac{D - T_E}{\sqrt{\sum \sigma_{cp}^2}} = \frac{56 - 54}{\sqrt{41}} = .312$$

$p(Z < -.156) = .5 - .1217 = \underline{.378}$ or $\underline{37.8 \%}$ (Appendix E)

Time-Cost Models

- *Basic Assumption:* Relationship between activity completion time and project cost.

- Time Cost Models: Determine the optimum point in time-cost tradeoffs.
  - Activity direct costs.
  - Project indirect costs.
  - Activity completion times.

CPM Assumptions/Limitations

- Project activities can be identified as entities. (There is a clear beginning and ending point for each activity.)
- Project activity sequence relationships can be specified and networked.
- Project control should focus on the critical path.
- The activity times follow the beta distribution, with the variance of the project assumed to equal the sum of the variances along the critical path. Project control should focus on the critical path.

CHASE ○ AQUILANO ○ JACOBS

Operations Management
For Competitive Advantage

Chapter 4

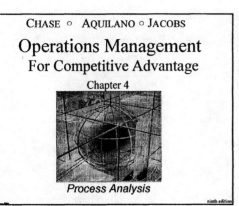

Process Analysis

ninth edition

Chapter 4

Process Analysis

- Process Analysis
- Process Flowcharting
- Types of Processes
- Process Performance Metrics

Process Analysis Terms

- Process: Is any part of an organization that takes inputs and transforms them into outputs.
- Cycle Time: Is the average successive time between completions of successive units.
- Utilization: Is the ratio of the time that a resource is actually activated relative to the time that it is available for use.

Process Flowcharting
Defined

- **Process flowcharting** is the use of a diagram to present the major elements of a process. The basic elements can include tasks or operations, flows of materials or customers, decision points, and storage areas or queues.
- It is an ideal methodology by which to begin analyzing a process.

Flowchart Symbols

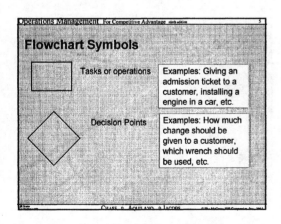

	Tasks or operations	Examples: Giving an admission ticket to a customer, installing a engine in a car, etc.
	Decision Points	Examples: How much change should be given to a customer, which wrench should be used, etc.

Flowchart Symbols (Continued)

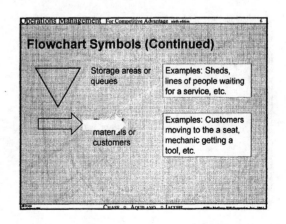

	Storage areas or queues	Examples: Sheds, lines of people waiting for a service, etc.
	materials or customers	Examples: Customers moving to the a seat, mechanic getting a tool, etc.

Example: Flowchart of Student Going to School

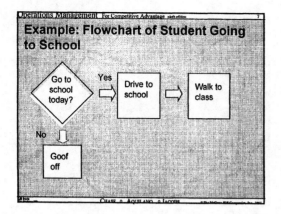

Multistage Process

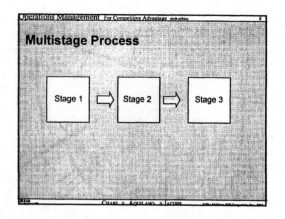

Multistage Process with Buffer

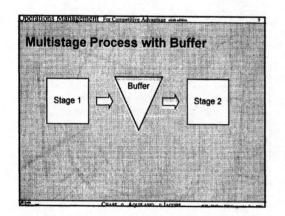

Other Types of Processes

- Make-to-order
  - Only activated in response to an actual order.
  - Both work-in-process and finished goods inventory kept to a minimum.
- Make-to-stock
  - Process activated to meet expected or forecast demand.
  - Customer orders are served from target stocking level.

Process Performance Metrics

- Operation time = Setup time
  Run time

- Throughput time = Average time for a unit to move through the system

- Velocity = $\dfrac{\text{Throughput time}}{\text{Value-added time}}$

Process Performance Metrics (Continued)

- Cycle time = Average time between completion of units

- Throughput rate = $\dfrac{1}{\text{Cycle time}}$

- Efficiency = $\dfrac{\text{Actual output}}{\text{Standard Output}}$

Process Performance Metrics (Continued)

- Productivity = $\dfrac{\text{Output}}{\text{Input}}$

- Utilization = $\dfrac{\text{Time Activated}}{\text{Time Available}}$

Cycle Time Example

- Suppose you had to produce 600 units in 80 hours to meet the demand requirements of a product. What is the cycle time to meet this demand requirement?
- Answer: There are 4,800 minutes (60 minutes/hour x 80 hours) in 80 hours. So the average time between completions would have to be: Cycle time = 4,800/600 units = 8 minutes.

Process Throughput Time Reduction

- Perform activities in parallel.

- Change the sequence of activities.

- Reduce interruptions.

CHASE ○ AQUILANO ○ JACOBS

Operations Management
For Competitive Advantage

Technical Note 4

Job Design and Work Measurement

ninth edition

Technical Note 4

Job Design and Work Measurement

- Job Design Defined
- Job Design Decisions
- Trends in Job Design
- Work Measurement
- Basic Compensation Systems
- Financial Incentive Plans

CHASE ○ AQUILANO ○ JACOBS

What is Job Design?
Defined

- **Job design** is the function of specifying the work activities of an individual or group in an organizational setting.
- The objective of job design is to develop jobs that meet the requirements of the organization and its technology and that satisfy the jobholder's personal and individual requirements.

CHASE ○ AQUILANO ○ JACOBS

Job Design Decisions

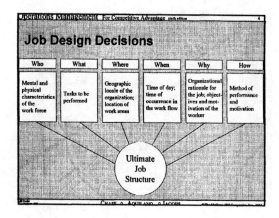

Who	What	Where	When	Why	How
Mental and physical characteristics of the work force	Tasks to be performed	Geographic locale of the organization; location of work areas	Time of day; time of occurrence in the work flow	Organizational rationale for the job; objectives and motivation of the worker	Method of performance and motivation

Ultimate Job Structure

CHASE ○ AQUILANO ○ JACOBS

Trends in Job Design

- Quality control as part of the worker's job.
- Cross-training workers to perform multiskilled jobs.
- Employee involvement and team approaches to designing and organizing work.
- "Informating" ordinary workers through telecommunication networks and computers.

CHASE ○ AQUILANO ○ JACOBS

Trends in Job Design (Continued)

- Extensive use of temporary workers.
- Automation of heavy manual work.
- Organizational commitment to providing meaningful and rewarding jobs for all employees.

CHASE ○ AQUILANO ○ JACOBS

Behavioral Considerations in Job Design

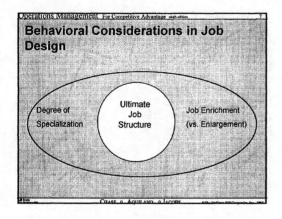

Degree of Specialization — Ultimate Job Structure — Job Enrichment (vs. Enlargement)

Sociotechnical Systems

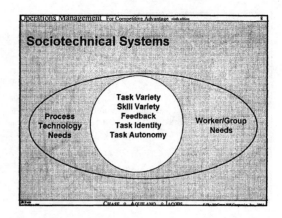

Process Technology Needs — Task Variety, Skill Variety, Feedback, Task Identity, Task Autonomy — Worker/Group Needs

Work Methods

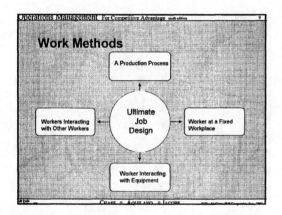

A Production Process

Ultimate Job Design

Workers Interacting with Other Workers

Worker at a Fixed Workplace

Worker Interacting with Equipment

Work Measurement
Defined

- **Work measurement** is a process of analyzing jobs for the purpose of setting time standards.
- Why use it?
  - Schedule work and allocate capacity
  - Motivate and measure work performance
  - Evaluate performance
  - Provide benchmarks

Time Study Normal Time Formulas

- Normal time (NT) = Observed performance time per unit x (1+Performance rating)

- $NT = \dfrac{\text{Time worked}}{\text{Number of units produced}} \times (1+\text{Performance rating})$

Time Study Standard Time Formulas

- Standard time = Normal time + (Allowances x Normal times)

- Standard time = NT(1 + Allowances)

- $\text{Standard time} = \dfrac{NT}{1 - \text{Allowances}}$

Time Study Example Problem

- You want to determine the standard time for a job. The employee selected for the time study has produced 20 units of product in an 8 hour day. Your observations made the employee nervous and you estimate that the employee worked about 10 percent faster than what is a normal pace for the job. Allowances for the job represent 25 percent of the normal time.

- Question: What are the normal and standard times for this job?

Time Study Example Solution

$$\text{Normal time} = \frac{\text{Time worked}}{\text{Number of units produced}} \times (1+ \text{Performance rating})$$

$$= (480 \text{ minutes}/20) \times (1.10)$$

$$= 26.4 \text{ minutes}$$

$$\text{Standard time} = \frac{NT}{1 - \text{Allowances}}$$

$$= (26.4)/(1-0.25)$$

$$= 35.2 \text{ minutes}$$

Work Sampling

- Use inference to make statements about work activity based on a sample of the activity.
- Ratio Delay
  - Activity time percentage for workers or equipment
- Performance Measurement
  - Relates work time to output (performance index)
- Time Standards
  - Standard task times

Advantage of Work Sampling over Time Study

- Several work sampling studies may be conducted simultaneously by one observer.

- The observer need not be a trained analyst unless the purpose of the study is to determine a time standard.

- No timing devices are required.

- Work of a long cycle time may be studied with fewer observer hours.

Advantage of Work Sampling over Time Study (Continued)

- The duration of the study is longer, which minimizes effects of short-period variations.

- The study may be temporarily delayed at any time with little effect.

- Because work sampling needs only instantaneous observations (made over a longer period), the operator has less chance to influence the findings by changing work method.

Basic Compensation Systems

- Hourly Pay

- Straight Salary

- Piece Rate

- Commissions

Financial Incentive Plans

- Individual and Small-Group Plans
  - Output measures
  - Quality measures
  - Pay for knowledge
- Organization-wide Plans
  - Profit-sharing
  - Gain-sharing
    - Bonus based on controllable costs or units of output
    - Involve participative management

Scanlon Plan
Basic Elements

$$Ratio = \frac{Total\ labor\ cost}{Sales\ value\ of\ production}$$

- The ratio
  - Standard for judging business performance

- The bonus
  - Depends on reduction in costs below the preset ratio

- The production committee

- The screening committee

Pay-for-Performance

- Paying employees based on their performance works--improvements in productivity and quality.

- Pay-for-performance will become increasingly common components of performance management strategies and systems.

CHASE ○ AQUILANO ○ JACOBS

Operations Management
For Competitive Advantage

Chapter 5

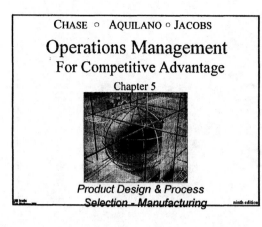

*Product Design & Process
Selection - Manufacturing*

ninth edition

Chapter 5

Product Design & Process Selection-Manufacturing

- Typical Phases of Product Design Development
  - Concurrent Engineering
- Designing for the Customer
  - QFD
- Design for Manufacturability
- Types of Processes
- Process Flow Structures
- Process Flow Design
- Global Product Design and Manufacturing

Typical Phases of Product Design Development

- Concept Development

- Product Planning

- Product/Process Engineering

- Pilot Production/Ramp-Up

Concurrent Engineering
Defined

- **Concurrent engineering** can be defined as the simultaneous development of project design functions, with open and interactive communication existing among all team members for the purposes of reducing time to market, decreasing cost, and improving quality and reliability.

Designing for the Customer

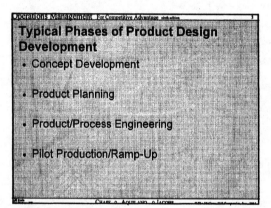

Designing for the Customer:
Quality Function Deployment

- Interfunctional teams from marketing, design engineering, and manufacturing

- Voice of the customer

- House of Quality

Designing for the Customer: Value Analysis/Value Engineering (VA/VE)

- Achieve equivalent or better performance at a lower cost while maintaining all functional requirements defined by the customer.
  - Does the item have any design features that are not necessary?
  - Can two or more parts be combined into one?
  - How can we cut down the weight?
  - Are there nonstandard parts that can be eliminated?

Design for Manufacturability

- Traditional Approach
  - "We design it, you build it" or "Over the wall"

- Concurrent Engineering
  - "Let's work together simultaneously"

Design for Manufacturing and Assembly

- Greatest improvements related to DFMA arise from simplification of the product by reducing the number of separate parts:
  » 1. During the operation of the product, does the part move relative to all other parts already assembled?
  » 2. Must the part be of a different material or be isolated from other parts already assembled?
  » 3. Must the part be separate from all other parts to allow the disassembly of the product for adjustment or maintenance?

Types of Processes

- Conversion
- Fabrication
- Assembly
- Testing

Process Flow Structures

- Job shop
- Batch shop
- Assembly Line
- Continuous Flow

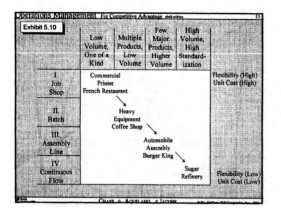

Exhibit 5.10

	Low Volume, One of a Kind	Multiple Products, Low Volume	Few Major Products, Higher Volume	High Volume, High Standard-ization	
I. Job Shop	Commercial Printer French Restaurant				Flexibility (High) Unit Cost (High)
II. Batch		Heavy Equipment Coffee Shop			
III. Assembly Line			Automobile Assembly Burger King		
IV. Continuous Flow				Sugar Refinery	Flexibility (Low) Unit Cost (Low)

Virtual Factory
Defined

A **virtual factory** can be defined as a manufacturing operation where activities are carried out not in one central plant, but in multiple locations by suppliers and partner firms as part of a strategic alliance.

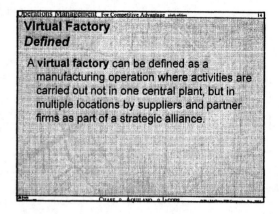

Process Flow Design
Defined

- A **process flow design** can be defined as a mapping of the specific processes that raw materials, parts, and subassemblies follow as they move through a plant.

- The most common tools to conduct a process flow design include assembly drawings, assembly charts, and operation and route sheets.

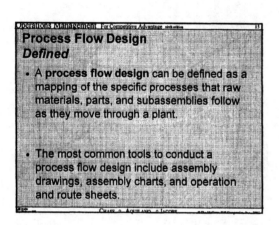

From Exhibit 5.14

Example: Assembly Chart (Gozinto)

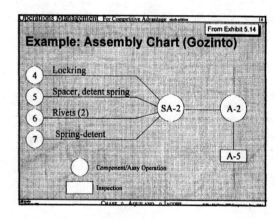

Example: Process Flow Chart

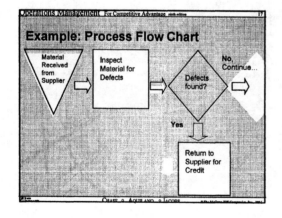

Global Product Design and Manufacturing Strategies

- Joint Ventures

- Global Product Design Strategy

Measuring Product Development Performance

- Time-to-market

- Productivity

- Quality

CHASE ○ AQUILANO ○ JACOBS

Operations Management
For Competitive Advantage
Technical Note 5

Facility Layout

Technical Note 5
Facility Layout

- Facility Layout and Basic Formats
- Process Layout
- Layout Planning
- Assembly Line balancing
- Service Layout

Facility Layout
Defined

Facility layout can be defined as the process by which the placement of departments, workgroups within departments, workstations, machines, and stock-holding points within a facility are determined.

This process requires the following inputs:

- Specification of objectives of the system in terms of output and flexibility.
- Estimation of product or service demand on the system.
- Processing requirements in terms of number of operations and amount of flow between departments and work centers.
- Space requirements for the elements in the layout.
- Space availability within the facility itself.

Basic Production Layout Formats

- Process Layout
- Product Layout
- Group Technology (Cellular) Layout
- Fixed-Position Layout

Process Layout: *Interdepartmental Flow*

- Given
  - The flow (number of moves) to and from all departments
  - The cost of moving from one department to another
  - The existing or planned physical layout of the plant
- Determine
  - The "best" locations for each department, where best means interdepartmental transportation, or flow, costs

---

Process Layout:
CRAFT Approach

- It is a heuristic program; it uses a simple rule of thumb in making evaluations:
  - "Compare two departments at a time and exchange them if it reduces the total cost of the layout."
- It does not guarantee an optimal solution.
- CRAFT assumes the existence of variable path material handling equipment such as forklift trucks.

Process Layout:
Systematic Layout Planning

- Numerical flow of items between departments
  - Can be impractical to obtain
  - Does not account for the qualitative factors that may be crucial to the placement decision
- Systematic Layout Planning
  - Accounts for the importance of having each department located next to every other department
  - Is also guided by trial and error
    - Switching departments then checking the results of the "closeness" score

Example of Systematic Layout Planning: Reasons for Closeness

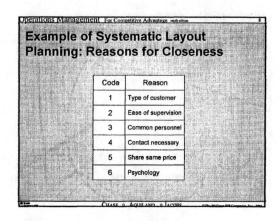

Code	Reason
1	Type of customer
2	Ease of supervision
3	Common personnel
4	Contact necessary
5	Share same price
6	Psychology

Example of Systematic Layout Planning: Importance of Closeness

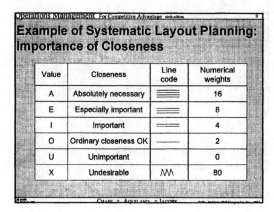

Value	Closeness	Line code	Numerical weights
A	Absolutely necessary	≡≡≡	16
E	Especially important	≡≡	8
I	Important	===	4
O	Ordinary closeness OK	———	2
U	Unimportant		0
X	Undesirable	﹀﹀﹀	80

Example of Systematic Layout Planning: Relating Reasons and Importance

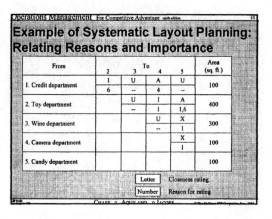

From	To 2	To 3	To 4	To 5	Area (sq. ft.)
1. Credit department	1	U	A	U	100
	6	--	4	--	
2. Toy department		U	1	A	400
		--	1	1,6	
3. Wine department			U	X	300
			--	1	
4. Camera department				X	100
				1	
5. Candy department					100

Letter	Closeness rating
Number	Reason for rating

Example of Systematic Layout Planning:
Initial Relationship Diagram

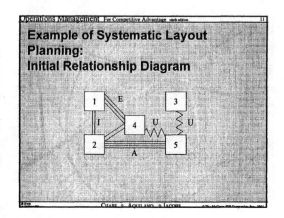

Example of Systematic Layout Planning:
Initial and Final Layouts

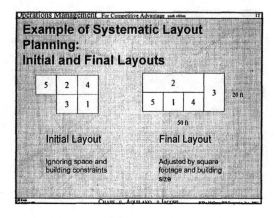

Initial Layout

Ignoring space and building constraints

Final Layout

Adjusted by square footage and building size

Assembly Lines Balancing Concepts

Question: Suppose you load work into the three work stations below such that each will take the corresponding number of minutes as shown. What is the cycle time of this line?

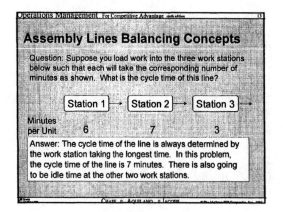

| Station 1 | → | Station 2 | → | Station 3 | → |

Minutes per Unit   6   7   3

Answer: The cycle time of the line is always determined by the work station taking the longest time. In this problem, the cycle time of the line is 7 minutes. There is also going to be idle time at the other two work stations.

Example of Line Balancing

- You've just been assigned the job a setting up an electric fan assembly line with the following tasks:

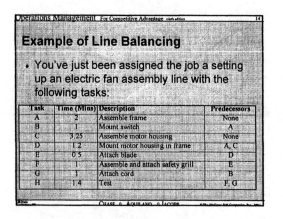

Task	Time (Mins)	Description	Predecessors
A	2	Assemble frame	None
B	1	Mount switch	A
C	3.25	Assemble motor housing	None
D	1.2	Mount motor housing in frame	A, C
E	0.5	Attach blade	D
F	1	Assemble and attach safety grill	E
G	1	Attach cord	B
H	1.4	Test	F, G

Example of Line Balancing:
Structuring the Precedence Diagram

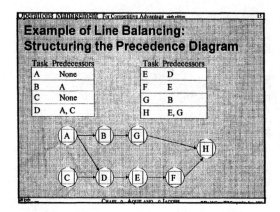

Task	Predecessors
A	None
B	A
C	None
D	A, C

Task	Predecessors
E	D
F	E
G	B
H	E, G

Example of Line Balancing:
Precedence Diagram

Question: Which process step defines the maximum rate of production?

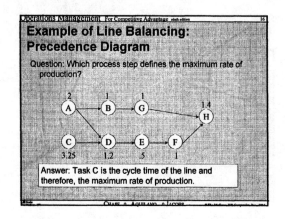

Answer: Task C is the cycle time of the line and therefore, the maximum rate of production.

Example of Line Balancing: The Bottleneck

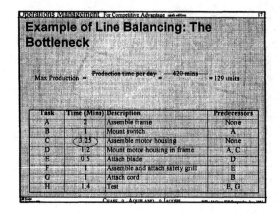

$$\text{Max Production} = \frac{\text{Production time per day}}{420\text{ mins}} = 129\text{ units}$$

Task	Time (Mins)	Description	Predecessors
A	2	Assemble frame	None
B	1	Mount switch	A
C	3.25	Assemble motor housing	None
D	1.2	Mount motor housing in frame	A, C
E	0.5	Attach blade	D
F	1	Assemble and attach safety grill	E
G	1	Attach cord	B
H	1.4	Test	E, G

Example of Line Balancing: Determine Cycle Time

Question: Suppose we want to assemble 100 fans per day. What would our cycle time have to be?

Answer:

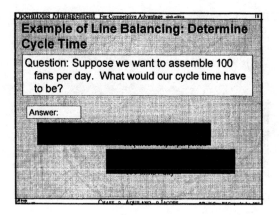

Example of Line Balancing: Determine Theoretical Minimum Number of Workstations

Question: What is the theoretical minimum number of workstations for this problem?

Answer:

Example of Line Balancing: Rules To Follow for Loading Workstations

- *Primary:* Assign tasks in order the the largest number of following tasks.

- *Secondary (tie-breaking):* Assign tasks in order of the longest operating time

---

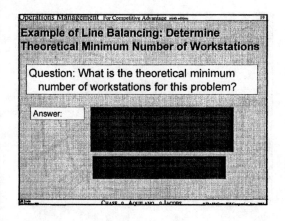

Task	Followers	Time (Mins)
A	6	2
C	4	3.25
D	3	1.2
B	2	1
E	2	0.5
F	1	1
G	1	1
H	0	1.4

Station 1 → Station 2 → Station 3 →

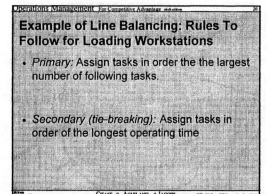

Task	Followers	Time (Mins)
A	6	2
C	4	3.25
D	3	1.2
B	2	1
E	2	0.5
F	1	1
G	1	1
H	0	1.4

Station 1 → Station 2 → Station 3 →

A (4.2-2=2.2)

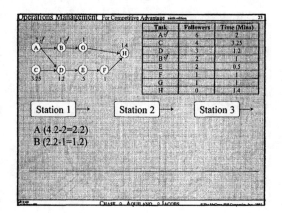

Task	Followers	Time (Mins)
A	6	2
C	4	3.25
D	3	1.2
B	2	1
E	2	0.5
F	1	1
G	1	1
H	0	1.4

Station 1 → Station 2 → Station 3 →

A (4.2-2=2.2)
B (2.2-1=1.2)

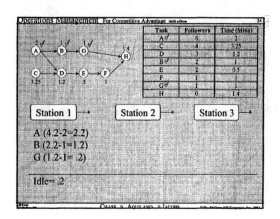

Task	Followers	Time (Mins)
A	6	2
C	4	3.25
D	3	1.2
B	2	1
E	2	0.5
F	1	1
G	1	1
H	0	1.4

Station 1 → Station 2 → Station 3 →

A (4.2-2=2.2)
B (2.2-1=1.2)
G (1.2-1= .2)

Idle= .2

Slide 25

Task	Followers	Time (Mins)
A	6	2
C	4	3.25
D	3	1.2
B	2	1
E	2	0.5
F	1	1
G	1	1
H	0	1.4

Station 1 → Station 2 → Station 3 →

A (4.2-2=2.2)
B (2.2-1=1.2)
G (1.2-1= .2)

C (4.2-3.25)=.95

Idle= .2

Slide 26

Task	Followers	Time (Mins)
A	6	2
C	4	3.25
D	3	1.2
B	2	1
E	2	0.5
F	1	1
G	1	1
H	0	1.4

Station 1 → Station 2 → Station 3 →

A (4.2-2=2.2)
B (2.2-1=1.2)
G (1.2-1= .2)

C (4.2-3.25)=.95

Idle= .2   Idle = .95

Slide 27

Task	Followers	Time (Mins)
A	6	2
C	4	3.25
D	3	1.2
B	2	1
E	2	0.5
F	1	1
G	1	1
H	0	1.4

Station 1 → Station 2 → Station 3 →

A (4.2-2=2.2)
B (2.2-1=1.2)
G (1.2-1= .2)

C (4.2-3.25)=.95

D (4.2-1.2)=3

Idle= .2   Idle = .95

Slide 28

Task	Followers	Time (Mins)
A	6	2
C	4	3.25
D	3	1.2
B	2	1
E	2	0.5
F	1	1
G	1	1
H	0	1.4

Station 1 → Station 2 → Station 3 →

A (4.2-2=2.2)
B (2.2-1=1.2)
G (1.2-1= .2)

C (4.2-3.25)=.95

D (4.2-1.2)=3
E (3-.5)=2.5

Idle= .2   Idle = .95

Slide 29

Task	Followers	Time (Mins)
A	6	2
C	4	3.25
D	3	1.2
B	2	1
E	2	0.5
F	1	1
G	1	1
H	0	1.4

Station 1 → Station 2 → Station 3 →

A (4.2-2=2.2)
B (2.2-1=1.2)
G (1.2-1= .2)

C (4.2-3.25)=.95

D (4.2-1.2)=3
E (3-.5)=2.5
F (2.5-1)=1.5

Idle= .2   Idle = .95

Slide 30

Task	Followers	Time (Mins)
A	6	2
C	4	3.25
D	3	1.2
B	2	1
E	2	0.5
F	1	1
G	1	1
H	0	1.4

Station 1 → Station 2 → Station 3 →

A (4.2-2=2.2)
B (2.2-1=1.2)
G (1.2-1= .2)

C (4.2-3.25)=.95

D (4.2-1.2)=3
E (3-.5)=2.5
F (2.5-1)=1.5
H (1.5-1.4)=.1

Idle= .2   Idle = .95   Idle = .1

Which station is the bottleneck? What is the _effective_ cycle time?

Example of Line Balancing: Determine the Efficiency of the Assembly Line

$$\text{Efficiency} = \frac{\text{Sum of task times (T)}}{\text{Actual number of workstations (Na) x Cycle time (C)}}$$

$$\text{Efficiency} = \frac{11.35 \text{ mins / unit}}{(3)(4.2 \text{mins / unit})} = .901$$

Group Technology: Benefits

1. Better human relations

2. Improved operator expertise

3. Less in-process inventory and material handling

4. Faster production setup

Group Technology: Transition from Process Layout

1. Grouping parts into families that follow a common sequence of steps.

2. Identifying dominant flow patterns of parts families as a basis for location or relocation of processes.

3. Physically grouping machines and processes into cells.

Fixed Position Layout

Question: What are our primary considerations for a fixed position layout?

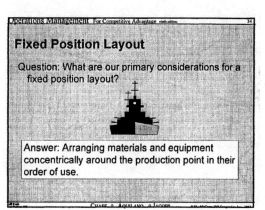

Answer: Arranging materials and equipment concentrically around the production point in their order of use.

Retail Service Layout

- Goal--maximize net profit per square foot of floor space.
- Servicescapes
  - Ambient Conditions
  - Spatial Layout and Functionality
  - Signs, Symbols, and Artifacts

CHASE ○ AQUILANO ○ JACOBS

Operations Management
For Competitive Advantage
Chapter 6

Product Design & Process Selection - Services

ninth edition

Chapter 6

Product Design and process Selection – Services

- Service Generalizations
- Service Strategy: Focus & Advantage
- Service-System Design Matrix
- Service Blueprinting
- Service Fail-safing
- Characteristics of a Well-Designed Service Delivery System

CHASE ○ AQUILANO ○ JACOBS

Service Generalizations

1. Everyone is an expert on services.

2. Services are idiosyncratic.

3. Quality of work is not quality of service.

4. Most services contain a mix of tangible and intangible attributes.

CHASE ○ AQUILANO ○ JACOBS

Service Generalizations (Continued)

5. High-contact services are experienced, whereas goods are consumed.

6. Effective management of services requires an understanding of marketing and personnel, as well as operations.

7. Services often take the form of cycles of encounters involving face-to-face, phone, internet, electromechanical, and/or mail interactions.

CHASE ○ AQUILANO ○ JACOBS

Service Businesses

- Facilities-based services

- Field-based services

CHASE ○ AQUILANO ○ JACOBS

Internal Services

Internal Supplier

Internal Supplier

Internal Customer

External Customer

CHASE ○ AQUILANO ○ JACOBS

The Service Triangle

Exhibit 6.1

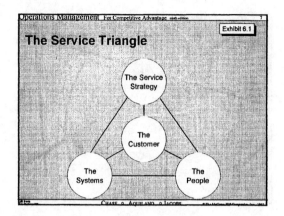

Service Strategy: Focus and Advantage
Performance Priorities

- Treatment of the customer
- Speed and convenience of service delivery
- Price
- Variety
- Quality of the tangible goods
- Unique skills that constitute the service offering

Service-System Design Matrix

Exhibit 6.6

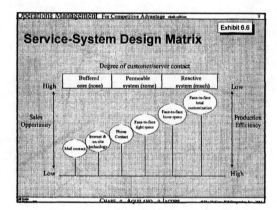

Example of Service Blueprinting

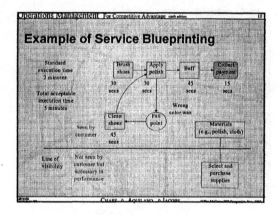

Service Fail-safing
Poka-Yokes (A Proactive Approach)

- Keeping a mistake from becoming a service defect.
- How can we fail-safe the three Ts?

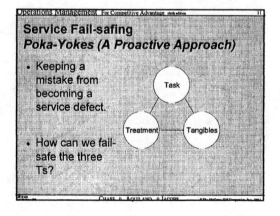

Have we compromised one of the 3 Ts?

Three Contrasting Service Designs

- The production line approach

- The self-service approach

- The personal attention approach

Characteristics of a Well-Designed Service System

1. Each element of the service system is consistent with the *operating focus* of the firm.

2. It is *user-friendly*.

3. It is *robust*.

4. It is structured so that *consistent performance* by its people and systems is easily maintained.

Characteristics of a Well-Designed Service System (Continued)

5. It provides effective *links* between the back office and the front office so that nothing falls between the cracks.

6. It manages the *evidence* of service quality in such a way that customers see the value of the service provided.

7. It is *cost-effective*.

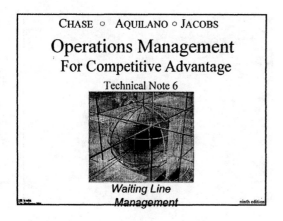

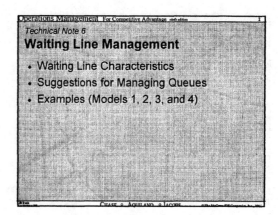

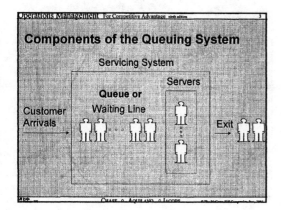

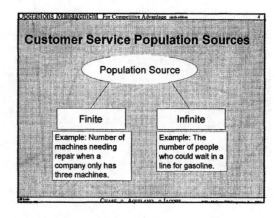

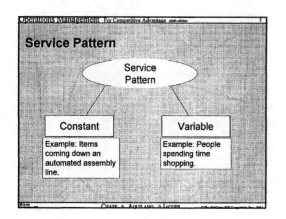

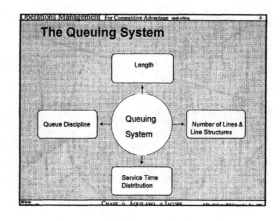

Examples of Line Structures

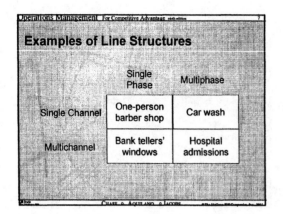

	Single Phase	Multiphase
Single Channel	One-person barber shop	Car wash
Multichannel	Bank tellers' windows	Hospital admissions

Degree of Patience

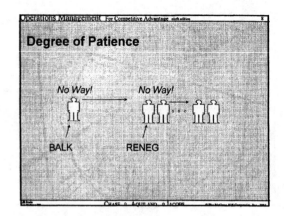

No Way!   No Way!

BALK   RENEG

Suggestions for Managing Queues

1. Determine an acceptable waiting time for your customers.
2. Try to divert your customer's attention when waiting.
3. Inform your customers of what to expect.
4. Keep employees not serving the customers out of sight.
5. Segment customers.

Suggestions for Managing Queues (Continued)

6. Train your servers to be friendly.
7. Encourage customers to come during the slack periods.
8. Take a long-term perspective toward getting rid of the queues.

Waiting Line Models

Model	Layout	Source Population	Service Pattern
1	Single channel	Infinite	Exponential
2	Single channel	Infinite	Constant
3	Multichannel	Infinite	Exponential
4	Single or Multi	Finite	Exponential

These four models share the following characteristics:
- Single phase
- Poisson arrival
- FCFS
- Unlimited queue length

Example: Model 1

Drive-up window at a fast food restaurant.
Customers arrive at the rate of 25 per hour.
The employee can serve one customer every two minutes.
Assume Poisson arrival and exponential service rates.

A) What is the average utilization of the employee?
B) What is the average number of customers in line?
C) What is the average number of customers in the system?
D) What is the average waiting time in line?
E) What is the average waiting time in the system?
F) What is the probability that exactly two cars will be in the system?

Example: Model 1

A) What is the average utilization of the employee?

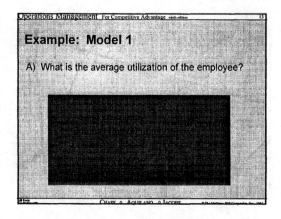

Example: Model 1

B) What is the average number of customers in line?

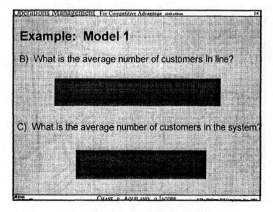

C) What is the average number of customers in the system?

Example: Model 1

D) What is the average waiting time in line?

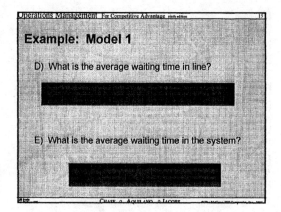

E) What is the average waiting time in the system?

Example: Model 1

F) What is the probability that exactly two cars will be in the system (one being served and the other waiting in line)?

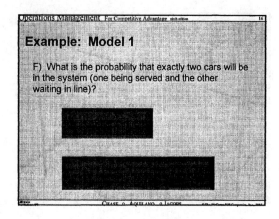

Example: Model 2

An automated pizza vending machine heats and dispenses a slice of pizza in 4 minutes.

Customers arrive at a rate of one every 6 minutes with the arrival rate exhibiting a Poisson distribution.

Determine:

A) The average number of customers in line.
B) The average total waiting time in the system.

Example: Model 2

A) The average number of customers in line.

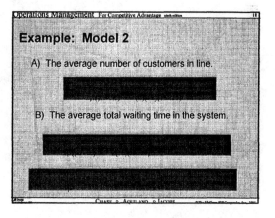

B) The average total waiting time in the system.

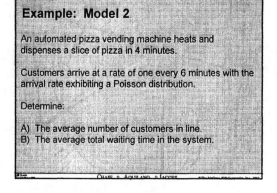

Example: Model 3

Recall the Model 1 example:
Drive-up window at a fast food restaurant.
Customers arrive at the rate of 25 per hour.
The employee can serve one customer every two minutes.
Assume Poisson arrival and exponential service rates.

If an identical window (and an identically trained server) were added, what would the effects be on the average number of cars in the system and the total time customers wait before being served?

Example: Model 3

Average number of cars in the system

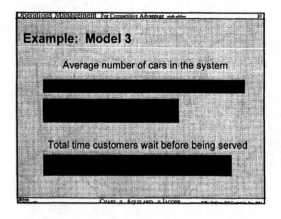

Total time customers wait before being served

Example: Model 4

The copy center of an electronics firm has four copy machines that are all serviced by a single technician.

Every two hours, on average, the machines require adjustment. The technician spends an average of 10 minutes per machine when adjustment is required.

Assuming Poisson arrivals and exponential service, how many machines are "down" (on average)?

Example: Model 4

N, the number of machines in the population = 4
M, the number of repair people = 1
T, the time required to service a machine = 10 minutes
U, the average time between service = 2 hours

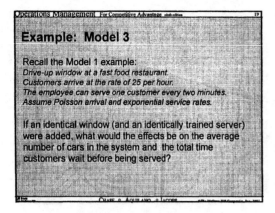

From Table TN6.11, F = .980 (Interpolation)

L, the number of machines waiting to be serviced = N(1-F) = 4(1-.980) = .08 machine

H, the number of machines being serviced = FNX = .980(4)(.077) = .302 machines

Number of machines down = L + H = **.382 machines**

CHASE ○ AQUILANO ○ JACOBS

Operations Management
For Competitive Advantage
Chapter 7

Quality Management

ninth edition

Chapter 7
Quality Management

- Total Quality Management Defined
- Malcolm Baldrige National Quality Award
- Quality Specifications
- Costs of Quality
- Continuous Improvement
- SPC Tools
- Benchmarking
- Fail-safing
- ISO 9000

Total Quality Management (TQM)
Defined

- **Total quality management** is defined as managing the entire organization so that it excels on all dimensions of products and services that are important to the customer.

1999 Malcolm Baldrige National Quality Award

- 1.0 Leadership (125 points)
- 2.0 Strategic Planning (85 points)
- 3.0 Customer and Market Focus (85 points)
- 4.0 Information and Analysis (85 points)
- 5.0 Human Resource Focus (85 Points)
- 6.0 Process Management (85 points)
- 7.0 Business Results (450 points)

Categories for the Baldrige Award

- Manufacturing companies or subsidiaries that
  - produce and sell manufactured products or manufacturing processes or
  - produce agricultural, mining, or construction products.
- Service companies or subsidiaries that sell service
- Small businesses
- Health care organizations
- Educational institutions

Characteristics of a Baldrige Award Winner

- The companies formulated a vision of what they thought quality was and how they would achieve it.
- Senior management was actively involved.
- Companies carefully planned and organized their quality effort to be sure it would be effectively initiated.
- They vigorously controlled the overall process.

Quality Specifications

- **Design quality**: Inherent value of the product in the marketplace

  - Dimensions include: Performance, Features, Reliability, Durability, Serviceability, Response, Aesthetics, and Reputation.

- **Conformance quality**: Degree to which the product or service design specifications are met

Costs of Quality

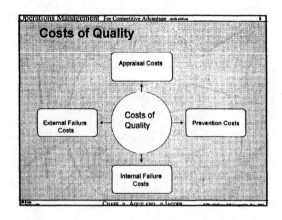

Continuous Improvement (CI)

- Management's view of performance standards of the organization
  - performance level of the firm as something to be "continuously challenged and incrementally upgraded."

- The way management views the contribution and role of its workforce
  - believe employee involvement and team efforts are the key to improvement

CI Methodology: PDCA Cycle (Deming Wheel)

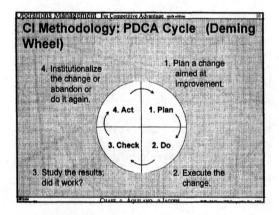

4. Institutionalize the change or abandon or do it again.

1. Plan a change aimed at Improvement.

3. Study the results; did it work?

2. Execute the change.

Example: Process Flow Chart

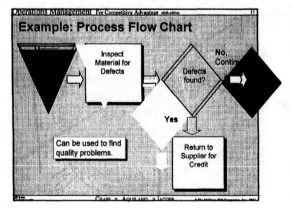

Example: Pareto Analysis

Can be used to find when 80% of the problems may be attributed to 20% of the causes.

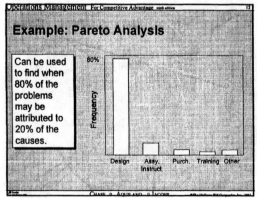

Example: Run Chart

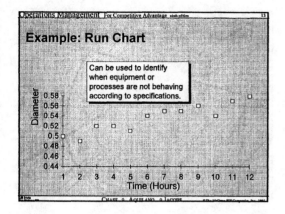

Can be used to identify when equipment or processes are not behaving according to specifications.

Example: Histogram

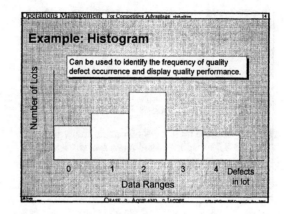

Can be used to identify the frequency of quality defect occurrence and display quality performance.

Example: Scatter Diagram

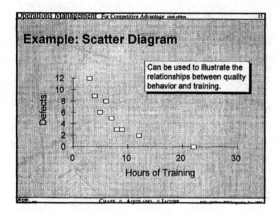

Can be used to illustrate the relationships between quality behavior and training.

Example: Checksheet

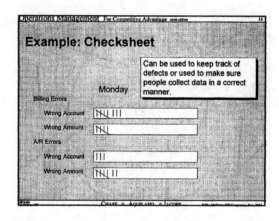

Can be used to keep track of defects or used to make sure people collect data in a correct manner.

Example: Cause & Effect Diagram

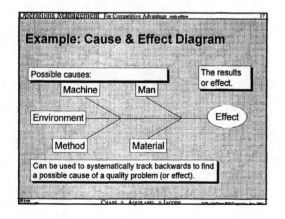

Can be used to systematically track backwards to find a possible cause of a quality problem (or effect).

Example: Control Charts

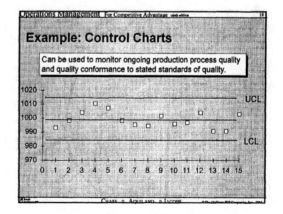

Can be used to monitor ongoing production process quality and quality conformance to stated standards of quality.

Benchmarking

1. Identify those processes needing improvement.

2. Identify a firm that is the world leader in performing the process.

3. Contact the managers of that company and make a personal visit to interview managers and workers.

4. Analyze data.

The Shingo System: Fail-Safe Design

- Shingo's argument:
  - SQC methods do not prevent defects
  - Defects arise when people make errors
  - Defects can be prevented by providing workers with feedback on errors

- Poka-Yoke includes:
  - Checklists
  - Special tooling that prevents workers from making errors

ISO 9000

- Series of standards agreed upon by the International Organization for Standardization (ISO)

- Adopted in 1987

- More than 100 countries

- A prerequisite for global competition?

- ISO 9000 directs you to "document what you do and then do as you documented."

Three Forms of ISO Certification

First party: A firm audits itself against ISO 9000 standards.

Second party: A customer audits its supplier.

Third party: A "qualified" national or international standards or certifying agency serves as auditor.

ISO 9000 versus the Baldrige Award

- Which should we pursue first?

- What are the differences between the two?

- Do you have to be ISO 9000 certified before going for the Baldrige Award?

CHASE ○ AQUILANO ○ JACOBS

Operations Management
For Competitive Advantage

Technical Note 7

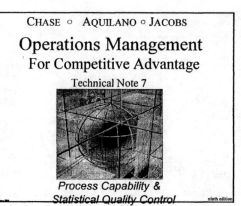

Process Capability &
Statistical Quality Control

ninth edition

Technical Note 7
Process Capability and Statistical Quality Control

- Process Variation
- Process Capability
- Process Control Procedures
  - Variable data
  - Attribute data
- Acceptance Sampling
  - Operating Characteristic Curve

Basic Forms of Variation

- **Assignable variation** is caused by factors that can be clearly identified and possibly managed.

- **Common variation** is inherent in the production process.

Taguchi's View of Variation

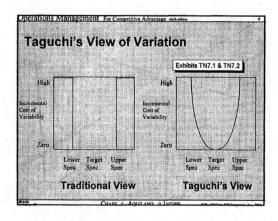

Exhibits TN7.1 & TN7.2

Traditional View   **Taguchi's View**

Process Capability

- Process limits

- Tolerance limits

- How do the limits relate to one another?

Process Capability Index, C_{pk}

Capability Index shows how well parts being produced fit into design limit specifications.

$$C_{pk} = \min\left(\frac{\overline{X}-LTL}{3\sigma} \text{ or } \frac{UTL-\overline{X}}{3\sigma}\right)$$

As a production process produces items small shifts in equipment or systems can cause differences in production performance from differing samples.

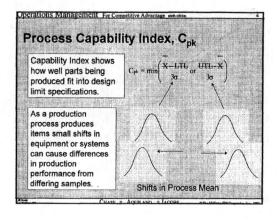

Shifts in Process Mean

Types of Statistical Sampling

- Attribute (Go or no-go information)
  - **Defectives** refers to the acceptability of product across a range of characteristics.
  - **Defects** refers to the number of defects per unit which may be higher than the number of defectives.
  - *p*-chart application
- Variable (Continuous)
  - Usually measured by the mean and the standard deviation.
  - X-bar and R chart applications

Statistical Process Control (SPC) Charts

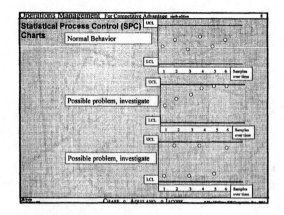

Normal Behavior

Possible problem, investigate

Possible problem, investigate

Control Limits are based on the Normal Curve

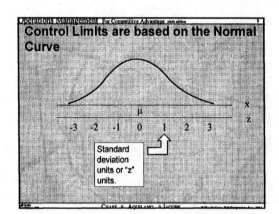

Standard deviation units or "z" units.

Control Limits

We establish the Upper Control Limits (UCL) and the Lower Control Limits (LCL) with plus or minus 3 standard deviations. Based on this we can expect 99.7% of our sample observations to fall within these limits.

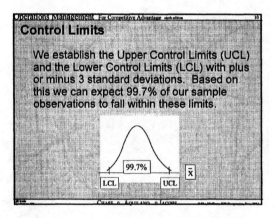

99.7%

LCL   UCL $\bar{x}$

Example of Constructing a *p*-Chart: Required Data

Sample	No.	Defectives
1	100	4
2	100	2
3	100	5
4	100	3
5	100	6
6	100	4
7	100	3
8	100	7
9	100	1
10	100	2
11	100	3
12	100	2
13	100	2
14	100	8
15	100	3

Statistical Process Control Formulas: Attribute Measurements (*p*-Chart)

Given:

$$\bar{p} = \frac{\text{Total Number of Defectives}}{\text{Total Number of Observations}}$$

$$s_p = \sqrt{\frac{\bar{p}\,(1-\bar{p})}{n}}$$

Compute control limits:

Example of Constructing a *p*-chart: Step 1

1. Calculate the sample proportions, p (these are what can be plotted on the *p*-chart) for each sample.

Sample	n	Defectives	p
1	100	4	0.04
2	100	2	0.02
3	100	5	0.05
4	100	3	0.03
5	100	6	0.06
6	100	4	0.04
7	100	3	0.03
8	100	7	0.07
9	100	1	0.01
10	100	2	0.02
11	100	3	0.03
12	100	2	0.02
13	100	2	0.02
14	100	8	0.08
15	100	3	0.03

Example of Constructing a *p*-chart: Steps 2&3

2. Calculate the average of the sample proportions.

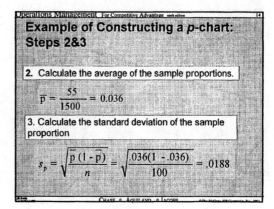

$$\bar{p} = \frac{55}{1500} = 0.036$$

3. Calculate the standard deviation of the sample proportion

$$s_p = \sqrt{\frac{\bar{p}(1-\bar{p})}{n}} = \sqrt{\frac{.036(1-.036)}{100}} = .0188$$

Example of Constructing a *p*-chart: Step 4

4. Calculate the control limits.

$$UCL = \bar{p} + z\, s_p$$
$$LCL = \bar{p} - z\, s_p$$

$$.036 \pm 3(.0188)$$

UCL = 0.0924
LCL = -0.0204 (or 0)

Example of Constructing a *p*-Chart: Step 5

5. Plot the individual sample proportions, the average of the proportions, and the control limits

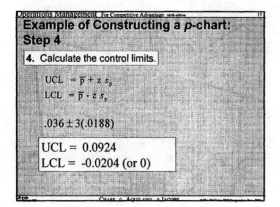

Example of x-Bar and R Charts: Required Data

Sample	Obs 1	Obs 2	Obs 3	Obs 4	Obs 5
1	10.68	10.689	10.776	10.798	10.714
2	10.79	10.86	10.601	10.746	10.779
3	10.78	10.667	10.838	10.785	10.723
4	10.59	10.727	10.812	10.775	10.73
5	10.69	10.708	10.79	10.758	10.671
6	10.75	10.714	10.738	10.719	10.606
7	10.79	10.713	10.689	10.877	10.603
8	10.74	10.779	10.11	10.737	10.75
9	10.77	10.773	10.641	10.644	10.725
10	10.72	10.671	10.708	10.85	10.712
11	10.79	10.821	10.764	10.658	10.708
12	10.62	10.802	10.818	10.872	10.727
13	10.66	10.822	10.893	10.544	10.75
14	10.81	10.749	10.859	10.801	10.701
15	10.86	10.881	10.644	10.747	10.728

Example of x-bar and R charts: Step 1. Calculate sample means, sample ranges, mean of means, and mean of ranges.

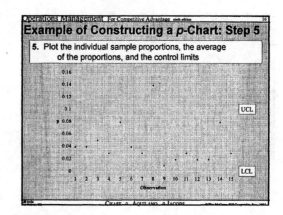

Sample	Obs 1	Obs 2	Obs 3	Obs 4	Obs 5	Avg	Range
1	10.68	10.689	10.776	10.798	10.714	10.732	0.116
2	10.79	10.86	10.601	10.746	10.779	10.755	0.259
3	10.78	10.667	10.838	10.785	10.723	10.759	0.171
4	10.59	10.727	10.812	10.775	10.73	10.727	0.221
5	10.69	10.708	10.79	10.758	10.671	10.724	0.119
6	10.75	10.714	10.738	10.719	10.606	10.705	0.143
7	10.79	10.713	10.689	10.877	10.603	10.735	0.274
8	10.74	10.779	10.11	10.737	10.75	10.624	0.669
9	10.77	10.773	10.641	10.644	10.725	10.710	0.132
10	10.72	10.671	10.708	10.85	10.712	10.732	0.179
11	10.79	10.821	10.764	10.658	10.708	10.748	0.163
12	10.62	10.802	10.818	10.872	10.727	10.768	0.250
13	10.66	10.822	10.893	10.544	10.75	10.733	0.349
14	10.81	10.749	10.859	10.801	10.701	10.783	0.158
15	10.86	10.881	10.644	10.747	10.728	10.692	0.103
					Averages	10.728	0.220400

Example of x-bar and R charts: Step 2. Determine Control Limit Formulas and Necessary Tabled Values

From Exhibit TN7.7

$\bar{x}$ **Chart Control Limits**

$$UCL = \bar{\bar{x}} + A_2\bar{R}$$

$$LCL = \bar{\bar{x}} - A_2\bar{R}$$

R Chart Control Limits

$$UCL = D_4\bar{R}$$

$$LCL = D_3\bar{R}$$

n	A2	D3	D4
2	1.88	0	3.27
3	1.02	0	2.57
4	0.73	0	2.28
5	0.58	0	2.11
6	0.48	0	2.00
7	0.42	0.08	1.92
8	0.37	0.14	1.86
9	0.34	0.18	1.82
10	0.31	0.22	1.78
11	0.29	0.26	1.74

Example of x-bar and R charts: Steps 3&4. Calculate x-bar Chart and Plot Values

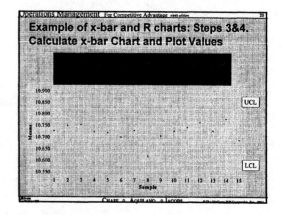

Example of x-bar and R charts: Steps 5&6. Calculate R-chart and Plot Values

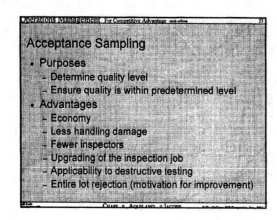

Basic Forms of Statistical Sampling for Quality Control

- Sampling to accept or reject the immediate lot of *product* at hand (Acceptance Sampling).

- Sampling to determine if the process is within acceptable limits (Statistical Process Control)

Acceptance Sampling

- Purposes
  - Determine quality level
  - Ensure quality is within predetermined level
- Advantages
  - Economy
  - Less handling damage
  - Fewer inspectors
  - Upgrading of the inspection job
  - Applicability to destructive testing
  - Entire lot rejection (motivation for improvement)

Acceptance Sampling

- Disadvantages
  - Risks of accepting "bad" lots and rejecting "good" lots
  - Added planning and documentation
  - Sample provides less information than 100-percent inspection

Acceptance Sampling: Single Sampling Plan

A simple goal

Determine (1) how many units, *n*, to sample from a lot, and (2) the maximum number of defective items, *c*, that can be found in the sample before the lot is rejected.

Risk

- Acceptable Quality Level (AQL)
  - Max. acceptable percentage of defectives defined by producer.
- α (Producer's risk)
  - The probability of rejecting a good lot.
- Lot Tolerance Percent Defective (LTPD)
  - Percentage of defectives that defines consumer's rejection point.
- β (Consumer's risk)
  - The probability of accepting a bad lot.

Operating Characteristic Curve

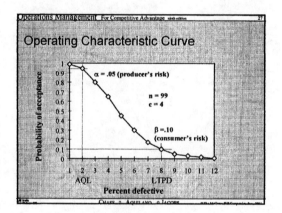

Example: Acceptance Sampling Problem

Zypercom, a manufacturer of video interfaces, purchases printed wiring boards from an outside vender, Procard. Procard has set an acceptable quality level of 1% and accepts a 5% risk of rejecting lots at or below this level. Zypercom considers lots with 3% defectives to be unacceptable and will assume a 10% risk of accepting a defective lot.

Develop a sampling plan for Zypercom and determine a rule to be followed by the receiving inspection personnel.

Example: Step 1. What is given and what is not?

In this problem, AQL is given to be 0.01 and LTDP is given to be 0.03. We are also given an alpha of 0.05 and a beta of 0.10.

What you need to determine your sampling plan is "c" and "n."

Example: Step 2. Determine "c"

First divide LTPD by AQL.

Then find the value for "c" by selecting the value in the TN7.10 "n(AQL)"column that is equal to or just greater than the ratio above.

Exhibit TN 7.10			So, c = 6.	
c	LTPD/AQL	n AQL	c	LTPD/AQL	n AQL
0	44.890	0.052	5	3.549	2.613
1	10.946	0.355	6	3.206	3.286
2	6.509	0.818	7	2.957	3.981
3	4.890	1.366	8	2.768	4.695
4	4.057	1.970	9	2.618	5.426

Example: Step 3. Determine Sample Size

Now given the information below, compute the sample size in units to generate your sampling plan.

c = 6, from Table
n (AQL) = 3.286, from Table
AQL = .01, given in problem

n(AQL/AQL) = 3.286/.01 = 328.6, or 329 (always round up)

Sampling Plan:
Take a random sample of 329 units from a lot.
Reject the lot if *more than* 6 units are defective.

CHASE ○ AQUILANO ○ JACOBS

Operations Management
For Competitive Advantage
Chapter 8

Supply Chain Strategy

ninth edition

Chapter 8
Supply-Chain Strategy

- Supply-Chain Management Defined?
- Measuring Supply-Chain Performance
- Bullwhip Effect
- Outsourcing Defined
- Value Density Defined
- Mass Customization Defined

CHASE ○ AQUILANO ○ JACOBS

What is Supply-Chain Management?
Defined

- **Supply-chain** is a term that describes how organizations (suppliers, manufacturers, distributors, and customers) are linked together.
- **Supply-chain management** is a total system approach to managing the entire flow of information, materials, and services from raw-material suppliers through factories and warehouses to the end customer.

CHASE ○ AQUILANO ○ JACOBS

Formulas for Measuring Supply-Chain Performance

- Inventory Turnover $= \dfrac{\text{Cost of goods sold}}{\text{Average aggregate inventory value}}$

- Weeks of Supply $= \left[\dfrac{\text{Average aggregate Inventory value}}{\text{Cost of goods sold}}\right](52\ \text{Weeks})$

CHASE ○ AQUILANO ○ JACOBS

Example of Measuring Supply-Chain Performance

- Suppose a company's new annual report claims their costs of goods sold for the year is $160 million and their total average inventory (production materials + work-in-process) is worth $35 million. This company is used to having any inventory turn ratio of 10.
- What is this year's Inventory Turnover ratio? What does it mean?

CHASE ○ AQUILANO ○ JACOBS

Example of Measuring Supply-Chain Performance (Continued)

Inventory Turnover

= Cost of goods sold/Average aggregate inventory value

= $160/$35

= 4.57

Since the company is used to an inventory turnover of 10, a drop to 4.57 means that the inventory is not turning over as quickly as it had in the past. Without knowing the industry average of turns for this company it is not possible to comment on how they are competitively doing in the industry.

CHASE ○ AQUILANO ○ JACOBS

Bullwhip Effect

The magnification of variability in orders in the supply-chain.

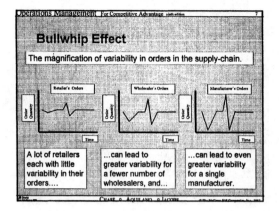

| A lot of retailers each with little variability in their orders.... | ...can lead to greater variability for a fewer number of wholesalers, and... | ...can lead to even greater variability for a single manufacturer. |

Matching Supply-Chains with Products

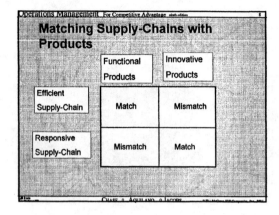

	Functional Products	Innovative Products
Efficient Supply-Chain	Match	Mismatch
Responsive Supply-Chain	Mismatch	Match

What Is Outsourcing?
Defined

Outsourcing is defined as the act of moving a

firm's internal activities and decision

responsibility to outside providers.

Reasons to Outsource

- Organizationally-driven
- Improvement-driven
- Financially-driven
- Revenue-driven
- Cost-driven
- Employee-driven

Value Density
Defined

- **Value density** is defined as the value of an item per pound of weight.

- It is used as an important measure when deciding where items should be stocked geographically and how they should be shipped.

Mass Customization
Defined

- **Mass customization** is a term used to describe the ability of a company to deliver highly customized products and services to different customers.

- The key to mass customization is effectively postponing the tasks of differentiating a product for a specific customer until the latest possible point in the supply-chain network.

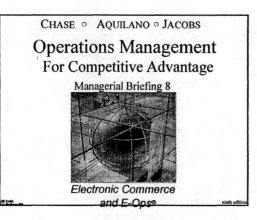

CHASE ○ AQUILANO ○ JACOBS

Operations Management
For Competitive Advantage
Managerial Briefing 8

*Electronic Commerce
and E-Ops®*

ninth edition

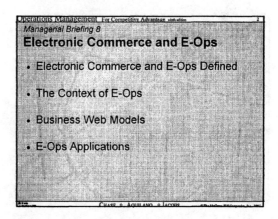

Managerial Briefing 8
Electronic Commerce and E-Ops

- Electronic Commerce and E-Ops Defined
- The Context of E-Ops
- Business Web Models
- E-Ops Applications

CHASE ○ AQUILANO ○ JACOBS

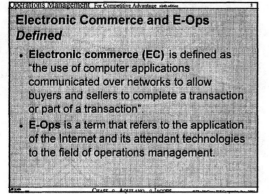

Electronic Commerce and E-Ops
Defined

- **Electronic commerce (EC)** is defined as "the use of computer applications communicated over networks to allow buyers and sellers to complete a transaction or part of a transaction".
- **E-Ops** is a term that refers to the application of the Internet and its attendant technologies to the field of operations management.

CHASE ○ AQUILANO ○ JACOBS

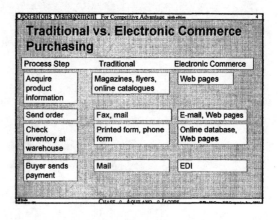

Traditional vs. Electronic Commerce Purchasing

Process Step	Traditional	Electronic Commerce
Acquire product information	Magazines, flyers, online catalogues	Web pages
Send order	Fax, mail	E-mail, Web pages
Check inventory at warehouse	Printed form, phone form	Online database, Web pages
Buyer sends payment	Mail	EDI

CHASE ○ AQUILANO ○ JACOBS

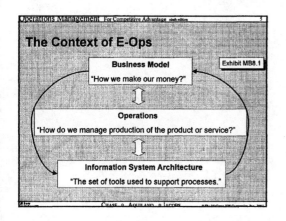

The Context of E-Ops

Exhibit MB8.1

Business Model
"How we make our money?"

Operations
"How do we manage production of the product or service?"

Information System Architecture
"The set of tools used to support processes."

CHASE ○ AQUILANO ○ JACOBS

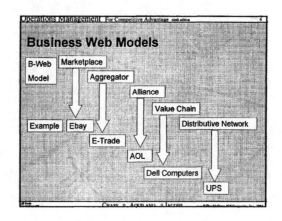

Business Web Models

B-Web Model

Marketplace
Aggregator
Alliance
Value Chain
Distributive Network

Example
Ebay
E-Trade
AOL
Dell Computers
UPS

CHASE ○ AQUILANO ○ JACOBS

E-Ops Applications

- Supply-Chain Management
- Project Management
- Product and Process Design
- Purchasing
- Manufacturing Processes

E-Ops Applications (Continued)

- Inventory Management
- Quality Management
- Forecasting
- Operations Scheduling
- Reengineering and Consulting

CHASE ○ AQUILANO ○ JACOBS

Operations Management
For Competitive Advantage

Chapter 9

Strategic Capacity
Management

ninth edition

Chapter 9
Strategic Capacity Planning

- Strategic Capacity Planning Defined
- Capacity Utilization & Best Operating Level
- Economies & Diseconomies of Scale
- The Experience Curve
- Capacity Focus, Flexibility & Planning
- Determining Capacity Requirements
- Decision Trees
- Capacity Utilization & Service Quality

CHASE ○ AQUILANO ○ JACOBS

Strategic Capacity Planning
Defined

- **Capacity** can be defined as the ability to hold, receive, store, or accommodate.

- **Strategic capacity planning** is an approach for determining the overall capacity level of capital intensive resources, including facilities, equipment, and overall labor force size.

CHASE ○ AQUILANO ○ JACOBS

Capacity Utilization

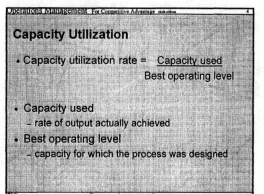

- Capacity utilization rate = $\dfrac{\text{Capacity used}}{\text{Best operating level}}$

- Capacity used
  - rate of output actually achieved
- Best operating level
  - capacity for which the process was designed

CHASE ○ AQUILANO ○ JACOBS

Best Operating Level

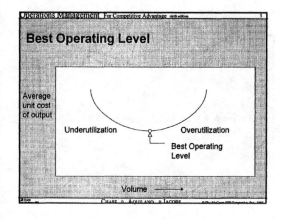

Example of Capacity Utilization

- During one week of production, a plant produced 83 units of a product. Its historic highest or best utilization recorded was 120 units per week. What is this plant's capacity utilization rate?

- Answer:
  Capacity utilization rate = $\dfrac{\text{Capacity used}}{\text{Best operating level}}$

  = 83/120
  = 0.69 or 69%

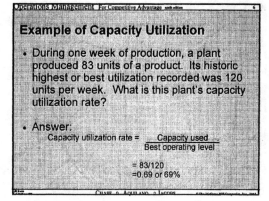

CHASE ○ AQUILANO ○ JACOBS

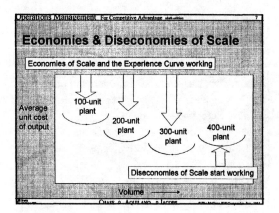

Economies & Diseconomies of Scale

Economies of Scale and the Experience Curve working

Average unit cost of output

100-unit plant

200-unit plant

300-unit plant

400-unit plant

Diseconomies of Scale start working

Volume ——→

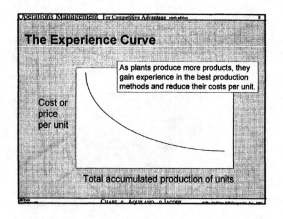

The Experience Curve

As plants produce more products, they gain experience in the best production methods and reduce their costs per unit.

Cost or price per unit

Total accumulated production of units

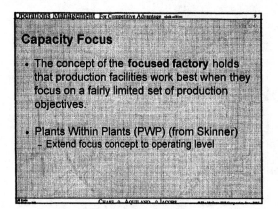

Capacity Focus

- The concept of the **focused factory** holds that production facilities work best when they focus on a fairly limited set of production objectives.

- Plants Within Plants (PWP) (from Skinner)
  - Extend focus concept to operating level

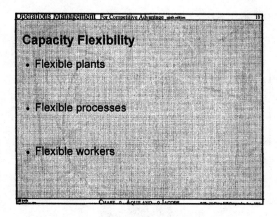

Capacity Flexibility

- Flexible plants

- Flexible processes

- Flexible workers

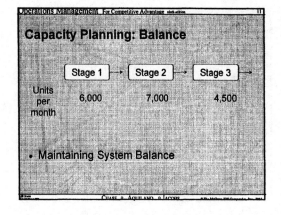

Capacity Planning: Balance

Stage 1 →	Stage 2 →	Stage 3 →
6,000	7,000	4,500

Units per month

- Maintaining System Balance

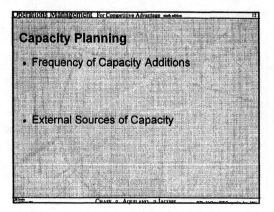

Capacity Planning

- Frequency of Capacity Additions

- External Sources of Capacity

Determining Capacity Requirements

- Forecast sales within each individual product line.

- Calculate equipment and labor requirements to meet the forecasts.

- Project equipment and labor availability over the planning horizon.

Example of Capacity Requirements

A manufacturer produces two lines of mustard, FancyFine and Generic line. Each is sold in small and family-size plastic bottles.

The following table shows forecast demand for the next four years.

Year:	1	2	3	4
FancyFine				
Small (000s)	50	60	80	100
Family (000s)	35	50	70	90
Generic				
Small (000s)	100	110	120	140
Family (000s)	80	90	100	110

Example of Capacity Requirements: The Product from a Capacity Viewpoint

- Question: Are we really producing two different types of mustards from the standpoint of capacity requirements?

- Answer: No, it's the same product just packaged differently.

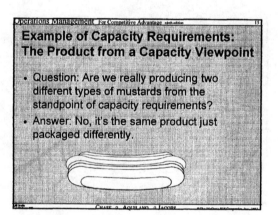

Example of Capacity Requirements: Equipment and Labor Requirements

Year:	1	2	3	4
Small (000s)	150	170	200	240
Family (000s)	115	140	170	200

Three 100,000 units-per-year machines are available for small-bottle production. Two operators required per machine.

Two 120,000 units-per-year machines are available for family-sized-bottle production. Three operators required per machine.

Question: What are the Year 1 values for capacity, machine, and labor?

Year:	1	2	3	4
Small (000s)	150	170	200	240
Family (000s)	115	140	170	200
Small	Mach. Cap.	300,000	Labor	6
Family-size	Mach. Cap.	240,000	Labor	6

150,000/300,000=50%

At 1 machine for 100,000, it takes 1.5 machines for 150,000

Small				
Percent capacity used	50.00%			
Machine requirement	1.50			
Labor requirement	3.00			
Family-size				
Percent capacity used	47.92%			
Machine requirement	0.96			
Labor requirement	2.88			

At 2 operators for 100,000, it takes 3 operators for 150,000

Question: What are the values for columns 2, 3 and 4 in the table below?

Year:	1	2	3	4
Small (000s)	150	170	200	240
Family (000s)	115	140	170	200
Small	Mach. Cap.	300,000	Labor	6
Family-size	Mach. Cap.	240,000	Labor	6

Small				
Percent capacity used	50.00%	56.67%	66.67%	80.00%
Machine requirement	1.50	1.70	2.00	2.40
Labor requirement	3.00	3.40	4.00	4.80
Family-size				
Percent capacity used	47.92%	58.33%	70.83%	83.33%
Machine requirement	0.96	1.17	1.42	1.67
Labor requirement	2.88	3.50	4.25	5.00

Example of a Decision Tree Problem

A glass factory specializing in crystal is experiencing a substantial backlog, and the firm's management is considering three courses of action:

A) Arrange for subcontracting,
B) Construct new facilities.
C) Do nothing (no change)

The correct choice depends largely upon demand, which may be low, medium, or high. By consensus, management estimates the respective demand probabilities as .10, .50, and .40.

Example of a Decision Tree Problem: The Payoff Table

The management also estimates the profits when choosing from the three alternatives (A, B, and C) under the differing probable levels of demand. These costs, in thousands of dollars are presented in the table below:

	0.1 Low	0.5 Medium	0.4 High
A	10	50	90
B	-120	25	200
C	20	40	60

Example of a Decision Tree Problem: Step 1. We start by drawing the three decisions

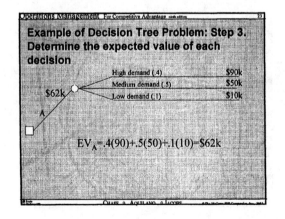

Example of Decision Tree Problem: Step 2. Add our possible states of nature, probabilities, and payoffs

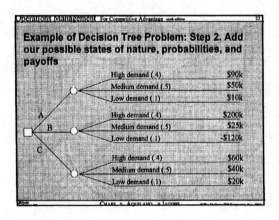

Example of Decision Tree Problem: Step 3. Determine the expected value of each decision

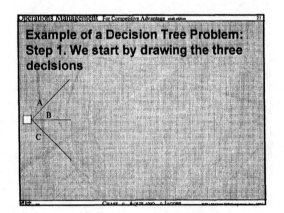

$$EV_A = .4(90) + .5(50) + .1(10) = \$62k$$

Example of Decision Tree Problem: Step 4. Make decision

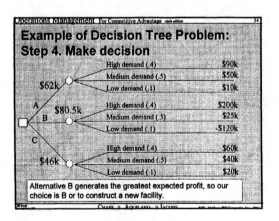

Alternative B generates the greatest expected profit, so our choice is B or to construct a new facility.

Planning Service Capacity

- Time

- Location

- Volatility of Demand

Capacity Utilization & Service Quality

- Best operating point is near 70% of capacity

- From 70% to 100% of service capacity, what do you think happens to service quality?

CHASE ○ AQUILANO ○ JACOBS

Operations Management
For Competitive Advantage

Technical Note 9

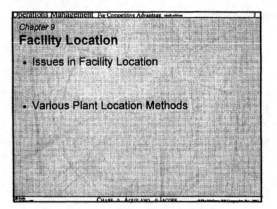

Facility Location

ninth edition

Chapter 9

Facility Location

- Issues in Facility Location

- Various Plant Location Methods

Competitive Imperatives Impacting Location

- The need to produce close to the customer due to time-based competition, trade agreements, and shipping costs.

- The need to locate near the appropriate labor pool to take advantage of low wage costs and/or high technical skills.

Issues in Facility Location

- Proximity to Customers
- Business Climate
- Total Costs
- Infrastructure
- Quality of Labor
- Suppliers
- Other Facilities

Issues in Facility Location

- Free Trade Zones
- Political Risk
- Government Barriers
- Trading Blocs
- Environmental Regulation
- Host Community
- Competitive Advantage

Plant Location Methodology: Factor Rating Method Example

Two refineries sites (A and B) are assigned the following range of point values and respective points, where the more points the better for the site location.

Major factors for site location	Pt. Range	A	B
Fuels in region	0 to 330	123	156
Power availability and reliability	0 to 200	150	100
Labor climate	0 to 100	54	63
Living conditions	0 to 100	24	96
Transportation	0 to 50	45	55
Water supply	0 to 10	34	14
Climate	0 to 50	8	4
Supplies	0 to 60	45	50
Tax policies and laws	0 to 20	45	20
Total pts.		528	558

Sites

Best Site is B

Plant Location Methodology: Transportation Method of Linear Programming

- Transportation method of linear programming seeks to minimize costs of shipping n units to m destinations or its seeks to maximize profit of shipping n units to m destinations.

Plant Location Methodology: Center of Gravity Method

- The center of gravity method is used for locating single facilities that considers existing facilities, the distances between them, and the volumes of goods to be shipped between them.
- This methodology involves formulas used to compute the coordinates of the two-dimensional point that meets the distance and volume criteria stated above.

Plant Location Methodology: Center of Gravity Method Formulas

$$C_x = \frac{\sum d_{ix} V_i}{\sum V_i} \qquad C_y = \frac{\sum d_{iy} V_i}{\sum V_i}$$

C_x = X coordinate of center of gravity

C_y = X coordinate of center of gravity

d_{ix} = X coordinate of the ith location

d_{iy} = Y coordinate of the ith location

V_i = volume of goods moved to or from ith location

Plant Location Methodology: Example of Center of Gravity Method

- Center of gravity method example
  - Several automobile showrooms are located according to the following grid which represents coordinate locations for each showroom.

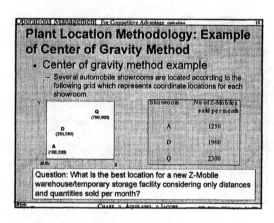

Question: What is the best location for a new Z-Mobile warehouse/temporary storage facility considering only distances and quantities sold per month?

Plant Location Methodology: Example of Center of Gravity Method: Determining Existing Facility Coordinates

To begin, you must identify the existing facilities on a two-dimensional plane or grid and determine their coordinates.

You must also have the volume information on the business activity at the existing facilities.

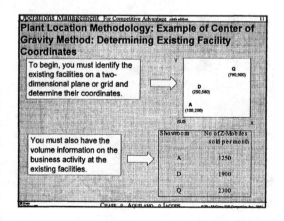

Plant Location Methodology: Example of Center of Gravity Method: Determining the Coordinates of the New Facility

You then compute the new coordinates using the formulas:

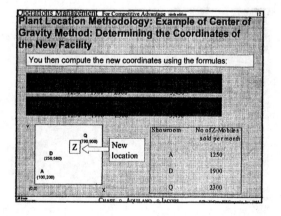

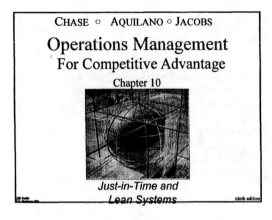

CHASE ○ AQUILANO ○ JACOBS

Operations Management
For Competitive Advantage
Chapter 10

Just-in-Time and
Lean Systems

ninth edition

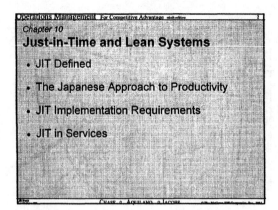

Chapter 10

Just-in-Time and Lean Systems

- JIT Defined
- The Japanese Approach to Productivity
- JIT Implementation Requirements
- JIT in Services

CHASE ○ AQUILANO ○ JACOBS

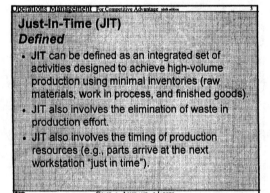

Just-In-Time (JIT)
Defined

- JIT can be defined as an integrated set of activities designed to achieve high-volume production using minimal inventories (raw materials, work in process, and finished goods).
- JIT also involves the elimination of waste in production effort.
- JIT also involves the timing of production resources (e.g., parts arrive at the next workstation "just in time").

CHASE ○ AQUILANO ○ JACOBS

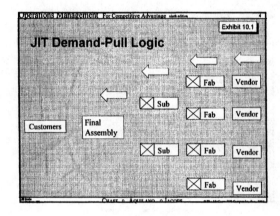

Exhibit 10.1

JIT Demand-Pull Logic

Customers — Final Assembly — Sub — Fab — Vendor

CHASE ○ AQUILANO ○ JACOBS

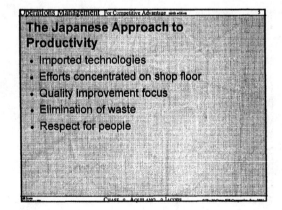

The Japanese Approach to Productivity

- Imported technologies
- Efforts concentrated on shop floor
- Quality improvement focus
- Elimination of waste
- Respect for people

CHASE ○ AQUILANO ○ JACOBS

Waste In Operations

(1) Waste from overproduction

(2) Waste of waiting time

(3) Transportation waste

(4) Inventory waste

(5) Processing waste

(6) Waste of motion

(7) Waste from product defects

CHASE ○ AQUILANO ○ JACOBS

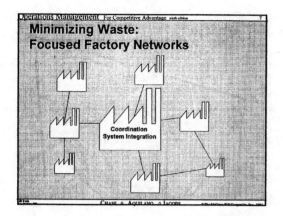

Minimizing Waste:
Focused Factory Networks

Coordination System Integration

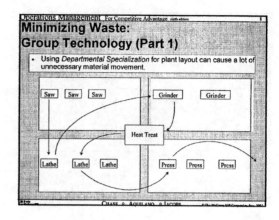

Minimizing Waste:
Group Technology (Part 1)

- Using *Departmental Specialization* for plant layout can cause a lot of unnecessary material movement.

| Saw | Saw | Saw | | Grinder | Grinder |

Heat Treat

| Lathe | Lathe | Lathe | | Press | Press | Press |

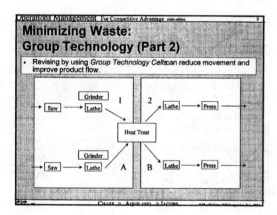

Minimizing Waste:
Group Technology (Part 2)

- Revising by using *Group Technology Cells* can reduce movement and improve product flow.

Grinder — Saw → Lathe — 1 — 2 — Lathe → Press
Heat Treat
Grinder — Saw → Lathe — A — B — Lathe → Press

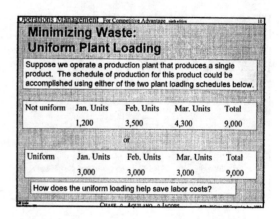

Minimizing Waste:
Uniform Plant Loading

Suppose we operate a production plant that produces a single product. The schedule of production for this product could be accomplished using either of the two plant loading schedules below.

Not uniform	Jan. Units	Feb. Units	Mar. Units	Total
	1,200	3,500	4,300	9,000

or

Uniform	Jan. Units	Feb. Units	Mar. Units	Total
	3,000	3,000	3,000	9,000

How does the uniform loading help save labor costs?

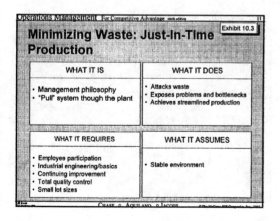

Minimizing Waste: Just-In-Time Production   Exhibit 10.3

WHAT IT IS	WHAT IT DOES
• Management philosophy • "Pull" system though the plant	• Attacks waste • Exposes problems and bottlenecks • Achieves streamlined production

WHAT IT REQUIRES	WHAT IT ASSUMES
• Employee participation • Industrial engineering/basics • Continuing improvement • Total quality control • Small lot sizes	• Stable environment

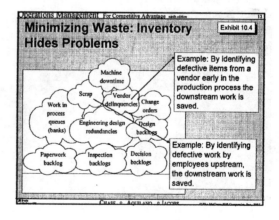

Minimizing Waste: Inventory Hides Problems   Exhibit 10.4

Example: By identifying defective items from a vendor early in the production process the downstream work is saved.

Example: By identifying defective work by employees upstream, the downstream work is saved.

Machine downtime, Scrap, Vendor delinquencies, Change orders, Work in process queues (banks), Engineering design redundancies, Design backlogs, Paperwork backlog, Inspection backlogs, Decision backlogs

Minimizing Waste: Kanban Production Control Systems

Exhibit 10.6

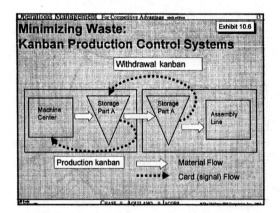

Determining the Number of Kanbans Needed

- Setting up a kanban system requires determining the number of kanbans (or containers) needed.

- Each container represents the minimum production lot size.

- An accurate estimate of the lead time required to produce a container is key to determining how many kanbans are required.

The Number of Kanban Card Sets

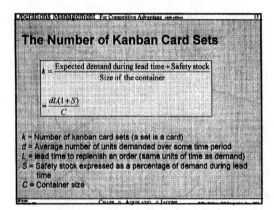

$$k = \frac{\text{Expected demand during lead time} + \text{Safety stock}}{\text{Size of the container}}$$

$$= \frac{dL(1+S)}{C}$$

k = Number of kanban card sets (a set is a card)
d = Average number of units demanded over some time period
L = lead time to replenish an order (same units of time as demand)
S = Safety stock expressed as a percentage of demand during lead time
C = Container size

Example of Kanban Card Determination: Problem Data

- A switch assembly is assembled in batches of 4 units from an "upstream" assembly area and delivered in a special container to a "downstream" control-panel assembly operation.

- The control-panel assembly area requires 5 switch assemblies per hour.

- The switch assembly area can produce a container of switch assemblies in 2 hours.

- Safety stock has been set at 10% of needed inventory.

Example of Kanban Card Determination: Calculations

$$k = \frac{\text{Expected demand during lead time} + \text{Safety stock}}{\text{Size of the container}}$$

$$= \frac{dL(1+S)}{C} = \frac{5(2)(1.1)}{4} = 2.75, \text{ or } 3$$

Always round up!

Respect for People

- Level payrolls

- Cooperative employee unions

- Subcontractor networks

- Bottom-round management style

- Quality circles (Small group involvement activities)

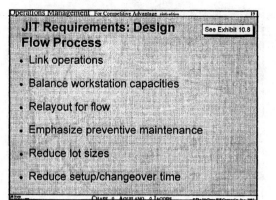

JIT Requirements: Design Flow Process

See Exhibit 10.8

- Link operations
- Balance workstation capacities
- Relayout for flow
- Emphasize preventive maintenance
- Reduce lot sizes
- Reduce setup/changeover time

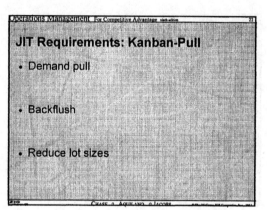

JIT Requirements: Total Quality Control

- Worker responsibility
- Measure SQC
- Enforce compliance
- Fail-safe methods
- Automatic inspection

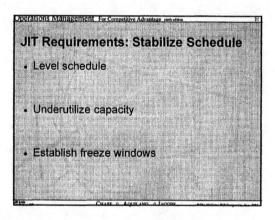

JIT Requirements: Stabilize Schedule

- Level schedule
- Underutilize capacity
- Establish freeze windows

JIT Requirements: Kanban-Pull

- Demand pull
- Backflush
- Reduce lot sizes

JIT Requirements: Work with Vendors

- Reduce lead times
- Frequent deliveries
- Project usage requirements
- Quality expectations

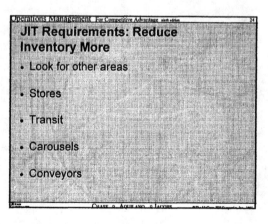

JIT Requirements: Reduce Inventory More

- Look for other areas
- Stores
- Transit
- Carousels
- Conveyors

JIT Requirements: Improve Product Design

- Standard product configuration

- Standardize and reduce number of parts

- Process design with product design

- Quality expectations

JIT in Services (Examples)

- Organize Problem-Solving Groups

- Upgrade Housekeeping

- Upgrade Quality

- Clarify Process Flows

- Revise Equipment and Process Technologies

JIT in Services (Examples)

- Level the Facility Load

- Eliminate Unnecessary Activities

- Reorganize Physical Configuration

- Introduce Demand-Pull Scheduling

- Develop Supplier Networks

CHASE ○ AQUILANO ○ JACOBS

Operations Management
For Competitive Advantage
Chapter 11

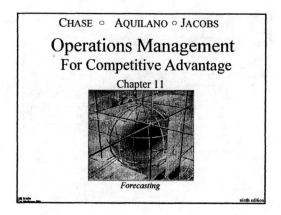

Forecasting

ninth edition

Chapter 11

Forecasting

- Demand Management

- Qualitative Forecasting Methods

- Simple & Weighted Moving Average Forecasts

- Exponential Smoothing

- Simple Linear Regression

Demand Management

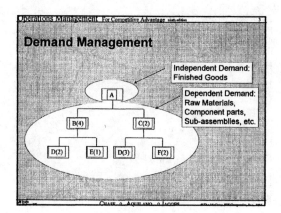

Independent Demand: Finished Goods

Dependent Demand: Raw Materials, Component parts, Sub-assemblies, etc.

Independent Demand: What a firm can do to manage it.

- Can take an active role to influence demand.

- Can take a passive role and simply respond to demand.

Types of Forecasts

- Qualitative (Judgmental)

- Quantitative
  - Time Series Analysis
  - Causal Relationships
  - Simulation

Components of Demand

- Average demand for a period of time
- Trend
- Seasonal element
- Cyclical elements
- Random variation
- Autocorrelation

Finding Components of Demand

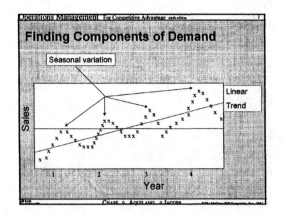

Qualitative Methods

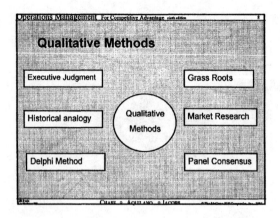

Delphi Method

1. Choose the experts to participate. There should be a variety of knowledgeable people in different areas.
2. Through a questionnaire (or E-mail), obtain forecasts (and any premises or qualifications for the forecasts) from all participants.
3. Summarize the results and redistribute them to the participants along with appropriate new questions.
4. Summarize again, refining forecasts and conditions, and again develop new questions.
5. Repeat Step 4 if necessary. Distribute the final results to all participants.

Time Series Analysis

- Time series forecasting models try to predict the future based on past data.
- You can pick models based on:
1. Time horizon to forecast
2. Data availability
3. Accuracy required
4. Size of forecasting budget
5. Availability of qualified personnel

Simple Moving Average Formula

- The simple moving average model assumes an average is a good estimator of future behavior.
- The formula for the simple moving average is:

$$F_t = \frac{A_{t-1} + A_{t-2} + A_{t-3} + \ldots + A_{t-n}}{N}$$

F_t = Forecast for the coming period

N = Number of periods to be averaged

A_{t-1} = Actual occurrence in the past period for up to "n" periods

Simple Moving Average Problem (1)

$$F_t = \frac{A_{t-1} + A_{t-2} + A_{t-3} + \ldots + A_{t-n}}{N}$$

Week	Demand
1	650
2	678
3	720
4	785
5	859
6	920
7	850
8	758
9	892
10	920
11	789
12	844

- *Question: What are the 3-week and 6-week moving average forecasts for demand?*
- Assume you only have 3 weeks and 6 weeks of actual demand data for the respective forecasts

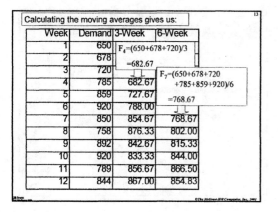

Week	Demand	3-Week	6-Week
1	650	$F_4=(650+678+720)/3$ $=682.67$	
2	678		
3	720	$F_7=(650+678+720$ $+785+859+920)/6$ $=768.67$	
4	785	682.67	
5	859	727.67	
6	920	788.00	
7	850	854.67	768.67
8	758	876.33	802.00
9	892	842.67	815.33
10	920	833.33	844.00
11	789	856.67	866.50
12	844	867.00	854.83

Plotting the moving averages and comparing them shows how the lines smooth out to reveal the overall upward trend in this example.

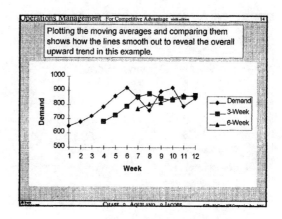

Simple Moving Average Problem (2) Data

Week	Demand
1	820
2	775
3	680
4	655
5	620
6	600
7	575

- Question: What is the 3 week moving average forecast for this data?
- Assume you only have 3 weeks and 5 weeks of actual demand data for the respective forecasts

Simple Moving Average Problem (2) Solution

Week	Demand	3-Week	5-Week
1	820		
2	775		
3	680		
4	655	758.33	
5	620	703.33	
6	600	651.67	710.00
7	575	625.00	666.00

Weighted Moving Average Formula

While the moving average formula implies an equal weight being placed on each value that is being averaged, the weighted moving average permits an unequal weighting on prior time periods.

The formula for the moving average is:

$$F_t = w_1A_{t-1} + w_2A_{t-2} + w_3A_{t-3}+...+w_nA_{t-n}$$

w_t = weight given to time period "t" occurrence. (Weights must add to one.) $\sum_{i=1}^{n}w_i = 1$

Weighted Moving Average Problem (1) Data

Question: Given the weekly demand and weights, what is the forecast for the 4th period or Week 4?

Week	Demand
1	650
2	678
3	720
4	

Weights:	
t-1	.5
t-2	.3
t-3	.2

Note that the weights place more emphasis on the most recent data, that is time period "t-1".

Weighted Moving Average Problem (1) Solution

Week	Demand	Forecast
1	650	
2	678	
3	720	
4		693.4

$$F_4 = 0.5(720)+0.3(678)+0.2(650)=693.4$$

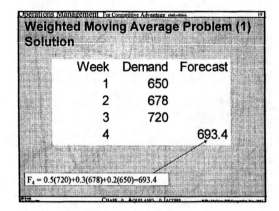

Weighted Moving Average Problem (2) Data

Question: Given the weekly demand information and weights, what is the weighted moving average forecast of the 5th period or week?

Week	Demand
1	820
2	775
3	680
4	655

Weights:
t-1	.7
t-2	.2
t-3	.1

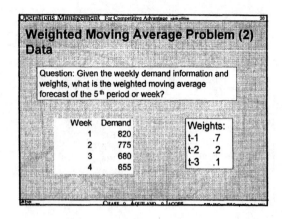

Weighted Moving Average Problem (2) Solution

Week	Demand	Forecast
1	820	
2	775	
3	680	
4	655	
5		672

$$F_5 = (0.1)(755)+(0.2)(680)+(0.7)(655)= 672$$

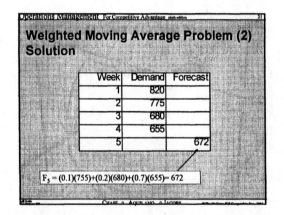

Exponential Smoothing Model

$$F_t = F_{t-1} + \alpha(A_{t-1} - F_{t-1})$$

α = smoothing constant

- Premise: The most recent observations might have the highest predictive value.
- Therefore, we should give more weight to the more recent time periods when forecasting.

Exponential Smoothing Problem (1) Data

Week	Demand
1	820
2	775
3	680
4	655
5	750
6	802
7	798
8	689
9	775
10	

- Question: Given the weekly demand data, what are the exponential smoothing forecasts for periods 2-10 using $\alpha=0.10$ and $\alpha=0.60$?
- Assume $F_1=D_1$

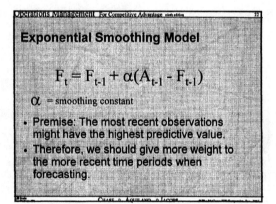

Answer: The respective alphas columns denote the forecast values. Note that you can only forecast one time period into the future.

Week	Demand	0.1	0.6
1	820	820.00	820.00
2	775	820.00	820.00
3	680	815.50	820.00
4	655	801.95	817.30
5	750	787.26	808.09
6	802	783.53	795.59
7	798	785.38	788.35
8	689	786.64	786.57
9	775	776.88	786.61
10		776.69	780.77

Exponential Smoothing Problem (1) Plotting

Note how that the smaller alpha the smoother the line in this example.

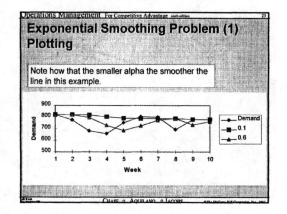

Exponential Smoothing Problem (2) Data

Week	Demand
1	820
2	775
3	680
4	655
5	

Question: What are the exponential smoothing forecasts for periods 2-5 using a =0.5?

Assume $F_1 = D_1$

Exponential Smoothing Problem (2) Solution

$F_2 = 820 + (0.5)(820 - 820) = 820$

$F_3 = 820 + (0.5)(775 - 820) = 797.75$

Week	Demand	0.5
1	820	820.00
2	775	820.00
3	680	797.50
4	655	738.75
5		696.88

The MAD Statistic to Determine Forecasting Error

$$MAD = \frac{\sum_{t=1}^{n} |A_t - F_t|}{n}$$

1 MAD ≈ 0.8 standard deviation

1 standard deviation ≈ 1.25 MAD

- The ideal MAD is zero. That would mean there is no forecasting error.

- The larger the MAD, the less the desirable the resulting model.

MAD Problem Data

Question: What is the MAD value given the forecast values in the table below?

Month	Sales	Forecast
1	220	n/a
2	250	255
3	210	205
4	300	320
5	325	315

MAD Problem Solution

Month	Sales	Forecast	Abs Error
1	220	n/a	
2	250	255	5
3	210	205	5
4	300	320	20
5	325	315	10
			40

Note that by itself, the MAD only lets us know the mean error in a set of forecasts.

Tracking Signal Formula

- The TS is a measure that indicates whether the forecast average is keeping pace with any genuine upward or downward changes in demand.
- Depending on the number of MAD's selected, the TS can be used like a quality control chart indicating when the model is generating too much error in its forecasts.
- The TS formula is:

$$TS = \frac{RSFE}{MAD} = \frac{\text{Running sum of forecast errors}}{\text{Mean absolute deviation}}$$

Simple Linear Regression Model

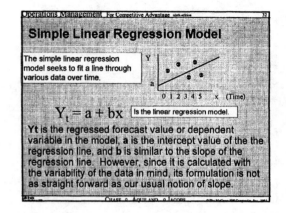

The simple linear regression model seeks to fit a line through various data over time.

$$Y_t = a + bx \quad \text{Is the linear regression model.}$$

Yt is the regressed forecast value or dependent variable in the model, a is the intercept value of the the regression line, and b is similar to the slope of the regression line. However, since it is calculated with the variability of the data in mind, its formulation is not as straight forward as our usual notion of slope.

Simple Linear Regression Formulas for Calculating "a" and "b"

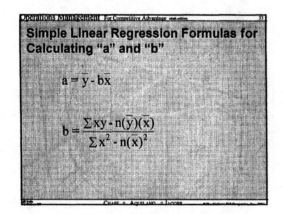

$$a = \bar{y} - b\bar{x}$$

$$b = \frac{\sum xy - n(\bar{y})(\bar{x})}{\sum x^2 - n(\bar{x})^2}$$

Simple Linear Regression Problem Data

Question: Given the data below, what is the simple linear regression model that can be used to predict sales?

Week	Sales
1	150
2	157
3	162
4	166
5	177

Answer: First, using the linear regression formulas, we can compute "a" and "b".

Week	Week*Week	Sales	Week*Sales
1	1	150	150
2	4	157	314
3	9	162	486
4	16	166	664
5	25	177	885
3	55	162.4	2499
Average	Sum	Average	Sum

The resulting regression model is:

$$Y_t = 143.5 + 6.3x$$

Now if we plot the regression generated forecasts against the actual sales we obtain the following chart:

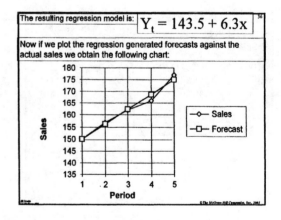

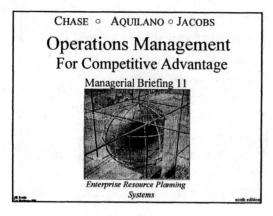

CHASE ○ AQUILANO ○ JACOBS

Operations Management
For Competitive Advantage

Managerial Briefing 11

Enterprise Resource Planning Systems

ninth edition

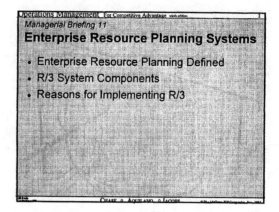

Managerial Briefing 11

Enterprise Resource Planning Systems

- Enterprise Resource Planning Defined
- R/3 System Components
- Reasons for Implementing R/3

Enterprise Resource Planning (ERP) Systems *Defined*

- **Enterprise Resource Planning Systems** is a computer system that integrates application programs in accounting, sales, manufacturing, and other functions in the firm.
- This integration is accomplished through a database shared by all the application programs.

R/3 System Functional Components

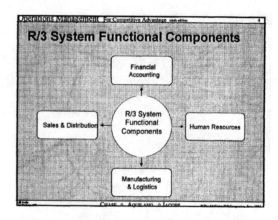

Financial Accounting

- Financials
- Controlling
- Asset management

Human Resources

- Payroll
- Benefits administration
- Applicant data administration
- Personnel development planning
- Workforce planning
- Schedule & shift planning
- Time management
- Travel expense accounting

Manufacturing & Logistics

- Materials management
- Plant maintenance
- Quality management
- Production planning & control
- Project management system

Sales and Distribution

- Prospect & customer management
- Sales order management
- Configuration management
- Distribution
- Export controls
- Shipping and transportation management
- Billing, invoicing, and rebate processing

Reasons for Implementing SAP R/3

- Desire to standardize and improve processes
- To improve the level of systems integration
- To improve information quality

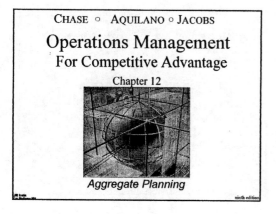

CHASE ○ AQUILANO ○ JACOBS

Operations Management
For Competitive Advantage
Chapter 12

Aggregate Planning

ninth edition

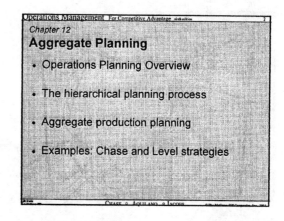

Chapter 12
Aggregate Planning

- Operations Planning Overview
- The hierarchical planning process
- Aggregate production planning
- Examples: Chase and Level strategies

CHASE ○ AQUILANO ○ JACOBS

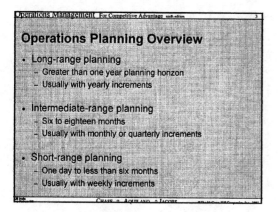

Operations Planning Overview

- Long-range planning
  - Greater than one year planning horizon
  - Usually with yearly increments
- Intermediate-range planning
  - Six to eighteen months
  - Usually with monthly or quarterly increments
- Short-range planning
  - One day to less than six months
  - Usually with weekly increments

CHASE ○ AQUILANO ○ JACOBS

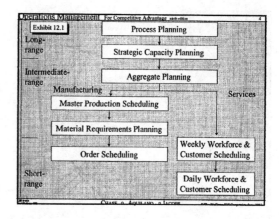

Exhibit 12.1

Long-range: Process Planning → Strategic Capacity Planning

Intermediate-range: Aggregate Planning

Manufacturing — Master Production Scheduling → Material Requirements Planning → Order Scheduling

Services — Weekly Workforce & Customer Scheduling

Short-range: Daily Workforce & Customer Scheduling

CHASE ○ AQUILANO ○ JACOBS

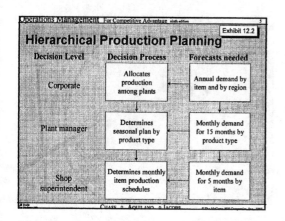

Hierarchical Production Planning

Exhibit 12.2

Decision Level	Decision Process	Forecasts needed
Corporate	Allocates production among plants	Annual demand by item and by region
Plant manager	Determines seasonal plan by product type	Monthly demand for 15 months by product type
Shop superintendent	Determines monthly item production schedules	Monthly demand for 5 months by item

CHASE ○ AQUILANO ○ JACOBS

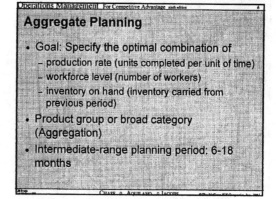

Aggregate Planning

- Goal: Specify the optimal combination of
  - production rate (units completed per unit of time)
  - workforce level (number of workers)
  - inventory on hand (inventory carried from previous period)
- Product group or broad category (Aggregation)
- Intermediate-range planning period: 6-18 months

CHASE ○ AQUILANO ○ JACOBS

Balancing Aggregate Demand and Aggregate Production Capacity

Suppose the figure to the right represents forecast demand in units.

Now suppose this lower figure represents the aggregate capacity of the company to meet demand.

What we want to do is balance out the production rate, workforce levels, and inventory to make these figures match up.

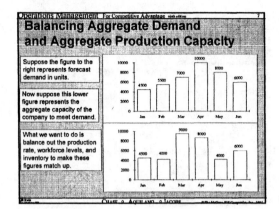

CHASE ○ AQUILANO ○ JACOBS

Key Strategies for Meeting Demand

- Chase

- Level

- Some combination of the two

CHASE ○ AQUILANO ○ JACOBS

Aggregate Planning Examples: Unit Demand and Cost Data

Suppose we have the following unit demand and cost information:

Demand/mo	Jan	Feb	Mar	Apr	May	Jun
	4500	5500	7000	10000	8000	6000

Materials	$5/unit
Holding costs	$1/unit per mo.
Marginal cost of stockout	$1.25/unit per mo.
Hiring and training cost	$200/worker
Layoff costs	$250/worker
Labor hours required	15 hrs/unit
Straight time labor cost	$8/hour
Beginning inventory	250 units
Productive hours/worker/day	7.25
Paid straight hrs/day	8

CHASE ○ AQUILANO ○ JACOBS

Cut-and-Try Example: Determining Straight Labor Costs and Output

Given the demand and cost information below, what are the aggregate hours/worker/month, units/worker, and dollars/worker?

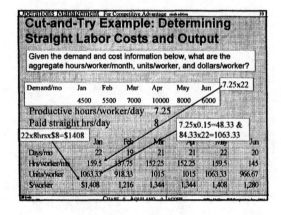

Demand/mo	Jan	Feb	Mar	Apr	May	Jun
	4500	5500	7000	10000	8000	6000

Productive hours/worker/day 7.25
Paid straight hrs/day 8

7.25x22

7.25x0.15=48.33 &
84.33x22=1063.33

22x8hrsx$8=$1408

	Jan	Feb	Mar	Apr	May	Jun
Days/mo	22	19	21	21	22	20
Hrs/worker/mo	159.5	137.75	152.25	152.25	159.5	145
Units/worker	1063.33	918.33	1015	1015	1063.33	966.67
$/worker	$1,408	1,216	1,344	1,344	1,408	1,280

CHASE ○ AQUILANO ○ JACOBS

Chase Strategy (Hiring & Firing to meet demand)

	Jan
Days/mo	22
Hrs/worker/mo	159.5
Units/worker	1,063.33
$/worker	$1,408

	Jan
Demand	4,500
Beg. inv.	250
Net req.	4,250
Req. workers	3.997
Hired	
Fired	3
Workforce	4
Ending inventory	0

Lets assume our current workforce is 7 workers.

First, calculate net requirements for production, or 4500-250=4250 units

Then, calculate number of workers needed to produce the net requirements, or 4250/1063.33=3.997 or 4 workers

Finally, determine the number of workers to hire/fire. In this case we only need 4 workers, we have 7, so 3 can be fired.

CHASE ○ AQUILANO ○ JACOBS

Below are the complete calculations for the remaining months in the six month planning horizon.

	Jan	Feb	Mar	Apr	May	Jun
Days/mo	22	19	21	21	22	20
Hrs/worker/mo	159.5	137.75	152.25	152.25	159.5	145
Units/worker	1,063	918	1,015	1,015	1,063	967
$/worker	$1,408	1,216	1,344	1,344	1,408	1,280

	Jan	Feb	Mar	Apr	May	Jun
Demand	4,500	5,500	7,000	10,000	8,000	6,000
Beg. inv.	250					
Net req.	4,250	5,500	7,000	10,000	8,000	6,000
Req. workers	3.997	5.989	6.897	9.852	7.524	6.207
Hired		2	1	3		
Fired	3				2	1
Workforce	4	6	7	10	8	7
Ending inventory	0	0	0	0	0	0

CHASE ○ AQUILANO ○ JACOBS

Below are the complete calculations for the remaining months in the six month planning horizon with the other costs included.

	Jan	Feb	Mar	Apr	May	Jun
Demand	4,500	5,500	7,000	10,000	8,000	6,000
Beg. inv.	250					
Net req.	4,250	5,500	7,000	10,000	8,000	6,000
Req. workers	3.997	5.989	6.897	9.852	7.524	6.207
Hired		2	1	3		
Fired	3				2	1
Workforce	4	6	7	10	8	7
Ending inventory	0	0	0	0	0	0

	Jan	Feb	Mar	Apr	May	Jun	Costs
Material	$21,250.00	$27,500.00	$35,000.00	$50,000.00	$40,000.00	$30,000.00	203,750.00
Labor	5,627.59	7,282.76	9,268.97	13,241.38	10,593.10	7,944.83	53,958.62
Hiring cost		400.00	200.00	600.00			1,200.00
Firing cost	750.00				500.00	250.00	1,500.00
							$260,408.62

Level Workforce Strategy (Surplus and Shortage Allowed)

Lets take the same problem as before but this time use the Level Workforce strategy.

This time we will seek to use a workforce level of 6 workers.

	Jan
Demand	4,500
Beg. inv.	250
Net req.	4,250
Workers	6
Production	6,380
Ending inventory	2,130
Surplus	2,130
Shortage	

Below are the complete calculations for the remaining months in the six month planning horizon.

	Jan	Feb	Mar	Apr	May	Jun
Demand	4,500	5,500	7,000	10,000	8,000	6,000
Beg. inv.	250	2,130	2,140	1,230	-2,680	-1,300
Net req.	4,250	3,370	4,860	8,770	10,680	7,300
Workers	6	6	6	6	6	6
Production	6,380	5,510	6,090	6,090	6,380	5,800
Ending inventory	2,130	2,140	1,230	-2,680	-1,300	-1,500
Surplus	2,130	2,140	1,230			
Shortage				2,680	1,300	1,500

Note, if we recalculate this sheet with 7 workers we would have a surplus.

Below are the complete calculations for the remaining months in the six month planning horizon with the other costs included.

Jan	Feb	Mar	Apr	May	Jun		
4,500	5,500	7,000	10,000	8,000	6,000		
250	2,130	10	-910	-3,910	-1,620		
4,250	3,370	4,860	8,770	10,680	7,300		
6	6	6	6	6	6		
6,380	5,510	6,090	6,090	6,380	5,800		
2,130	2,140	1,230	-2,680	-1,300	-1,500		
2,130	2,140	1,230					
			2,680	1,300	1,500		

Jan	Feb	Mar	Apr	May	Jun		
$8,448	$7,296	$6,064	$8,064	$8,448	$7,680	$48,000.00	Material
31,900	27,550	30,450	30,450	31,900	28,000	181,250.00	Storage
2,130	2,140	1,230				5,500.00	Stockout
			3,350	1,625	1,875	6,850.00	
						$241,600.00	

Note, the total costs under this strategy are less than under Chase.

CHASE ○ AQUILANO ○ JACOBS

Operations Management
For Competitive Advantage
Chapter 13

Inventory Control

ninth edition

Chapter 13
Inventory Control

- Inventory System Defined
- Inventory Costs
- Independent vs. Dependent Demand
- Basic Fixed-Order Quantity Models
- Basic Fixed-Time Period Model
- Miscellaneous Systems and Issues

CHASE ○ AQUILANO ○ JACOBS

Inventory System
Defined

- Inventory is the stock of any item or resource used in an organization. These items or resources can include: raw materials, finished products, component parts, supplies, and work-in-process.
- An inventory system is the set of policies and controls that monitor levels of inventory and determines what levels should be maintained, when stock should be replenished, and how large orders should be.

CHASE ○ AQUILANO ○ JACOBS

Purposes of Inventory

1. To maintain independence of operations.
2. To meet variation in product demand.
3. To allow flexibility in production scheduling.
4. To provide a safeguard for variation in raw material delivery time.
5. To take advantage of economic purchase-order size.

CHASE ○ AQUILANO ○ JACOBS

Inventory Costs

- Holding (or carrying) costs.
  - Costs for storage, handling, insurance, etc.
- Setup (or production change) costs.
  - Costs for arranging specific equipment setups, etc.
- Ordering costs.
  - Costs of someone placing an order, etc.
- Shortage costs.
  - Costs of canceling an order, etc.

CHASE ○ AQUILANO ○ JACOBS

Independent vs. Dependent Demand

Independent Demand (Demand not related to other items or the final end-product)

Dependent Demand (Derived demand items for component parts, subassemblies, raw materials, etc.)

CHASE ○ AQUILANO ○ JACOBS

Classifying Inventory Models

- Fixed-Order Quantity Models
  - Event triggered (Example: running out of stock)

- Fixed-Time Period Models
  - Time triggered (Example: Monthly sales call by sales representative)

Fixed-Order Quantity Models: Model Assumptions (Part 1)

- Demand for the product is constant and uniform throughout the period.

- Lead time (time from ordering to receipt) is constant.

- Price per unit of product is constant.

Fixed-Order Quantity Models: Model Assumptions (Part 2)

- Inventory holding cost is based on average inventory.

- Ordering or setup costs are constant.

- All demands for the product will be satisfied. (No back orders are allowed.)

Basic Fixed-Order Quantity Model and Reorder Point Behavior

Exhibit 13.3

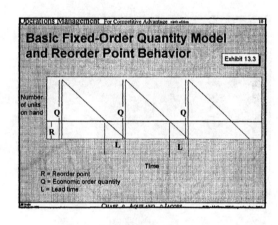

Number of units on hand

R = Reorder point
Q = Economic order quantity
L = Lead time

Cost Minimization Goal

By adding the item, holding, and ordering costs together, we determine the total cost curve, which in turn is used to find the Q_{opt} inventory order point that minimizes total costs.

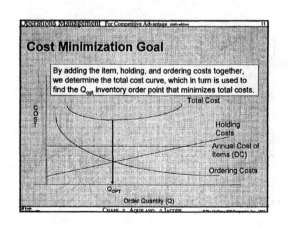

Basic Fixed-Order Quantity (EOQ) Model Formula

$$\text{Total Annual Cost} = \begin{array}{c}\text{Annual} \\ \text{Purchase} \\ \text{Cost}\end{array} + \begin{array}{c}\text{Annual} \\ \text{Ordering} \\ \text{Cost}\end{array} + \begin{array}{c}\text{Annual} \\ \text{Holding} \\ \text{Cost}\end{array}$$

$$TC = DC + \frac{D}{Q}S + \frac{Q}{2}H$$

TC	= Total annual cost
D	= Demand
C	= Cost per unit
Q	= Order quantity
S	= Cost of placing an order or setup cost
R	= Reorder point
L	= Lead time
H	= Annual holding and storage cost per unit of inventory

Deriving the EOQ

Using calculus, we take the first derivative of the total cost function with respect to Q, and set the derivative (slope) equal to zero, solving for the optimized (cost minimized) value of Q_{opt}.

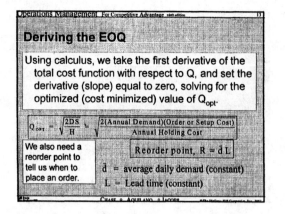

$$Q_{OPT} = \sqrt{\frac{2DS}{H}} = \sqrt{\frac{2(\text{Annual Demand})(\text{Order or Setup Cost})}{\text{Annual Holding Cost}}}$$

We also need a reorder point to tell us when to place an order.

Reorder point, $R = \bar{d}\,L$

$\bar{d}$ = average daily demand (constant)

L = Lead time (constant)

EOQ Example (1) Problem Data

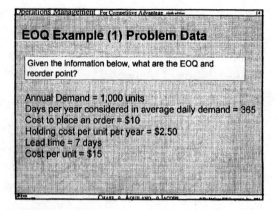

Given the information below, what are the EOQ and reorder point?

Annual Demand = 1,000 units
Days per year considered in average daily demand = 365
Cost to place an order = $10
Holding cost per unit per year = $2.50
Lead time = 7 days
Cost per unit = $15

EOQ Example (1) Solution

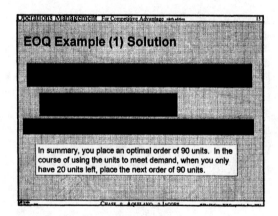

In summary, you place an optimal order of 90 units. In the course of using the units to meet demand, when you only have 20 units left, place the next order of 90 units.

EOQ Example (2) Problem Data

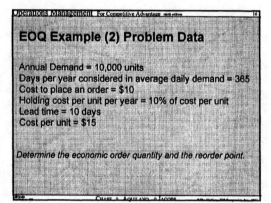

Annual Demand = 10,000 units
Days per year considered in average daily demand = 365
Cost to place an order = $10
Holding cost per unit per year = 10% of cost per unit
Lead time = 10 days
Cost per unit = $15

Determine the economic order quantity and the reorder point.

EOQ Example (2) Solution

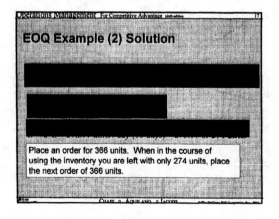

Place an order for 366 units. When in the course of using the inventory you are left with only 274 units, place the next order of 366 units.

Fixed-Time Period Model with Safety Stock Formula

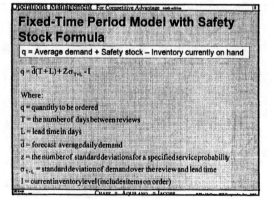

q = Average demand + Safety stock − Inventory currently on hand

$$q = \bar{d}(T+L) + Z\sigma_{T+L} - I$$

Where:

q = quantitity to be ordered

T = the number of days between reviews

L = lead time in days

$\bar{d}$ = forecast average daily demand

z = the number of standard deviations for a specified service probability

σ_{T+L} = standard deviation of demand over the review and lead time

I = current inventory level (includes items on order)

Fixed-Time Period Model: Determining the Value of σ_{T+L}

$$\sigma_{T+L} = \sqrt{\sum_{i=1}^{T+L}\left(\sigma_{d_i}\right)^2}$$

Since each day is independent and σ_d is constant,

$$\sigma_{T+L} = \sqrt{(T+L)\sigma_d^2}$$

- The standard deviation of a sequence of random events equals the square root of the sum of the variances.

Example of the Fixed-Time Period Model

Given the information below, how many units should be ordered?

Average daily demand for a product is 20 units. The review period is 30 days, and lead time is 10 days. Management has set a policy of satisfying 96 percent of demand from items in stock. At the beginning of the review period there are 200 units in inventory. The daily demand standard deviation is 4 units.

Example of the Fixed-Time Period Model: Solution (Part 1)

The value for "z" is found by using the Excel NORMSINV function, or as we will do here, using Appendix D. By adding 0.5 to all the values in Appendix D and finding the value in the table that comes closest to the service probability, the "z" value can be read by adding the column heading label to the row label.

So, by adding 0.5 to the value from Appendix D of 0.4599, we have a probability of 0.9599, which is given by a z = 1.75.

Example of the Fixed-Time Period Model: Solution (Part 2)

So, to satisfy 96 percent of the demand, you should place an order of 645 units at this review period.

Special Purpose Model: Price-Break Model Formula

Based on the same assumptions as the EOQ model, the price-break model has a similar Q_{opt} formula:

$$Q_{OPT} = \sqrt{\frac{2DS}{iC}} = \sqrt{\frac{2(\text{Annual Demand})(\text{Order or Setup Cost})}{\text{Annual Holding Cost}}}$$

i = percentage of unit cost attributed to carrying inventory
C = cost per unit

Since "C" changes for each price-break, the formula above will have to be used with each price-break cost value.

Price-Break Example Problem Data (Part 1)

A company has a chance to reduce their inventory ordering costs by placing larger quantity orders using the price-break order quantity schedule below. What should their optimal order quantity be if this company purchases this single inventory item with an e-mail ordering cost of $4, a carrying cost rate of 2% of the inventory cost of the item, and an annual demand of 10,000 units?

Order Quantity(units)	Price/unit($)
0 to 2,499	$1.20
2,500 to 3,999	1.00
4,000 or more	.98

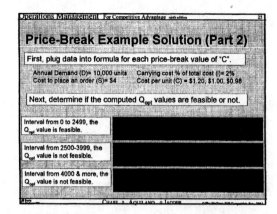

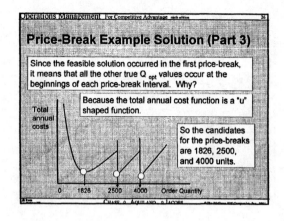

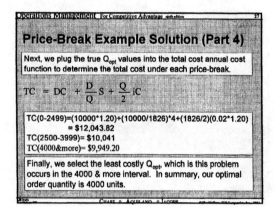

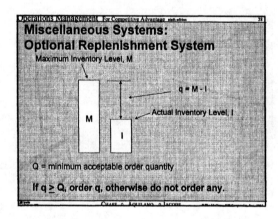

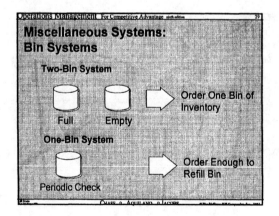

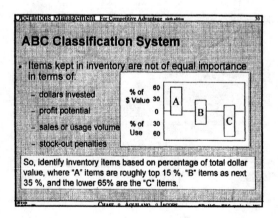

Inventory Accuracy and Cycle Counting Defined

- **Inventory accuracy** refers to how well the inventory records agree with physical count.

- **Cycle Counting** is a physical inventory-taking technique in which inventory is counted on a frequent basis rather than once or twice a year.

Slide 1

CHASE ○ AQUILANO ○ JACOBS

Operations Management
For Competitive Advantage
Chapter 14

Material Requirements Planning

ninth edition

Slide 2

Chapter 14

Materials Requirements Planning

- Material Requirements Planning (MRP)
- MRP Logic and Product Structure Trees
- Time Fences
- MRP Example
- MRP II
- Lot Sizing in MRP Programs

CHASE ○ AQUILANO ○ JACOBS

Slide 3

Material Requirements Planning
Defined

- Materials requirements planning (MRP) is the logic for determining the number of parts, components, and materials needed to produce a product.
- MRP provides time scheduling information specifying when each of the materials, parts, and components should be ordered or produced.
- Dependent demand drives MRP.
- MRP is a software system.

CHASE ○ AQUILANO ○ JACOBS

Slide 4

Example of MRP Logic and Product Structure Tree

Given the *product structure tree* for "A" and the lead time and demand information below, provide a materials requirements plan that defines the number of units of each component and when they will be needed.

Product Structure Tree for Assembly A

Lead Times	
A	1 day
B	2 days
C	1 day
D	3 days
E	4 days
F	1 day

A
→ B(4) → D(2), E(1)
→ C(2) → D(3), F(2)

Demand
Day 10 50 A
Day 8   20 B (Spares)
Day 6   15 D (Spares)

CHASE ○ AQUILANO ○ JACOBS

Slide 5

First, the number of units of "A" are scheduled backwards to allow for their lead time. So, in the materials requirement plan below, we have to place an order for 50 units of "A" in the 9th week to receive them in the 10th week.

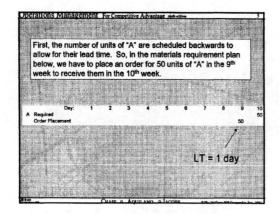

LT = 1 day

CHASE ○ AQUILANO ○ JACOBS

Slide 6

Next, we need to start scheduling the components that make up "A". In the case of component "B" we need 4 B's for each A. Since we need 50 A's, that means 200 B's. And again, we back the schedule up for the necessary 2 days of lead time.

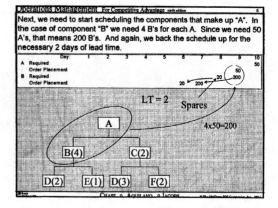

LT = 2   Spares

4x50=200

CHASE ○ AQUILANO ○ JACOBS

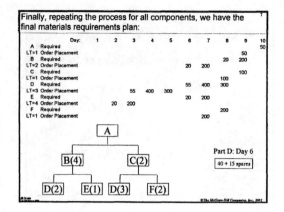

Finally, repeating the process for all components, we have the final materials requirements plan:

	Day:	1	2	3	4	5	6	7	8	9	10
A	Required										50
LT=1	Order Placement									50	
B	Required								20	200	
LT=2	Order Placement						20	200			
C	Required									100	
LT=1	Order Placement								100		
D	Required							55	400	300	
LT=3	Order Placement			55	400	300					
E	Required							20	200		
LT=4	Order Placement	20	200								
F	Required								200		
LT=1	Order Placement							200			

Tree:
- A
  - B(4)
    - D(2)
    - E(1)
  - C(2)
    - D(3)
    - F(2)

Part D: Day 6

40 + 15 spares

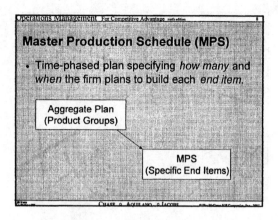

Master Production Schedule (MPS)

- Time-phased plan specifying *how many* and *when* the firm plans to build each *end item*.

Aggregate Plan (Product Groups) → MPS (Specific End Items)

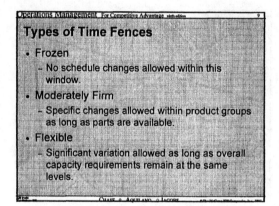

Types of Time Fences

- Frozen
  - No schedule changes allowed within this window.
- Moderately Firm
  - Specific changes allowed within product groups as long as parts are available.
- Flexible
  - Significant variation allowed as long as overall capacity requirements remain at the same levels.

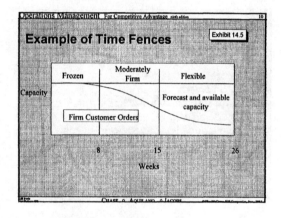

Example of Time Fences

Exhibit 14.5

	Frozen	Moderately Firm	Flexible
Capacity			Forecast and available capacity
	Firm Customer Orders		

8   15   26

Weeks

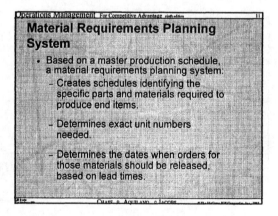

Material Requirements Planning System

- Based on a master production schedule, a material requirements planning system:
  - Creates schedules identifying the specific parts and materials required to produce end items.
  - Determines exact unit numbers needed.
  - Determines the dates when orders for those materials should be released, based on lead times.

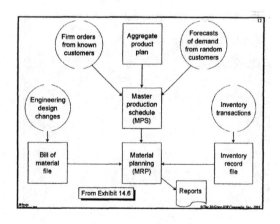

From Exhibit 14.6

Bill of Materials (BOM) File
A Complete Product Description

- Materials
- Parts
- Components
- Production sequence
- Modular BOM
  - Subassemblies
- Planning BOM
  - Fractional options

Inventory Records File

- Each inventory item carried as a separate file
  - Status according to "time buckets".

- Pegging
  - Identify each parent item that created demand.

Primary MRP Reports

- **Planned orders** to be released at a future time.
- **Order release notices** to execute the planned orders.
- **Changes in due dates** of open orders due to rescheduling.
- **Cancellations or suspensions** of open orders due to cancellation or suspension of orders on the master production schedule.
- **Inventory status data.**

Secondary MRP Reports

- **Planning reports,** for example, forecasting inventory requirements over a period of time.
- **Performance reports** used to determine agreement between actual and programmed usage and costs.
- **Exception reports** used to point out serious discrepancies, such as late or overdue orders.

Net Change System

- Activity driven
- Net change schedules
- Potential for system nervousness

Additional MRP Scheduling Terminology

- Gross Requirements
- On-hand
- Net requirements
- Planned order receipt
- Planned order release

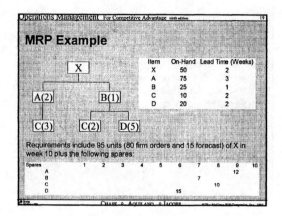

MRP Example

Item	On-Hand	Lead Time (Weeks)
X	50	2
A	75	3
B	25	1
C	10	2
D	20	2

Requirements include 95 units (80 firm orders and 15 forecast) of X in week 10 plus the following spares:

Spares	1	2	3	4	5	6	7	8	9	10
A									12	
B							7			
C								10		
D					15					

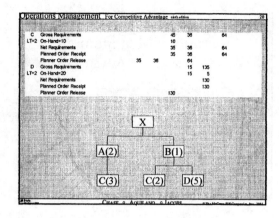

	Day	1	2	3	4	5	6	7	8	9	10
C	Gross Requirements						45	36			64
LT=2	On-Hand=10						10				
	Net Requirements						35	36			64
	Planned Order Receipt						35	36			64
	Planner Order Release				35	36		64			
D	Gross Requirements						15	135			
LT=2	On-Hand=20						15	5			
	Net Requirements							130			
	Planned Order Receipt							130			
	Planner Order Release					130					

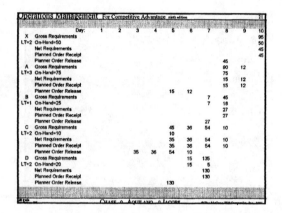

	Day:	1	2	3	4	5	6	7	8	9	10
X	Gross Requirements										95
LT=2	On-Hand=50										50
	Net Requirements										45
	Planned Order Receipt										45
	Planner Order Release								45		
A	Gross Requirements								90	12	
LT=3	On-Hand=75								75		
	Net Requirements								15	12	
	Planned Order Receipt								15	12	
	Planner Order Release					15	12				
B	Gross Requirements							7	45		
LT=1	On-Hand=25							7	18		
	Net Requirements								27		
	Planned Order Receipt								27		
	Planner Order Release							27			
C	Gross Requirements					45	36	54	10		
LT=2	On-Hand=10					10					
	Net Requirements					35	36	54	10		
	Planned Order Receipt					35	36	54	10		
	Planner Order Release			35	36	54	10				
D	Gross Requirements						15	135			
LT=2	On-Hand=20						15	5			
	Net Requirements							130			
	Planned Order Receipt							130			
	Planner Order Release					130					

Closed Loop MRP

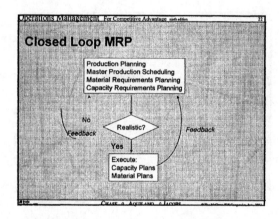

Manufacturing Resource Planning (MRP II)

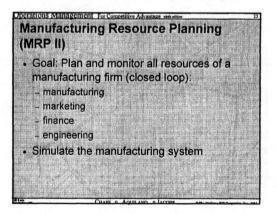

- Goal: Plan and monitor all resources of a manufacturing firm (closed loop):
  - manufacturing
  - marketing
  - finance
  - engineering
- Simulate the manufacturing system

Lot Sizing in MRP Programs

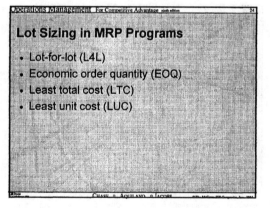

- Lot-for-lot (L4L)
- Economic order quantity (EOQ)
- Least total cost (LTC)
- Least unit cost (LUC)

CHASE ○ AQUILANO ○ JACOBS

Operations Management
For Competitive Advantage

Chapter 15

Operations Scheduling

ninth edition

Chapter 15

Operations Scheduling

- Work Center Defined
- Typical Scheduling and Control Functions
- Job-shop Scheduling
- Examples of Scheduling Rules
- Shop-floor Control
- Principles of Work Center Scheduling
- Issues in Scheduling Service Personnel

Work Center
Defined

- A work center is an area in a business in which productive resources are organized and work is completed.

- May be a single machine, a group of machines, or an area where a particular type of work is done.

Capacity and Scheduling

- Infinite loading (Example: MRP)
- Finite loading
- Forward scheduling
- Backward scheduling (Example: MRP)

Typical Scheduling and Control Functions

- Allocating orders, equipment, and personnel.

- Determining the sequence of order performance.

- Initiating performance of the scheduled work.

- Shop-floor control.

Work-Center Scheduling Objectives

- Meet due dates

- Minimize lead time

- Minimize setup time or cost

- Minimize work-in-process inventory

- Maximize machine utilization

Priority Rules for Job Sequencing

1. First-come, first-served (FCFS)

2. Shortest operating time (SOT)

3. Earliest due date first

4. Earliest start date first (due date-lead time)

5. Least slack time remaining (STR) first

Priority Rules for Job Sequencing (Continued)

6. Least slack time remaining (per operation as opposed to per job) first

7. Smallest critical ratio (CR) first
   (due date-current date)/(number of days remaining)

8. Smallest queue ratio (QR) first
   (slack time remaining in schedule)/(planned remaining queue time)

9. Last come, first served (LCFS)

10. Random order or whim

Schedule Performance Measures

- Meeting due dates of customers or downstream operations.

- Minimizing the flow time (the time a job spends in the process).

- Minimizing work-in-process inventory.

- Minimizing idle time of machines or workers.

Example of Job Sequencing: First-Come First-Served

Suppose you have the four jobs to the right arrive for processing on one machine.

What is the FCFS schedule?

Do all the jobs get done on time?

Jobs (in order of arrival)	Processing Time (days)	Due Date (days hence)
A	4	5
B	7	10
C	3	6
D	1	4

Answer: FCFS Schedule

Jobs (in order of arrival)	Processing Time (days)	Due Date (days hence)	Flow Time (days)
A	4	5	4
B	7	10	11
C	3	6	14
D	1	4	15

No, Jobs B, C, and D are going to be late.

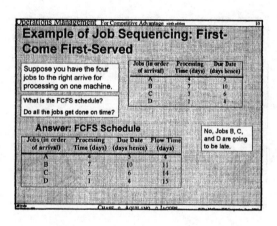

Example of Job Sequencing: Shortest Operating Time

Suppose you have the four jobs to the right arrive for processing on one machine.

What is the SOT schedule?

Do all the jobs get done on time?

Jobs (in order of arrival)	Processing Time (days)	Due Date (days hence)
A	4	5
B	7	10
C	3	6
D	1	4

Answer: Shortest Operating Time Schedule

Jobs (in order of arrival)	Processing Time (days)	Due Date (days hence)	Flow Time (days)
D	1	4	1
C	3	6	4
A	4	5	8
B	7	10	15

No, Jobs A and B are going to be late.

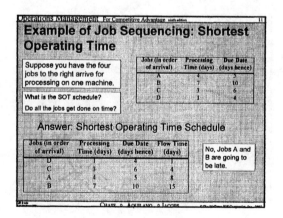

Example of Job Sequencing: Last-Come First-Served

Suppose you have the four jobs to the right arrive for processing on one machine.

What is the LCFS schedule?

Do all the jobs get done on time?

Jobs (in order of arrival)	Processing Time (days)	Due Date (days hence)
A	4	5
B	7	10
C	3	6
D	1	4

Answer: Last-Come First-Served Schedule

Jobs (in order of arrival)	Processing Time (days)	Due Date (days hence)	Flow Time (days)
D	1	4	1
C	3	6	4
B	7	10	11
A	4	5	15

No, Jobs B and A are going to be late.

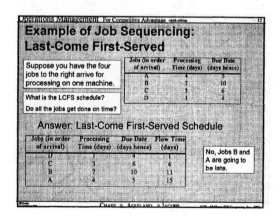

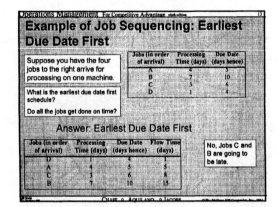

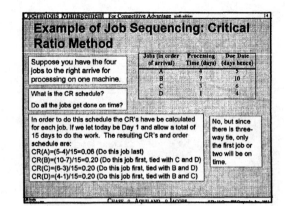

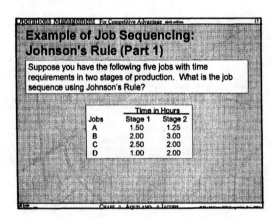

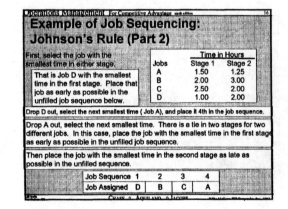

Shop-Floor Control: Major Functions

1. Assigning priority of each shop order.

2. Maintaining work-in-process quantity information.

3. Conveying shop-order status information to the office.

Shop-Floor Control: Major Functions (Continued)

4. Providing actual output data for capacity control purposes.

5. Providing quantity by location by shop order for WIP inventory and accounting purposes.

6. Providing measurement of efficiency, utilization, and productivity of manpower and machines.

Input/Output Control

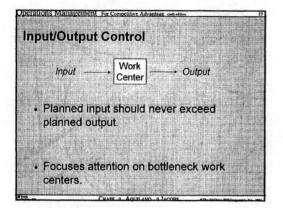

- Planned input should never exceed planned output.

- Focuses attention on bottleneck work centers.

Principles of Work Center Scheduling

1. There is a direct equivalence between work flow and cash flow.

2. The effectiveness of any job shop should be measured by speed of flow through the shop.

3. Schedule jobs as a string, with process steps back-to-back.

4. A job once started should not be interrupted.

Principles of Job Shop Scheduling (Continued)

5. Speed of flow is most efficiently achieved by focusing on bottleneck work centers and jobs.

6. Reschedule every day.

7. Obtain feedback each day on jobs that are not completed at each work center.

8. Match work center input information to what the worker can actually do.

Principles of Job Shop Scheduling (Continued)

9. When seeking improvement in output, look for incompatibility between engineering design and process execution.

10. Certainty of standards, routings, and so forth is not possible in a job shop, but always work towards achieving it.

Personnel Scheduling in Services

- Scheduling consecutive days off

- Scheduling daily work times

- Scheduling hourly work times

CHASE ○ AQUILANO ○ JACOBS

Operations Management
For Competitive Advantage
Technical Note 15

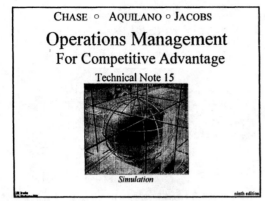

Simulation

ninth edition

Technical Note 15
Simulation

- Definition of Simulation
- Simulation Methodology
- Proposing a New Experiment
- Considerations When Using Computer Models
- Types of Simulations
- Desirable Features of Simulation Software
- Advantages & Disadvantages of Simulation

Simulation
Defined

- A computer-based model used to run experiments on a real system.
  - Typically done on a computer.
  - Determines reactions to different operating rules or change in structure.
  - Can be used in conjunction with traditional statistical and management science techniques.

From Exhibit TN15.1
Major Phases in a Simulation Study

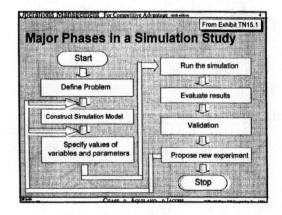

Simulation Methodology:
Problem Definition

- Specifying the objectives

- Identifying the relevant controllable and uncontrollable variables of the system to be studied

---

Constructing a Simulation Model

- Specification of Variables and Parameters

- Specification of Decision Rules

- Specification of Probability Distributions

- Specification of Time-Incrementing Procedure

Data Collection and Random Number Interval Example

Suppose you timed 20 athletes running the 100-yard dash and tallied the information into the four time intervals below.

You then count the tallies and make a frequency distribution.

Then convert the frequencies into percentages.

You then can add the frequencies into a cumulative distribution.

Finally, use the percentages to develop the random number intervals.

Seconds	Tallies	Frequency	%	Accum. %	RN Intervals
0-5.99	IIII	4	20	20	00-19
6-6.99	IN IN	10	50	70	20-69
7-7.99	IIII	4	20	90	70-89
8 or more	II	2	10	100	90-99

Evaluating Results

- Conclusions depend on
  - the degree to which the model reflects the real system
  - design of the simulation (in a statistical sense)

- The only true test of a simulation is how well the real system performs after the results of the study have been implemented.

Proposing a New Experiment

- Might want to change many of the factors:
  - parameters
  - variables
  - decision rules
  - starting conditions
  - run length
- If the initial rules led to poor results or if these runs yielded new insights into the problem, then a new decision rule may be worth trying.

Considerations When Using Computer Models

- Computer language selection

- Flowcharting

- Coding

- Data generation

- Output reports

- Validation

Types of Simulation Models

- Continuous
  - Based on mathematical equations.
  - Used for simulating continuous values for all points in time.
  - Example: The amount of time a person spends in a queue.
- Discrete
  - Used for simulating specific values or specific points.
  - Example: Number of people in a queue.

Desirable Features of Simulation Software

- Be capable of being used interactively as well as allowing complete runs.

- Be user-friendly and easy to understand.

- Allow modules to be built and then connected.

- Allow users to write and incorporate their own routines.

- Have building blocks that contain built-in commands.

- Have macro capability, such as the ability to develop machining cells.

Desirable Features of Simulation Software

- Have material-flow capability.

- Output standard statistics such as cycle times, utilization, and wait times.

- Allow a variety of data analysis alternatives for both input and output data.

- Have animation capabilities to display graphically the product flow through the system.

- Permit interactive debugging.

Advantages of Simulation

- Often leads to a better understanding of the real system.
- Years of experience in the real system can be compressed into seconds or minutes.
- Simulation does not disrupt ongoing activities of the real system.
- Simulation is far more general than mathematical models.
- Simulation can be used as a game for training experience.

Advantages of Simulation (Continued)

- Simulation provides a more realistic replication of a system than mathematical analysis.

- Simulation can be used to analyze transient conditions, whereas mathematical techniques usually cannot.

- Many standard packaged models, covering a wide range of topics, are available commercially.

- Simulation answers what-if questions.

Disadvantages of Simulation

- There is no guarantee that the model will, in fact, provide good answers.
- There is no way to prove reliability.
- Building a simulation model can take a great deal of time.
- Simulation may be less accurate than mathematical analysis because it is randomly based.
- A significant amount of computer time may be needed to run complex models.
- The technique of simulation still lacks a standardized approach.

CHASE ○ AQUILANO ○ JACOBS

Operations Management
For Competitive Advantage
Chapter 16

Consulting and Reengineering

ninth edition

Chapter 16
Consulting and Reengineering

- Operations Consulting Defined
- Operations Consulting and the 5 P's
- Hierarchy Within a Consulting Organization
- Stages of Operations Consulting
- Operations Consulting Tool Kit
- Reengineering Defined
- Principles of Reengineering

CHASE ○ AQUILANO ○ JACOBS

Operations Consulting
Defined

- **Operations consulting** involves assisting clients in developing operations strategies (i.e., product leadership, operational excellence, customer intimacy, etc.) and in improving production (and service delivery) processes.

CHASE ○ AQUILANO ○ JACOBS

Reasons Why Operations Consulting Industry is Growing

- Market pressures on clients to reengineer their core processes and eliminate non-core processes.

- Globalization.

- Need to better manage information technology.

CHASE ○ AQUILANO ○ JACOBS

Operations Consulting & the 5 Ps

- Plants
  - Adding and locating new plants
  - Expanding, contracting, or refocusing facilities
- Parts
  - Make or buy decisions
  - Vendor selection decisions
- Processes
  - Technology evaluation
  - Process improvement and reengineering

CHASE ○ AQUILANO ○ JACOBS

Operations Consulting & the 5 Ps (Continued)

- People
  - Quality improvement
  - Setting/revising work standards
  - Learning curve analysis
- Planning and Control Systems
  - Supply chain management
  - MRP
  - Shop floor control
  - Warehousing and distribution

CHASE ○ AQUILANO ○ JACOBS

Hierarchy within Consulting Firms

- Partners — *Finders*
- Managers — *Minders*
- Consultants — *Grinders*

Economics of Consulting Firms

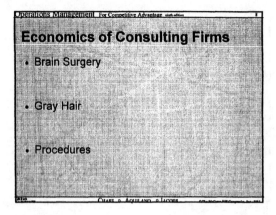

- Brain Surgery
- Gray Hair
- Procedures

When are Operations Consultants Needed

- When faced with major investment decision(s)

- When management believes it is not getting the maximum effectiveness from the organization's productive capability.

Stages in Operations Consulting Process

1. Sales & Development Proposal
2. Perform Problem Analysis
3. Design, Develop, and Test Alternative Solutions
4. Develop Systematic Performance Measures
5. Present Final Report
6. Implement Changes
7. Assure Client Satisfaction
8. Assemble Learnings from the Study

Operations Consulting Tool Kit: Category 1

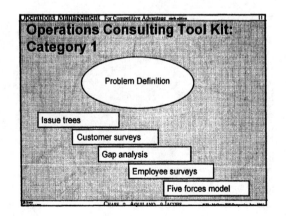

Problem Definition

- Issue trees
- Customer surveys
- Gap analysis
- Employee surveys
- Five forces model

Operations Consulting Tool Kit: Category 2

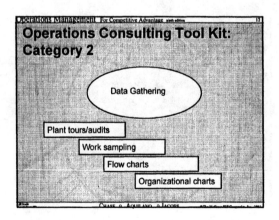

Data Gathering

- Plant tours/audits
- Work sampling
- Flow charts
- Organizational charts

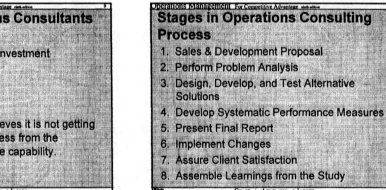

Operations Consulting Tool Kit: Category 3

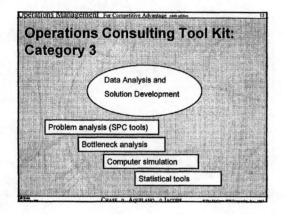

Operations Consulting Tool Kit: Category 4

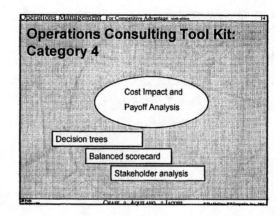

Operations Consulting Tool Kit: Category 5

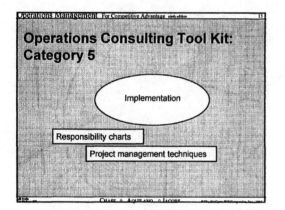

Reengineering
Defined

- **Reengineering** is defined as the fundamental rethinking and radical redesign of business processes to achieve dramatic improvements in critical, contemporary measures of performance such as cost, quality, service, and speed.
- **Business process reengineering** is focused on reengineering business processes.

Key Words in Reengineering Definition

- Fundamental
  - *Why* do we do what we do?
  - Ignore *what is* and concentrate on *what should be.*
- Radical
  - Business *reinvention* vs. business improvement

Key Words in Reengineering Definition (Continued)

- Dramatic
  - Reengineering should be brought in "when a need exits for heavy blasting."
    - Companies in deep trouble.
    - Companies that see trouble coming.
    - Companies that are in peak condition.
- Business Process
  - a collection of activities that takes one or more kinds of inputs and creates an output that is of value to a customer.

Principles of Reengineering

- Organize around outcomes, not tasks.

- Have those who use the output of the process perform the process.

- Merge information-processing work into the real work that produces the information.

- Treat geographically dispersed resources as though they were centralized.

Principles of Reengineering (Continued)

- Link parallel activities instead of integrating their results.

- Put the decision point where the work is performed, and build control into the process.

- Capture information once and at the source.

CHASE ○ AQUILANO ○ JACOBS

Operations Management
For Competitive Advantage
Chapter 17

Synchronous Manufacturing and Theory of Constraints

ninth edition

Chapter 17
Synchronous Manufacturing and the Theory of Constraints

- Goldratt's Rules

- Goldratt's *Goal* of the Firm

- Performance Measurement

- Capacity and Flow issues

- Synchronous Manufacturing

CHASE ○ AQUILANO ○ JACOBS

Goldratt's Rules of Production Scheduling

- Do not balance capacity balance the flow.
- The level utilization of a nonbottleneck resource is not determined by its own potential but by some other constraint in the system.
- Utilization and activation of a resource are not the same.
- An hour lost at a bottleneck is an hour lost for the entire system.
- An hour saved at a nonbottleneck is a mirage.

CHASE ○ AQUILANO ○ JACOBS

Goldratt's Rules of Production Scheduling (Continued)

- Bottlenecks govern both throughput and inventory in the system.
- Transfer batch may not and many times should not be equal to the process batch.
- A process batch should be variable both along its route and in time.
- Priorities can be set only by examining the system's constraints. Lead time is a derivative of the schedule.

CHASE ○ AQUILANO ○ JACOBS

Goldratt's Theory of Constraints (TOC)

- Identify the system constraints.
- Decide how to exploit the system constraints.
- Subordinate everything else to that decision.
- Elevate the system constraints.
- If, in the previous steps, the constraints have been broken, go back to Step 1, but do not let inertia become the system constraint.

CHASE ○ AQUILANO ○ JACOBS

Goldratt's Goal of the Firm

The goal of a firm is to make money.

CHASE ○ AQUILANO ○ JACOBS

Performance Measurement: Financial

- Net profit
  - an absolute measurement in dollars

- Return on investment
  - a relative measure based on investment

- Cash flow
  - a survival measurement

Performance Measurement: Operational

- 1. Throughput
  - the rate at which money is generated by the system through sales
- 2. Inventory
  - all the money that the system has invested in purchasing things it intends to sell
- 3. Operating expenses
  - all the money that the system spends to turn inventory into throughput

Productivity

- Does not guarantee profitability

  - Has throughput increased?

  - Has inventory decreased?

  - Have operational expenses decreased?

Unbalanced Capacity

- In earlier chapters, we discussed balancing assembly lines.
  - The goal was a constant cycle time across all stations.

- Synchronous manufacturing views constant workstation capacity as a bad decision.

The Statistics of Dependent Events

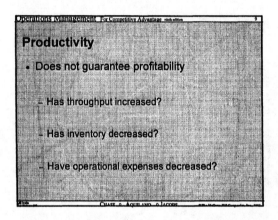

- Rather than balancing capacities, the flow of product through the system should be balanced.

Capacity Related Terminology

- Capacity is the available time for production.
- Bottleneck is what happens if capacity is less than demand placed on resource.
- Nonbottleneck is what happens when capacity is greater than demand placed on resource.
- Capacity-constrained resource (CCR) is a resource where the capacity is close to demand placed on the resource.

Capacity Example Situation 1

There is some idle production in this set up. How much?

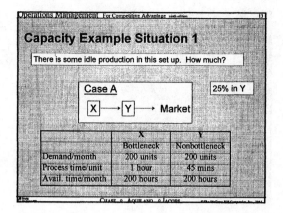

Case A | 25% in Y

X → Y → Market

	X Bottleneck	Y Nonbottleneck
Demand/month	200 units	200 units
Process time/unit	1 hour	45 mins
Avail. time/month	200 hours	200 hours

CHASE □ AQUILANO □ JACOBS

Capacity Example Situation 2

Is there is going to be a build up of unnecessary production in Y?

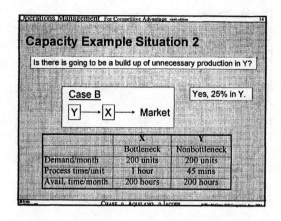

Case B | Yes, 25% in Y.

Y → X → Market

	X Bottleneck	Y Nonbottleneck
Demand/month	200 units	200 units
Process time/unit	1 hour	45 mins
Avail. time/month	200 hours	200 hours

CHASE □ AQUILANO □ JACOBS

Capacity Example Situation 3

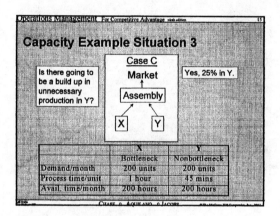

Is there going to be a build up in unnecessary production in Y?

Case C
Market
↑
Assembly
↑   ↑
X   Y

Yes, 25% in Y.

	X Bottleneck	Y Nonbottleneck
Demand/month	200 units	200 units
Process time/unit	1 hour	45 mins
Avail. time/month	200 hours	200 hours

CHASE □ AQUILANO □ JACOBS

Capacity Example Situation 4

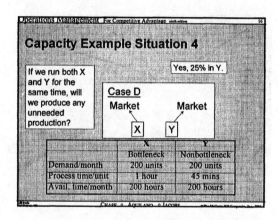

If we run both X and Y for the same time, will we produce any unneeded production?

Yes, 25% in Y.

Case D
Market   Market
↑   ↑
X   Y

	X Bottleneck	Y Nonbottleneck
Demand/month	200 units	200 units
Process time/unit	1 hour	45 mins
Avail. time/month	200 hours	200 hours

CHASE □ AQUILANO □ JACOBS

Time Components of Production Cycle

- Setup time is the time that a part spends waiting for a resource to be set up to work on this same part.
- Process time is the time that the part is being processed.
- Queue time is the time that a part waits for a resource while the resource is busy with something else.

CHASE □ AQUILANO □ JACOBS

Time Components of Production Cycle (Continued)

- Wait time is the time that a part waits not for a resource but for another part so that they can be assembled together.

- Idle time is the unused time. It represents the cycle time less the sum of the setup time, processing time, queue time, and wait time.

CHASE □ AQUILANO □ JACOBS

Saving Time

What are the consequences of saving time at each process?

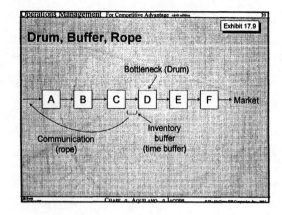

| Bottleneck | → | Nonbottleneck |

- Rule: Bottlenecks govern both throughput and inventory in the system.
- Rule: An hour lost at a bottleneck is an hour lost for the entire system.
- Rule: An hour saved at a nonbottleneck is a mirage.

Exhibit 17.9

Drum, Buffer, Rope

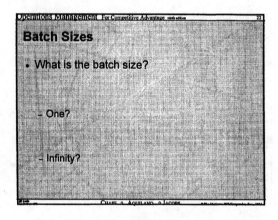

Bottleneck (Drum)

A → B → C → D → E → F → Market

Communication (rope)

Inventory buffer (time buffer)

Quality Implications

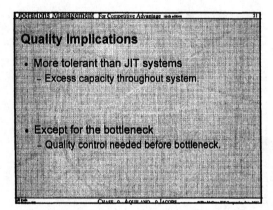

- More tolerant than JIT systems
  - Excess capacity throughout system.

- Except for the bottleneck
  - Quality control needed before bottleneck.

Batch Sizes

- What is the batch size?

  - One?

  - Infinity?

Bottlenecks and CCRs: Flow-Control Situations

- A bottleneck
  - (1) with no setup required when changing from one product to another.
  - (2) with setup times required to change from one product to another.
- A capacity constrained resource (CCR)
  - (3) with no setup required to change from one product to another.
  - (4) with setup time required when changing from one product to another.

Inventory Cost Measurement: Dollar Days

- Dollar Days is a measurement of the value of inventory and the time it stays within an area.

Example

Dollar Days = (value of inventory)(number of days within a department)

Benefits from Dollar Day Measurement

- Marketing
  - Discourages holding large amounts of finished goods inventory.
- Purchasing
  - Discourages placing large purchase orders that on the surface appear to take advantage of quantity discounts.
- Manufacturing
  - Discourage large work in process and producing earlier than needed.

Comparing Synchronous Manufacturing to MRP

- MRP uses *backward scheduling*.

- Synchronous manufacturing uses *forward scheduling*.

Comparing Synchronous Manufacturing to JIT

- JIT is limited to repetitive manufacturing

- JIT requires a stable production level

- JIT does not allow very much flexibility in the products produced

Comparing Synchronous Manufacturing to JIT (Continued)

- JIT still requires work in process when used with kanban so that there is "something to pull."

- Vendors need to be located nearby because the system depends on smaller, more frequent deliveries.

Relationship with Other Functional Areas

- Accounting's influence

- Marketing and production

CHASE ○ AQUILANO ○ JACOBS

Operations Management
For Competitive Advantage
Supplement A

Linear Programming Using Excel Solver

ninth edition

Supplement A
Linear Programming Using Excel Solver

- Linear Programming

- A Maximization Problem

- A Minimization Problem

Linear Programming

- Is used in problems where resources are constrained or limited.
- The model has an objective (function)
  - Generally maximizing profit or minimizing costs subject to resource-based, or other, constraints.
- *Linearity* is a requirement of the model in both objective function and constraints.
- Variables must be divisible (i.e., permit fractional values if need be) and non-negative.

Objective Function

$$\text{Maximize (or Minimize) } Z = C_1 X_1 + C_2 X_2 + \ldots + C_n X_n$$

- C_j is a constant that describes the rate of contribution to costs or profit of units being produced (X_j).

- Z is the total cost or profit from the given number of units being produced.

Constraints

$$A_{11} X_1 + A_{12} X_2 + \ldots + A_{1n} X_n \leq B_1$$
$$A_{21} X_1 + A_{22} X_2 + \ldots + A_{2n} X_n \geq B_2$$
$$\vdots$$
$$A_{M1} X_1 + A_{M2} X_2 + \ldots + A_{Mn} X_n = B_M$$

- A_{ij} are resource requirements for each of the related (X_j) decision variables.
- B_i are the available resource requirements.
- Note that the direction of the inequalities can be all or a combination of $\leq$, $\geq$, or $=$ linear mathematical expressions.

Non-Negativity Requirement

$$X_1, X_2, \ldots, X_n \geq 0$$

- All linear programming model formulations require their decision variables to be non-negative.
- While these non-negativity requirements take the form of a constraint, they are considered a mathematical requirement to complete the formulation of an LP model.

An Example of a Maximization Problem

LawnGrow Manufacturing Company must determine the mix of its commercial riding mower products to be produced next year. The company produces two product lines, the Max and the Multimax. The average profit is $400 for each Max and $800 for each Multimax. Fabrication and assembly are limited resources. There is a maximum of 5,000 hours of fabrication capacity available per month (Each Max requires 3 hours and each Multimax requires 5 hours). There is a maximum of 3,000 hours of assembly capacity available per month (Each Max requires 1 hour and each Multimax requires 4 hours). Question: How many of each riding mower should be produced each month in order to maximize profit?

Now let's formula this problem.

The Objective Function

If we define the Max and Multimax products as the two decision variables X_1 and X_2, and since we want to maximize profit, we can state the objective function as follows:

$$\text{Maximize } Z = 400X_1 + 800X_2$$

Where

Z = the monthly profit from Max and Multimax

X_1 = the number of Max produced each month

X_2 = the number of Multimax produced each month

Constraints

Given the resource information below from the problem:

Max (X1)	Multimax (X2)		
Required Time/Unit	Required Time/Unit	Available Time/Month	
3	5	5,000	Fab
1	4	3,000	Assy

We can now state the constraints and non-negativity requirement a:

$$3X_1 + 5X_2 \le 5,000 \quad \text{(Fab.)}$$
$$X_1 + 4X_2 \le 3,000 \quad \text{(Assy.)}$$
$$X_1, X_2 \ge 0 \quad \text{(Non-negativity)}$$

Note that the inequalities are less-than-or-equal since the time resources represent the total available resources for production.

Solution

Produce 715 Max and 571 Multimax per month for a profit of $742,800.

An Example of a Minimization Problem

HiTech Metal Company is developing a plan for buying scrap metal for its operations. HiTech receives scrap metal from two sources, Hasbeen Industries and Gentro. Scrap in daily shipments using large trucks. Each truckload of scrap from Hasbeen yields 1.5 tons of zinc and 1 ton of lead at a cost of $15,000. Each truckload of scrap from Gentro yields 1 ton of zinc and 3 tons of lead at a cost of $18,000. HiTech requires at least 6 tons of zinc and at least 10 tons of lead per day. Question: How many truckloads of scrap should be purchased per day from each source in order to minimize scrap metal cost?

Now let's formula this problem.

The Objective Function

If we define the Hasbeen truckloads and the Gentro truckloads as the two decision variables X_1 and X_2, and since we want to minimize cost, we can state the objective function as follows:

$$\text{Minimize } Z = 15,000 X_1 + 18,000 X_2$$

Where

Z = daily scrap cost

X_1 = truckloads from Hasbeen

X_2 = truckloads from Gentro

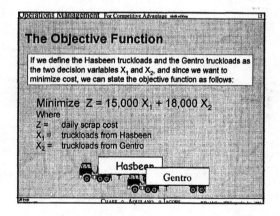

Constraints

Given the demand information below from the problem:

Hasbeen (X1) Tons	Gentro (X2) Tons	Min Tons	
1.5	1	6	Zinc
1	3	10	Lead

We can now state the constraints and non-negativity requirement a:

$$1.5X_1 + X_2 \geq 6 \quad \text{(Zinc/tons)}$$

$$X_1 + 3X_2 \geq 10 \quad \text{(Lead/tons)}$$

$$X_1, X_2 \geq 0 \quad \text{(Non-negativity)}$$

Note that the inequalities are greater-than-or-equal since the demand information represent the minimum necessary for production.

Solution

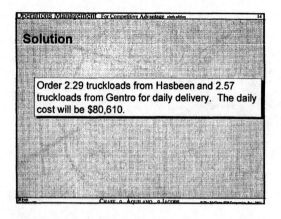

Order 2.29 truckloads from Hasbeen and 2.57 truckloads from Gentro for daily delivery. The daily cost will be $80,610.

CHASE ○ AQUILANO ○ JACOBS

Operations Management
For Competitive Advantage

Supplement B

Financial Analysis

Supplement B
Financial Analysis

- Cost Definitions
- Expected Value
- Depreciation
- Activity-Based Costing
- Investment Categories
- Cost of Capital
- Interest Rate Effects
- Methods of Ranking Investments

Cost Definitions

- **Fixed costs** are any expenses that remains constant regardless of the level of output.
- **Variable costs** are expenses that fluctuate directly with changes in the level of output.
- **Sunk costs** are past expenses or investments that have no salvage value and therefore should not be taken into account in considering investment alternatives.

Cost Definitions (Continued)

- **Opportunity cost** is the benefit forgone, or advantage lost, that results from choosing one action over the best alternative course of action.
- **Avoidable costs** include any expense that is not incurred if an investment is made but must be incurred if the investment is not made.

Expected Value

- This analysis is used to include risk factors (probabilities) with payoff values for decision making.
- Basic premise:

Expected Value= Expected outcome x Probability of outcome occurring

---

Economic Life and Obsolescence

- Economic life of a machine is the period time over which it provides the best method for performing its task.
- Obsolescence occurs when a machine is worn out.

Depreciation

- **Depreciation** is a method for allocating costs of capital investment, including buildings, machinery, etc.
- Depreciation procedures may not reflect an asset's true value because obsolescence may at any time cause a large difference between the true value and book value.

Depreciation Methods

- Straight-Line Method
- Sum-of-the-Years'-Digits (SYD) Method
- Declining-Balance Method
- Double-Declining-Balance Method
- Depreciation-by-Use Method

Traditional and Activity-Based Costing

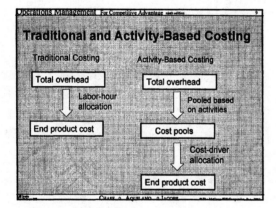

Choosing Among Investment Proposals: Investment Decision Categories

- Purchase of new equipment and/or facilities.
- Replacement of existing equipment or facilities.
- Make-or-buy decisions.
- Lease-or-buy decisions.
- Temporary shutdowns or plant-abandonment decisions.
- Addition or elimination of a product or product line.

Cost of Capital

- The **cost of capital** is calculated from a weighted average of debt and equity security costs.

- Short-term debt

- Long-term debt

Interest Rate Effects

- Compound value of a single amount
- Compound value of an annuity
- Present value of a future single payment
- Present value of an annuity
- Discounted cash flow

Methods of Ranking Investments

- Net present value
- Payback period
- Internal rate of return
- Ranking investments with uneven lives

CHASE ○ AQUILANO ○ JACOBS

Operations Management
For Competitive Advantage

Supplement C

Operations Technology

Supplement C
Operations Technology

- Hardware Systems

- Software Systems

- Formula for Evaluating Robots

- Computer Integrated Manufacturing

- Technologies in Services

- Benefits

- Risks

Hardware Systems

- Numerically controlled (NC) machines

- Machining centers

- Industrial robots

- Automated material handling (AMH) systems

  – Automated Storage and Retrieval Systems (AS/AR)

  – Automate Guided Vehicle (AGV)

- Flexible manufacturing systems (FMS)

Formula for Evaluating a Robot Investment

The payback formula for an investment in robots is:

$$P = \frac{I}{L - E + q(L + Z)}$$

Where
P = Payback period in years
I = Total capital investment required in robot and accessories
L = Annual labor costs replaced by the robot (wage and
  benefit costs per worker times the number of shifts per day)
E = Annual maintenance cost for the robot
Z = Annual depreciation
q = Fractional speedup (or slowdown) factor (in decimals).
Example: If robot produces 150 % of what the normal worker is
capable of doing, the fractional speedup factor is .5.

Example of Evaluating a Robot Investment

Suppose a company wants to buy a robot. The bank wants to know what the payback period is before they will lend them the $120,000 the robot will cost. You have determined that the robot will replace one worker per shift, for a one shift operation. The annual savings per worker is $35,000. The annual maintenance cost for the robot is estimated at $5,000, with an annual depreciation of $12,000. The estimated productivity of the robot over the typical worker is 110%. What is the payback period of this robot?

$$P = \frac{I}{L - E + q(L + Z)} = \frac{120{,}000}{35{,}000 - 5{,}000 + 1.1(35{,}000 + 12{,}000)} = 1.47 \text{ years}$$

Software Systems

- Computer-aided-design (CAD)
  – Computer-aided engineering (CAE)
  – Computer-aided process planning (CAPP)

- Automated manufacturing planning and control systems (MP & CS)

Computer Integrated Manufacturing (CIM)

- Product and process design

- Planning and control

- The manufacturing process

Technologies in Services

- Office automation

- Image processing systems

- Electronic data interchange (EDI)

- Decision support systems & expert systems

- Networked computer systems

Cost Reduction Benefits from Adopting New Technologies

- Labor costs
- Material costs
- Inventory costs
- Transportation or distribution costs
- Quality costs
- Other costs

Other Benefits....

- Increased product variety

- Improved product features and quality

- Shorter cycle times

Risks

- Technological risks

- Organizational risks

- Environmental risks

- Market risks

McGRAW-HILL/IRWIN/

Instructor's Resource Manual to accompany Operations Management for Competitive Advantage, 9/e by Chase, Aquilano, and Jacobs..

Please use this postage-paid form to report any errors that you find in this material. Be as complete as possible noting specifically which changes should be made. We will address them in subsequent printings and future editions. Thank You.

NOTE: Extra copies of this form appear at the end of this manual.

Attention: R. T. Hercher

Name _____   School _____

Office Phone _____

Please fold and seal so that our address is visible.

BUSINESS REPLY MAIL

FIRST-CLASS MAIL   PERMIT NO.204   OAKBROOK, IL

POSTAGE WILL BE PAID BY ADDRESSEE

ATTENTION: R. Hercher

THE McGRAW-HILL COMPANIES
1333 BURR RIDGE PKY.
BURR RIDGE, IL 60521-0085

(fold)

(fold)

McGRAW-HILL/IRWIN/

Instructor's Resource Manual to accompany Operations Management for Competitive Advantage, 9/e by Chase, Aquilano, and Jacobs..

Please use this postage-paid form to report any errors that you find in this material. Be as complete as possible noting specifically which changes should be made. We will address them in subsequent printings and future editions. Thank You.

NOTE: Extra copies of this form appear at the end of this manual.

Attention: R. T. Hercher

Name _____   School _____

Office Phone _____

Please fold and seal so that our address is visible.

BUSINESS REPLY MAIL
FIRST-CLASS MAIL   PERMIT NO.204   OAKBROOK, IL

POSTAGE WILL BE PAID BY ADDRESSEE

ATTENTION: R. Hercher

THE McGRAW-HILL COMPANIES
1333 BURR RIDGE PKY.
BURR RIDGE, IL 60521-0085

(fold)

McGRAW-HILL/IRWIN/

Instructor's Resource Manual to accompany Operations Management for Competitive Advantage, 9/e by Chase, Aquilano, and Jacobs..

Please use this postage-paid form to report any errors that you find in this material. Be as complete as possible noting specifically which changes should be made. We will address them in subsequent printings and future editions. Thank You.

NOTE: Extra copies of this form appear at the end of this manual.

Attention: R. T. Hercher

Name _____   School _____

Office Phone _____

Please fold and seal so that our address is visible.

BUSINESS REPLY MAIL
FIRST-CLASS MAIL   PERMIT NO.204   OAKBROOK, IL

POSTAGE WILL BE PAID BY ADDRESSEE

ATTENTION: R. Hercher

THE McGRAW-HILL COMPANIES
1333 BURR RIDGE PKY.
BURR RIDGE, IL 60521-0085

(fold)

(fold)